Switched Mode Power Supplies

Switched Mode Power Supplies

design and construction

SECOND EDITION

H W Whittington
B W Flynn
D E Macpherson

The University of Edinburgh, UK

Universities Press

UNIVERSITIES PRESS (INDIA) PRIVATE LIMITED

Registered Office
3-6-747/1/A & 3-6-754/1, Himayatnagar,
Hyderabad 500 029 (A.P.), India
e-mail: info@universitiespress.com

Distributed by
Orient Blackswan Private Limited

Registered Office
3-6-752 Himayatnagar, Hyderabad 500 029 (A.P.) India

Other Offices
Bangalore / Bhopal / Bhubaneshwar / Chennai
Ernakulam / Guwahati / Hyderabad / Jaipur / Kolkata
Lucknow / Mumbai / New Delhi / Patna

Second edition 1997

First published in India by
Universities Press (India) Private Limited 2009

ISBN 978 81 7371 664 5

Printed at
Graphica Printers
Hyderabad 500 013

Published by
Universities Press (India) Private Limited
3-6-747/1/A & 3-6-754/1, Himayatnagar,
Hyderabad 500 029 (A.P.), India

EDITORIAL FOREWORD

This is the second edition of Switched Mode Power Supplies: Design and Construction. The rapid world-wide expansion of the consumer electronics industry has brought about a requirement for manufacturers of switched mode power supplies to design and fabricate to new specifications which are both more onerous and more tightly framed.

This book extends the coverage of the first edition from basic design and manufacture to new techniques such as computer-aided design.

H.W. Whittington
June 1997

PREFACE

The "brain" of a computer is its microprocessor: most people are now aware of the key role played by the microprocessor and the specific reference to certain microprocessors has become part of standard advertising. At least as important is the "heart" of the computer: this book is concerned with the design and fabrication of the computer's heart - the electronic power supply.

In this second edition, the section on the electromagnetic compatibility of power supplies has been re-written. New regulations have been introduced in Europe governing the current harmonics that may be drawn from the mains supply. These are discussed in Section 4.4, together with various techniques for reducing these harmonic currents.

Computer simulation is now increasingly used to reduce design times, and a new section has therefore been included on simulation using SPICE. The bipolar transistor has all but disappeared from designs, and, as a consequence, it has been dropped from this edition. Section 2 on wound component design has been largely re-written.

This book aims to help engineers in designing and producing switched mode power supplies. Mathematics has been restricted to a minimum and "rules-of-thumb" have been used where appropriate.

The authors wish to express their gratitude to Richard Soh of Minebea Electronics (UK) Ltd. for all the invaluable discussions held with him during the preparation of this second edition. Thanks are also due to Frank Fisher of GEC Marconi in Edinburgh for his advice and comments on the first edition, and to Amarnath Reddy of Cortech Systems for his assistance with the section on SPICE simulation.

HWW, BWF, DEM
June 1997

CONTENTS

SECTION 1

INTRODUCTION AND BASIC CIRCUITS

SECTION 2

WOUND COMPONENT DESIGN AND PRODUCTION

SECTION 3

SEMICONDUCTOR DEVICES AND SMPS CONTROL

SECTION 4

PRACTICAL SMPS DESIGN CONSIDERATIONS

SECTION 1

INTRODUCTION AND BASIC CIRCUITS

1.1 INTRODUCTION

All electronic circuits need a supply of power. For low power consumption units or for portable operation, a battery is often used - a solar cell may even be enough. Higher power circuits are normally powered from the a.c. mains supply. In almost all cases the power requires conversion to the appropriate d.c. voltage by an electronic power unit, which is usually switched mode in operation.

Advances in power supply design and manufacture have had to keep pace with advances in the electronic systems they supply. The requirement for portability has led to demands for more compact units with reduced losses, and the trend towards lower operating voltages has proved particularly demanding. In addition, regulations relating to safety and electromagnetic compatibility are becoming increasingly more stringent. Designers and production engineers have proved to be up to the task and a wide range of innovative techniques are now standard in the electronic power supply industry. Size and unit costs have been reduced while reliability has been increased. Efficiency has been improved by the use of new active components, new circuit topologies and new ways of manufacture.

The switching frequency of units in bulk production at present is 100-200kHz, but new designs operating at much elevated frequencies are already being manufactured in prototype form and should soon appear in the market, competing with traditional circuits.

The engineer working in this field requires technical competence in several areas, including:

- design of power electronic switching circuits,
- design of wound components,
- understanding of control theory and its application to SMPS,
- design for electromagnetic compatibility (EMC),
- understanding of thermal management within power electronic circuits,
- use of computer-aids for system design,
- use of computer simulation tools for circuit verification.

It is estimated that the world market for SMPS is currently between 3.5 and 4 billion dollars. Paradoxically, despite this large market for power supplies, there still exists a shortage of experienced power supply design engineers. Those who take up the challenge will find it demanding but stimulating.

1.2 SPECIFICATION OF SMPS

Any electronic system requires a power source in order to function correctly, yet the power supply is normally the most neglected part of the complete system. It is often hastily designed (or bought in) after the rest of the system is complete, and placed in the leftover space, which is often too small and has inadequate ventilation for cooling purposes.

System designers naturally wish to avoid any system faults occurring due to the power supply, so the specifications for the power supply normally include large safety margins. As the power supply will have its own safety margins, it is often grossly over-specified, and as a result is considerably larger, heavier and more expensive than is necessary.

When the systems designer is specifying the power supply, he will initially consider the required voltage, together with the maximum current. However, voltage and current ratings are only the beginning of a long list of parameters which need to be specified.

Number of Outputs

Typically, +5 volts is required for logic circuits, but frequently other voltage levels are required as well, possibly including negative voltages. Each output should have a complete specification.

Current Rating

Each output should have a maximum steady state current rating. In addition, any possible current spikes or surges (eg. starting disc drives) should be fully specified, preferably with a current waveform diagram.

Input Voltage

The input voltage must be specified, whether a.c. or d.c., together with the voltage range.

Isolation

In many applications, electrical isolation is required between the input and output, and between outputs, necessitating the use of a transformer in the power supply circuit. However, in some applications isolation is not necessary, and a smaller, cheaper power supply may be possible by choosing a design which does not incorporate an isolating transformer.

Ripple Voltage

There are three main causes of ripple:

(a) 50 Hz a.c. mains,
(b) ripple from the transistor switching (at switching frequency),
(c) voltage spikes (usually caused by the transistors switching).

This is normally expressed as a peak-to-peak voltage, at a fundamental frequency; however, it is sometimes given as a percentage of the nominal output voltage, and sometimes as an r.m.s. voltage. The ripple content can be reduced either by increasing the filter capacity, or by increasing the ripple frequency.

Regulation

The output voltage regulation of a power supply is a measure of how close the output voltage stays to its nominal value over the full range of operating conditions. It is commonly split up into three components: line, load, and temperature regulation.

(a) *Line Regulation*
Line regulation is a measure of the effect of changes in the input voltage on the output voltage. Most manufacturers specify an input voltage range for which the power supply output will stay within specified limits.

(b) *Load Regulation*
Load regulation is the percentage change in the steady state output voltage when the load current is increased from its minimum value to the fully rated current (this does not include any transient effects which may occur).

(c) *Temperature Regulation*
Temperature regulation is the effect a change in ambient temperature has on the output voltage.

Many power supply manufacturers specify only an overall percentage regulation, together with limits for input voltage, output current, and temperature.

$$Regulation = \frac{(V_{max} - V_{min})}{V_{nom}} \times 100\ \%$$

However, this figure is very much a worst case, as it is very unlikely that the extremes of load, input voltage and temperature will all occur simultaneously.

A regulated power supply has a feedback circuit to compensate for such changes, keeping the output voltage within the specified limits.

Transient Response

An often neglected power supply parameter is the response to sudden changes in load current. If the full load current is suddenly switched on when the power supply is very lightly loaded, the output voltage will dip temporarily below the minimum allowable steady state voltage (as set by the specified regulation). Conversely, if the load is switched off, the output voltage will rise temporarily above the maximum steady state voltage.

Transient response is normally specified as:

$$\frac{V_{dev}}{V_{nom}} \times 100\ \% \quad \text{for } 100\ \%\ \textit{load change}$$

(V_{dev} = maximum deviation from nominal output voltage)

together with a "Recovery Time", the time it takes for the output to return within the specified regulation limits.

The transient response is affected by the type of power supply circuit used, the feedback loop and the output filter.

Efficiency

An inefficient power supply has two major disadvantages:

(a) Energy is wasted, which is particularly important when fed from a battery.

(b) Large heatsinks and good ventilation are required, which add to the size and weight of the power supply.

Protection

Power supplies can have many different forms of protection, but the most common are:

(a) *Overvoltage*
It is important to protect the load against an overvoltage at the output. It is normal to simply shut down the power supply if an overvoltage is detected (apart from transients). Alternatively, a "crowbar" thyristor may be used, where a thyristor is triggered if the voltage rises above a preset limit, putting a short circuit across the output, and hence clamping the output voltage low, with the current controlled by the current limit circuit.

(b) *Overcurrent*
Most power supplies have some form of current limit, such that if the load current rises above a preset level, the output voltage reduces to limit the current to a safe level.

(c) *Short Circuit*
This may be covered by the overcurrent protection, but a separate circuit is often used to shut down the power supply if a short circuit is seen across the output terminals.

(d) *Inrush Current*
SMPS normally have a large d.c. smoothing capacitor near the input, which is likely to cause a very high current spike at initial switch-on. Most SMPS incorporate some form of current limiting circuitry to keep this inrush current to a minimum.

Electromagnetic Interference (EMI)

This is not normally a problem with linear or low frequency (< 20 kHz) switched mode power supplies, but the problems associated with EMI increase with frequency. Adequate filtering of input and output leads should be provided as a minimum.

Hold-Up Time

It is highly desirable that the SMPS should continue to provide an output voltage within specification through short interruptions to the input lasting, typically, one or two cycles at 50 Hz.

Temperature Range

It should be noted that the ambient temperature is the temperature INSIDE the cabinet/box in which the system and the power supply are housed, which is likely to be considerably higher than the temperature outside. Allowance should also be made for the temperature rise due to the power dissipated by the power supply.

Physical Dimensions

The physical size and weight of the power supply are often the limiting factor in the choice of power supply, as it is usually situated in the leftover space. Recent advances in high frequency (> 100 kHz) switched mode power supplies have resulted in considerable reductions in size.

Certification

Many countries have their own regulatory bodies which produce standards that must be complied with if the power supply is to be sold in that country: for example, British Standards (BS) in the UK, Germany's Verband Deutscher Elektrotechniker (VDE), Underwriters Laboratory (UL) in the US, and Canadian Standards Association (CSA) in Canada.

There has been a move recently to try and pull together many of the various national standards into international standards, under the auspices of the IEC (International Electrotechnical Commission). This should simplify the present problems which manufacturers face when designing equipment to sell worldwide, where every country has its own set of standards, for which compliance and certification is required. In Europe, common European standards are now produced by CENELEC.

Of great significance to the power supply user are the various safety and electromagnetic interference (EMI) regulations. However, growing importance is now also attached to the input current waveform, where Europe and Japan are introducing stringent regulations.

Economics

As usual, the cost of the power supply is often the overriding consideration. Frequently, system designers underestimate (or ignore altogether) the cost of the power supply, while expecting very tight specifications to be met.

1.3 RECTIFIER CIRCUITS

The block diagram of a typical SMPS is shown in Figure 1.1. This section discusses the design of the two rectifiers included in most power supplies.

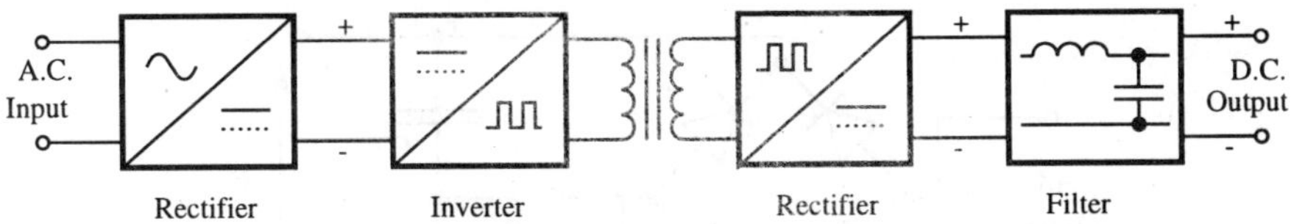

Figure 1.1 SMPS block diagram

There are two circuits used for converting single phase a.c. to d.c., the bridge rectifier and the centre-tapped transformer rectifier (shown in Figure 1.2). They both have the same output waveshape, shown for both sinusoidal and square wave inputs.

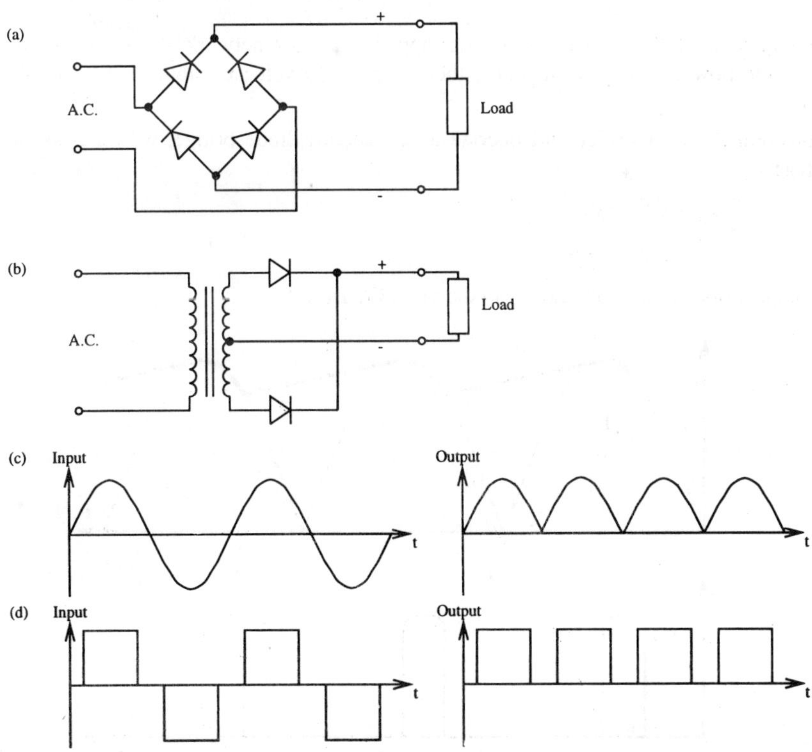

Figure 1.2 (a) Bridge rectifier (b) Centre-tapped transformer rectifier (c) Waveform for sinusoidal input (d) Waveform for square wave input

Input Rectifier

This rectifier converts the a.c. mains voltage to high voltage d.c. A bridge rectifier is normally used, to avoid the inclusion of a low frequency transformer, which would add considerably to the size and weight (and cost) of the power supply.

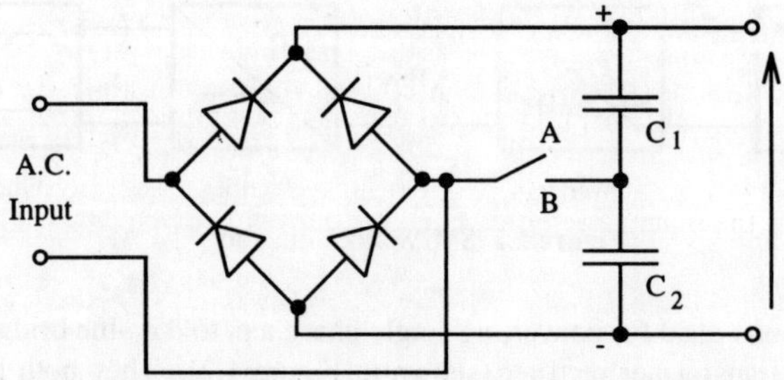

Figure 1.3 Input rectifier for 230 or 110 volt a.c. input

The inclusion of the switch and centre-tapped capacitor network shown in Figure 1.3 allows the power supply to operate either from a 230 volt a.c. input, or a 110 volt a.c. input.

In position A, the rectifier will operate as a standard diode bridge, with a peak output voltage V_o:

$$V_o = \sqrt{2} \times 230$$
$$\approx 325 \quad volts$$

The capacitors will smooth the V_o as shown in Figure 1.4.

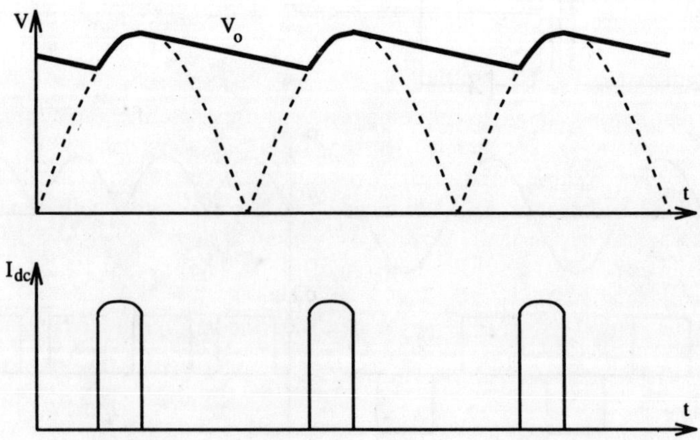

Figure 1.4 Rectifier output voltage and current waveforms

It can be shown that the value of capacitance is given by:

$$C = \frac{power}{V_{max}^2 - V_{min}^2} \times \frac{1}{f}$$

where:

$V_{max} =$ peak d.c. voltage
$V_{min} =$ minimum d.c. voltage
$f =$ a.c. mains frequency (50 Hz)

The charging current is also shown. It can be seen that this is a narrow current spike, which will become narrower and higher if V_{min} is increased by increasing the smoothing capacitor.

It can be shown that the magnitude of the charging current is given by:

$$i_{peak} = \frac{C}{t_c} \times (V_{max} - V_{min})$$

where:

$$t_c = \frac{1}{2\pi f} \times \cos^{-1}\left(\frac{V_{min}}{V_{max}}\right)$$

This current spike can introduce harmonics onto the mains supply, which may need filtering out. Legislation will shortly be introduced governing the waveshape of current drawn from the mains.

If a 110 volt input is used, then the switch should be moved to position B. In this case the upper capacitor will be charged during the positive half cycle, and the lower capacitor during the negative half cycle, giving a peak output voltage:

$$V_o = 2 \times \sqrt{2} \times 110 \quad volts$$
$$\sim 311 \quad volts$$

which is only 9% less than from a 230 volt supply, with the switch in position A.

Output Rectifier

The output rectifier is normally a centre-tapped transformer rectifier. In a bridge rectifier two diodes are always conducting, which would add considerably to the losses, particularly for low voltage outputs (e.g. 5 volt supplies), due to the relatively high diode on-state voltage. However in the centre-tapped transformer rectifier there is only ever one diode conducting at any instant. Most SMPS include a high frequency transformer for isolation, so an extra transformer is not required.

It should be noted that the diodes should be rated for twice the peak d.c. voltage.

1.4 BASIC CONVERTER CIRCUITS

Many different SMPS circuit topologies have been developed, most of which are derivatives of the following basic circuits:

(a) buck

(b) buck-boost

(c) boost

BUCK REGULATOR

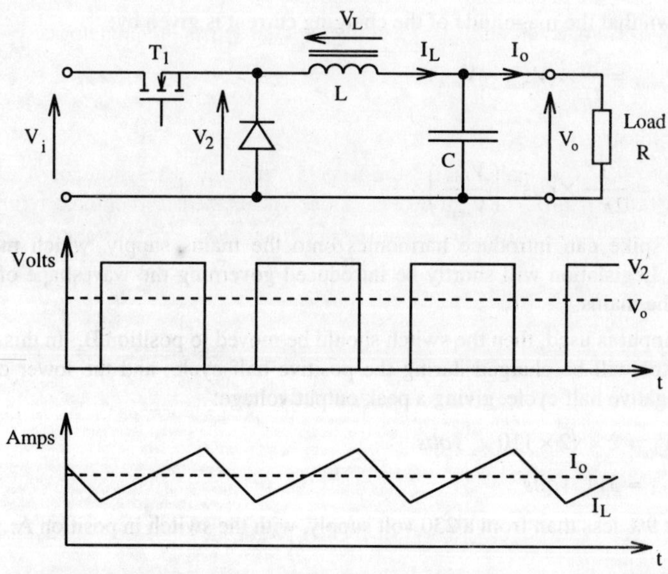

Figure 1.5 Buck regulator with associated voltage and current waveforms

In the basic buck circuit shown in Figure 1.5, transistor T_1 is switched at high frequency (20 kHz → 1 MHz) to produce a chopped output voltage V_2. This is then filtered by the L-C circuit to produce a smooth load voltage V_o. The output voltage can be controlled by varying the mark:space ratio of V_2.

The average output voltage is given by:

$$\frac{V_o}{V_i} = \frac{t_{on}}{T}$$

$$= D$$

where: T = total period $= \dfrac{1}{f}$

t_{on} = transistor on time

D = transistor duty ratio = $\frac{t_{on}}{T}$

Thus in the ideal case the output voltage is independent of load.

However, in a realistic circuit there will be losses associated with:

- transistor "on" state voltage drop
- transistor switching losses
- diode forward voltage drop
- inductor effective resistance,

all of which increase the dependency of V_o on load.

When transistor T_1 is switched on, $V_2 = V_i$, so the voltage across the inductor is:

$$V_L = L \cdot \frac{di}{dt} = V_i - V_o$$

So I_L increases linearly.

When transistor T_1 is switched off, the current through the inductor L cannot instantaneously fall to zero, so the "flywheel" diode is included to provide a return path for the current to circulate through the load. During this period, $V_2 = 0$, so:

$$V_L = L . \frac{di}{dt} = -V_o$$

So I_L decreases linearly.

The peak-to-peak current ripple is:

$$\Delta I = t_{on} \cdot \left(\frac{V_i - V_o}{L}\right)$$

$$= \left(\frac{V_o \cdot T}{L}\right) . (1 - D)$$

The maximum current is:

$$I_{max} = \frac{V_o}{R} + \frac{\Delta I}{2}$$

The minimum current is:

$$I_{min} = \frac{V_o}{R} - \frac{\Delta I}{2}$$

Discontinuous Mode Operation

The previous section analysed the buck converter for the *continuous current* mode, ie. when the inductor current never falls to zero in the cycle. However, many switched mode power supplies are designed to operate in the *discontinuous current* mode, where for a proportion of each cycle the inductor current is zero.

If the load on a buck regulator is slowly reduced, eventually $I_{min} = 0$ (case (ii) in Figure1.6). If the load is reduced still further, the inductor current is zero for a period, and the circuit is operating in the discontinuous mode (case (iii)).

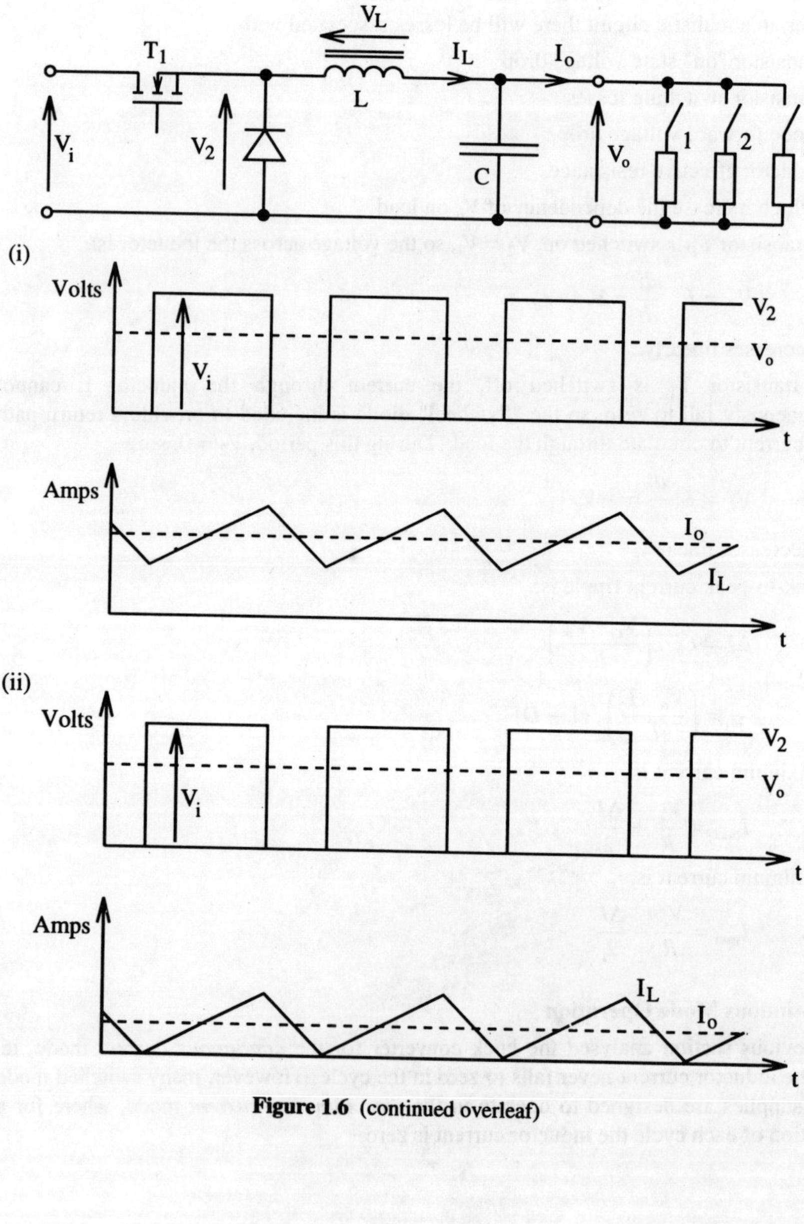

Figure 1.6 (continued overleaf)

(iii)

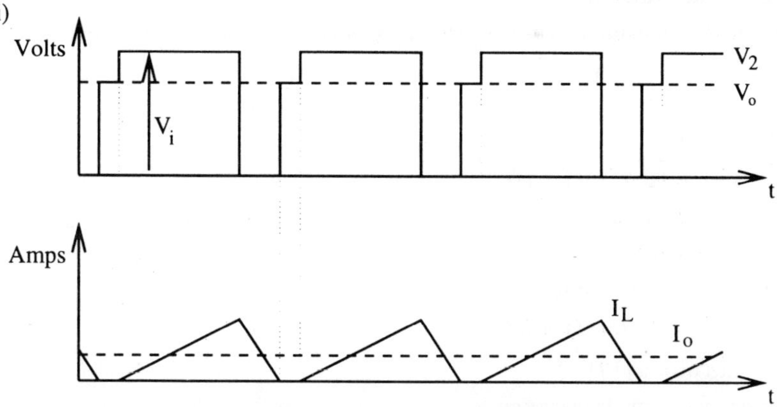

Figure 1.6 Effect of load on the buck regulator
(i) Continuous inductor current (full load)
(ii) Boundary between continuous and discontinuous inductor current
(iii) Discontinuous inductor current (light load)

For t_{on} , the inductor voltage $V_L = V_i - V_o$.
For the period the diode is conducting $(D_D . T)$, the inductor voltage $V_L = - V_o$.
Since the average voltage across an inductor over a complete cycle is zero (assuming steady state conditions),

$$(V_i - V_o) . D . T = V_o . D_D . T$$

Therefore:

$$\frac{V_o}{V_i} = \frac{D}{D + D_D}$$

The ripple current is:

$$\Delta I = \frac{(V_i - V_o) . D . T}{L}$$

$$= \frac{V_o . D_D . T}{L}$$

The output current = I_L averaged over one cycle, ie:

$$I_o = \frac{\Delta I}{2} \times (D . T + D_D . T) \times \frac{1}{T}$$

$$= \frac{V_o}{R}$$

Combining the above:

$$\frac{V_o}{V_i} = \frac{2 . D}{D + \sqrt{D^2 + (8 . L/R . T)}}$$

Choice of Filter Inductor

At the boundary condition between continuous and discontinuous mode of operation,

$$I = \frac{V_o}{R} = \frac{\Delta I}{2}$$

Therefore:

$$L = ½ . R . T . (1 - D)$$

The value of L decides whether the circuit will operate in the continuous mode or discontinuous mode.

For continuous mode operation:

$$L > ½ . R . T . (1 - D)$$

for all values of R and D.

For discontinuous mode operation:

$$L < ½ . R . T . (1 - D)$$

for all values of R and D.

Choice of Filter Capacitor

The output filter capacitor is chosen to minimise the output ripple voltage, ΔV_o.

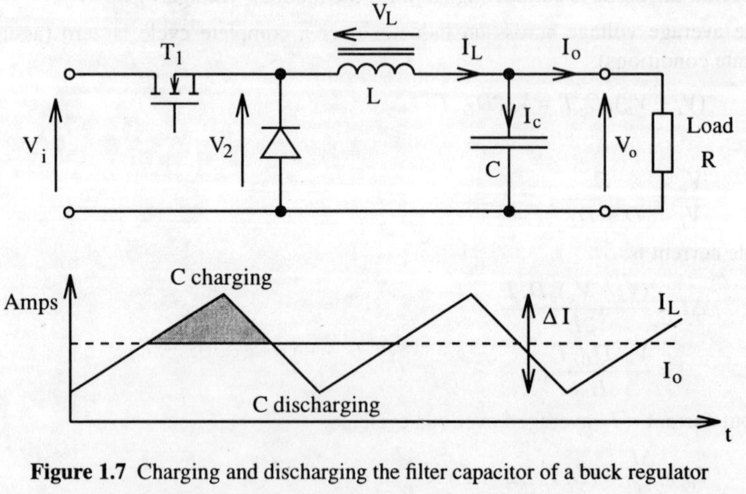

Figure 1.7 Charging and discharging the filter capacitor of a buck regulator

In Figure 1.7, capacitor C is charging during the period that $I_L > I_o$, the shaded area being the increase in charge on C ΔQ. When $I_L < I_o$, C is discharging. Thus:

$$\Delta Q = \frac{1}{2} . \frac{\Delta I}{2} . \frac{T}{2}$$

$$= \frac{T \cdot \Delta I}{8}$$

Thus:

$$\Delta V_o = \frac{\Delta Q}{C}$$

$$= \frac{T \cdot \Delta I}{8\,C}$$

$$= \frac{V_o \cdot T^2}{8\,L\,C} \cdot (1 - D)$$

or:

$$C = \frac{V_o}{\Delta V_o} \cdot \frac{T^2}{8\,L} \cdot (1 - D)$$

However, in most practical circuits, the output ripple voltage is more likely to be caused by the ripple current through the capacitor ESR (equivalent series resistance).

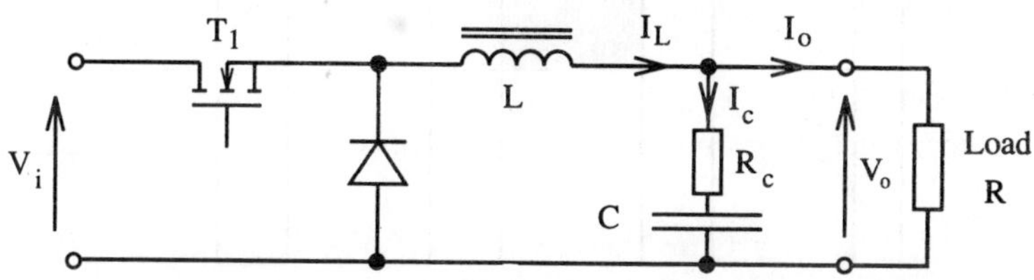

Figure 1.8 Buck regulator including capacitor ESR

The peak-to-peak ripple voltage is thus given by:

$$\Delta V_o = \Delta I \cdot R_c$$

where:

R_c = capacitor ESR

$$\Delta I = \frac{t_{on} \cdot (V_i - V_o)}{L}$$

It is, therefore, important to choose a filter capacitor with a low ESR value.

BUCK-BOOST REGULATOR

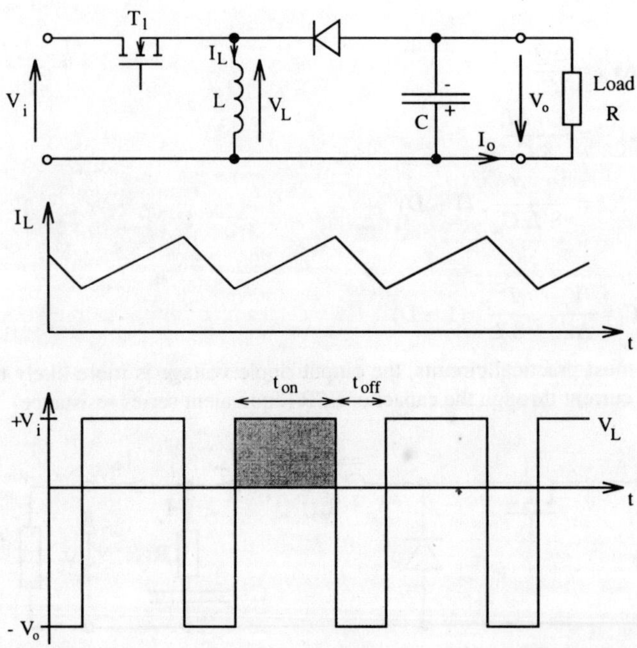

Figure 1.9 Buck-Boost regulator with inductor current and voltage waveforms

In the basic buck-boost regulator shown in Figure 1.9, energy is stored in inductor L during the on-time of transistor T_1. When T_1 is switched off, the voltage across L reverses as the inductor transfers the stored energy ($=\frac{1}{2}Li^2$) to the smoothing capacitor and to the load. Note that the output voltage is the opposite polarity to the input.

The basic equation for an inductor is:

$$V_L = L.\frac{di}{dt}$$

Integrating both sides over one complete cycle:

$$\int V_L.dt = \int L.di = L.(I_2 - I_1)$$

where I_1 is the current at the start of the cycle, and I_2 at the end of the cycle. Under steady state conditions, the current through the inductor at the start of a cycle equals the current at the end of the cycle; therefore, over one complete cycle:

$$\int V_L.dt = 0$$

ie. the *average* voltage across the inductor over one complete cycle is zero.

During the on-period, the inductor voltage $V_L = V_i$, while during the off-period, $V_L = -V_o$. Therefore:

$$V_i . t_{on} - V_o . (t_{off}) = 0$$

Therefore:

$$\frac{V_o}{V_i} = \frac{t_{on}}{t_{off}} = \frac{D.T}{(1-D).T}$$

$$= \frac{D}{1-D}$$

where D = transistor duty ratio.

Losses which have been neglected are the inductor resistance, the transistor on-state voltage drop, the forward volt drop across the diode, and the transistor switching losses. However, the formulae as presented are usually adequate as a first approximation.

The peak-to-peak current ripple is:

$$\Delta I = t_{on} . \left(\frac{V_i}{L}\right)$$

$$= D . T . \left(\frac{V_i}{L}\right)$$

The inductor current only goes to the load during t_{off}, therefore the average load current is the average inductor current *during the transistor off-period.*

At the boundary condition between continuous and discontinuous mode of operation the average current into the load is:

$$I = \frac{V_o}{R}$$

$$= \frac{\Delta I . t_{off}}{2} \times \frac{1}{T}$$

$$= \frac{D.T.V_i}{L} . \frac{(1-D).T}{T} . \frac{1}{2}$$

Thus:

$$L = ½. R.T.(1-D)^2$$

Therefore, for continuous mode operation:

$$L > ½. R.T.(1-D)^2$$

for all likely values of R and D.

Discontinuous Mode Operation

If load is slowly reduced, the buck-boost regulator will eventually be operating in the discontinuous mode (Figure 1.10 (iii)). The average voltage across an inductor over one complete cycle equals zero; therefore:

$$V_i.D.T = V_o.D_D.T$$

Hence:

$$\frac{V_o}{V_i} = \frac{D}{D_D}$$

In a similar fashion as earlier, it can be shown that:

$$\frac{V_o}{V_i} = D.\sqrt{\frac{R.T}{2L}}$$

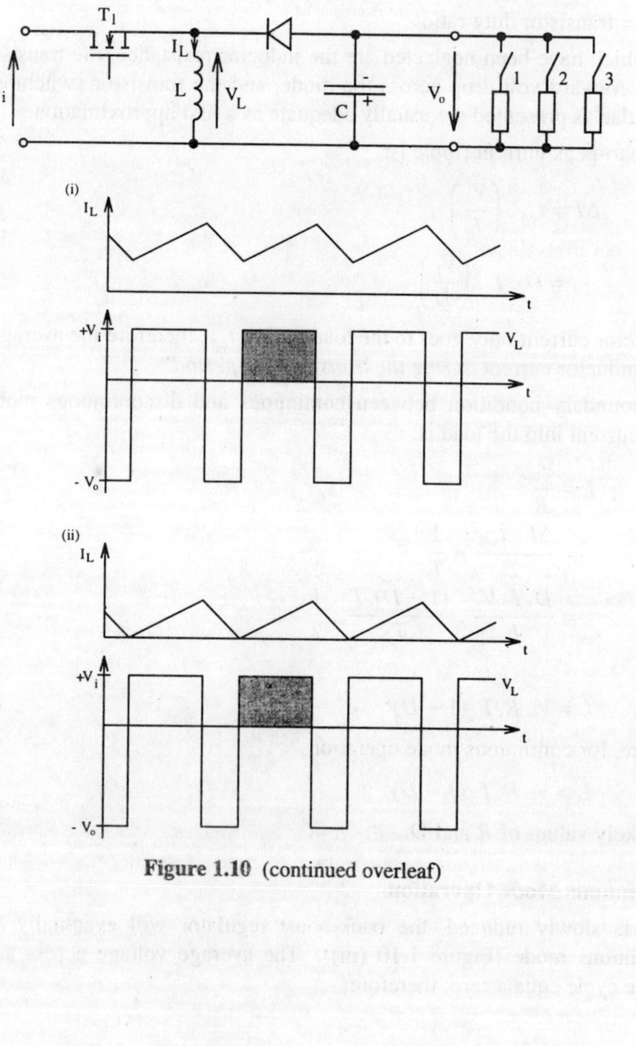

Figure 1.10 (continued overleaf)

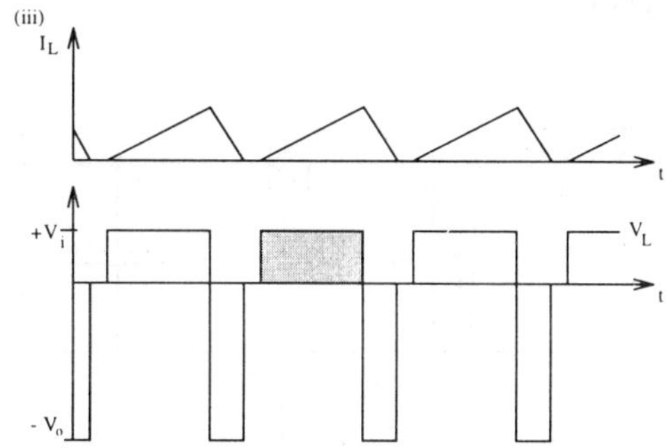

Figure 1.10 Effect of load on the buck-boost regulator
(i) Continuous inductor current (full load)
(ii) Boundary between continuous and discontinuous inductor current
(iii) Discontinuous inductor current (light load)

Choice of Filter Capacitor

The capacitor is chosen to limit the output ripple voltage. During the transistor on-time, the load current is supplied entirely by the filter capacitor. Thus:

$$I = -C \cdot \frac{dV_o}{dt} = \frac{V_o}{R}$$

or:

$$\frac{dV_o}{dt} = \frac{\Delta V_o}{\Delta t}$$

$$= -\frac{V_o}{RC}$$

$$\Delta t = t_{on} = D.T$$

so:

$$\frac{\Delta V_o}{V_o} = \frac{D.T}{R.C}$$

However, as with the buck regulator, the more important parameter for limiting the ripple voltage is usually the capacitor ESR.

Unlike the continuous mode buck regulator, the capacitor in the buck-boost regulator supplies *all* the load current during the period that the transistor is on. Therefore the capacitor in the buck-boost regulator sees a much higher ripple current, placing a more stringent ESR requirement on it.

It should be noted that the peak voltage across the transistor during t_{off} is $(V_i + V_o)$.

BOOST REGULATOR

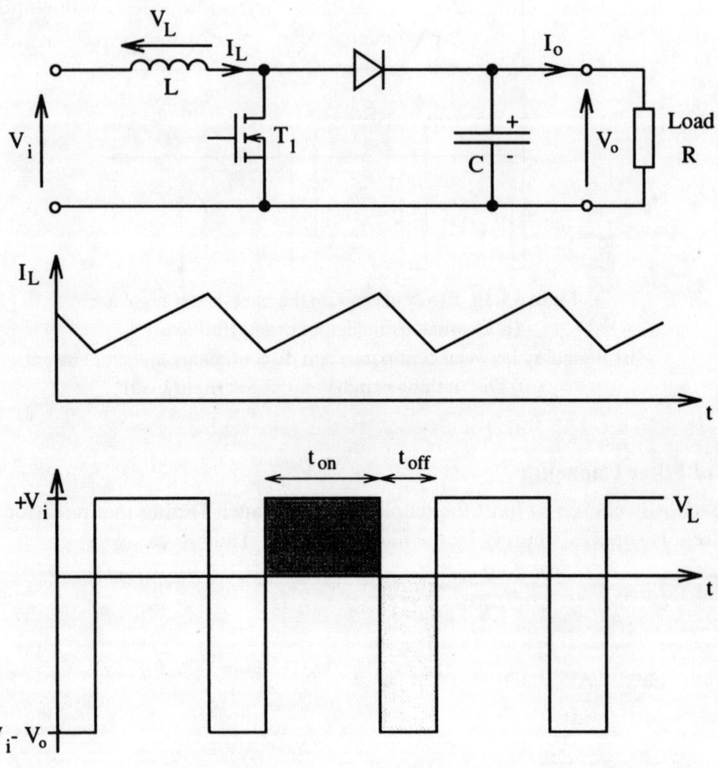

Figure 1.11 Boost regulator with inductor current and voltage waveforms

During the on-time of transistor T_1, the current builds up in inductor L due to the inductor voltage $V_L = V_i$. When T_1 is switched off, the voltage across L reverses ($V_L = V_i - V_o$) and adds to the input voltage, making the output voltage greater than the input voltage.

As before, the average voltage across the inductor over one complete cycle is zero, therefore:

$$V_i . t_{on} - (V_o - V_i). t_{off} = 0$$

Therefore:

$$V_i . D . T = (V_o - V_i).(1 - D). T$$

And:

$$\frac{V_o}{V_i} = \frac{1}{1 - D}$$

where D = transistor duty ratio.

Losses which have been neglected are the inductor resistance, the transistor on-state voltage drop, the forward volt drop across the diode, and the transistor switching losses. However, the formulae as presented are usually adequate as a first approximation. The effect of losses on the d.c. gain is shown in Figure 1.12.

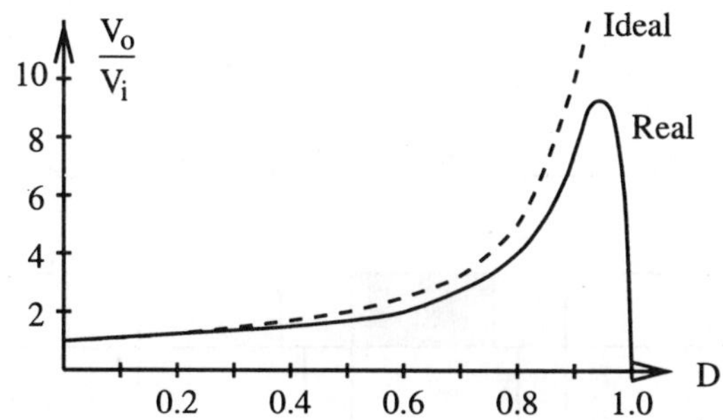

Figure 1.12 Effect of losses on the d.c. gain of a boost regulator

The current ripple is:

$$\Delta I = \left(\frac{V_i}{L}\right) . t_{on}$$

$$= \left(\frac{V_i}{L}\right) . D.T$$

Input power = output power,

$$V_i \; . \; I_{L(av)} = V_o \; . \; I_{load}$$

Therefore:

$$I_{load} = \frac{V_o}{R} = I_{L(av)} \cdot \frac{V_i}{V_o}$$

$$= I_{L(av)} \cdot (1 - D)$$

At the boundary condition between continuous and discontinuous mode of operation,

$$I_{L(av)} = \frac{\Delta I}{2}$$

Therefore:

$$\frac{V_o}{R} = \frac{\Delta I}{2} \cdot (1 - D) = \frac{V_i}{2. L} \; . \; D.T \; . \; (1 - D)$$

Therefore:

$$L = \tfrac{1}{2}. R. T. D. (1 - D)^2$$

Thus, for continuous mode of operation:

$$L > ½.R.T.D.(1-D)^2$$

for all likely values of R and D.

Discontinuous Mode of Operation

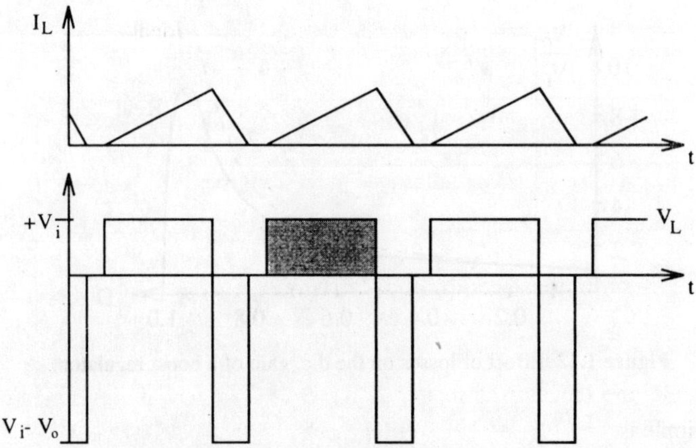

Figure 1.13 Inductor current and voltage waveforms in the discontinuous current mode

Again, the inductor volt-second relationship holds:

$$V_i.D.T = (V_o - V_i).D_D.T$$

So:

$$\frac{V_o}{V_i} = \frac{D + D_D}{D_D}$$

It can be shown that:

$$\frac{V_o}{V_i} = \frac{1 + \sqrt{1 + 2.D^2.T.R/L}}{2}$$

Choice of Filter Capacitor

As with the buck-boost regulator, the load is supplied by the filter capacitor during the transistor on-period. Hence, the output ripple voltage is the same as for the buck-boost regulator, ie.

$$\frac{\Delta V_o}{V_o} = \frac{D.T}{R.C}$$

Again, the capacitor ESR is likely to be of paramount importance in the choice of capacitor.

SUMMARY OF BASIC CONVERTER CIRCUITS

Circuit Summary

Topology	Polarity V_o wrt V_i	Magnitude V_o wrt V_i
Buck	same polarity	step-down
Buck-Boost	inverse polarity	step-up or step-down
Boost	same polarity	step-up

Continuous or Discontinuous Mode of Operation

(a) *Continuous Mode Operation*

In this mode, the inductor current, I_L , never falls to zero during any part of the switching cycle. To maintain the current, the inductance has to be considerably larger than is required with the discontinuous mode.

Although the inductor current is continuous, in the buck-boost and boost regulators the current into the regulator output stage (ie. the diode current) is discontinuous. However, in the buck regulator the inductor current is the current into the output stage, which is continuous and has a relatively small ripple value. The buck regulator is, therefore, easier to filter, and is the most popular switching configuration, particularly at high power levels.

Open Loop Regulation

The basic equations for continuous mode operation derived earlier are:
Buck:

$$\frac{V_o}{V_i} = D$$

Buck-Boost:

$$\frac{V_o}{V_i} = \frac{D}{1-D}$$

Boost:

$$\frac{V_o}{V_i} = \frac{1}{1-D}$$

It can be seen from the above that the output does not depend on the load resistance R (taking a first order approximation and neglecting the inductor resistance r_L).

Hence the open loop load regulation is very good. However, V_o does depend on the input voltage V_i , so the open loop line regulation is poor.

Closed Loop Response

The large inductor required for continuous mode operation, together with the filter capacitor, constitutes a 2nd order delay in the feedback control loop, resulting in poor closed loop response.

(b) *Discontinuous Mode Operation*

In this mode the inductor current falls to zero each cycle. This results in high inductor current peaks, placing an arduous duty on the switching transistor and the filter capacitor, as well as the inductor itself.

Open Loop Regulation

As shown earlier in this section, when a buck, buck-boost or boost regulator operates in the discontinuous mode the output voltage depends on the load resistance R. Hence the open loop load regulation is poor.

As in the continuous mode, the output voltage depends on the input voltage, so the open loop line regulation in the discontinuous mode is also poor.

Closed Loop Response

As the inductor starts each cycle with zero stored energy, it is possible for the control circuit to obtain any energy level and hence output current on a cycle-by-cycle basis. The inductor, therefore, has no effect on the small signal closed loop characteristic, leaving only the capacitor as the delay element in the loop. Regulators operating in the discontinuous mode, therefore, are very stable and have a very good closed loop response.

General

It can be seen from the above that each of the three types of regulator has very different open loop and closed loop characteristics, depending on whether operation is in the continuous or discontinuous current mode. It is important that a regulator designed for one mode of operation is not used in the other, as the different feedback characteristic is likely to lead to instability.

If the current in a continuous mode regulator is reduced below a minimum value (ie. a high value of R), discontinuous mode operation will result. Thus a continuous mode regulator should not be run on very light loading.

1.5 ISOLATED SWITCHED MODE POWER SUPPLIES

Most SMPS are required to have transformer-coupling between the input and the output(s). Transformer coupling provides the following advantages over the basic regulators so far described:

- The output is electrically isolated from the input. This is usually a requirement when operating from a 230 volt or 110 volt mains supply, to keep the mains voltages well apart from a low voltage load. It also allows the output to be earthed, if required.
- The transformer turns ratio can be chosen to give an output voltage widely different from the input voltage. The basic buck, buck-boost and boost circuits have the output voltage limited to within approximately a factor of 10 of the input voltage.
- With transformer coupling the polarity and step-up/step-down restrictions of the basic circuits no longer apply.
- By having more than one transformer secondary, multiple outputs at different voltage levels can be obtained.

However, the introduction of a transformer adds considerably to the size and weight of the SMPS, and introduces further losses into the circuit. In addition, the transformer leakage inductances may lead to severe voltage spikes in the circuit.

Transformer Saturation

To avoid excessive core losses, the transformer should operate in the linear region of the B-H curve in Figure 1.14(b), between $-B_{max}$ and $+B_{max}$. In the positive ½ cycle B increases to just below $+B_{max}$, and in the negative ½ cycle it returns to its starting point above $-B_{max}$.

On the transformer primary in Figure 1.14(a):

$$V_1 = N_1 . \frac{d\phi}{dt}$$

$$= N_1 A \frac{dB}{dt}$$

Therefore over one cycle:

$$B_2 - B_1 = \frac{1}{N_1 . A} \int V_1 . dt$$

In steady state operation $B_1 = B_2$ (see Figure 1.14(d)). Therefore:

$$\int V_1 . dt = 0 \quad \text{over one complete cycle}$$

ie. the average voltage over one cycle equals zero.

If the average voltage across the primary does not equal zero, the transformer will "walk" into saturation, as shown in Figure 1.14(e). Here B is steadily increasing, and will eventually rise above B_{max}, leading to excessive losses and circuit failure.

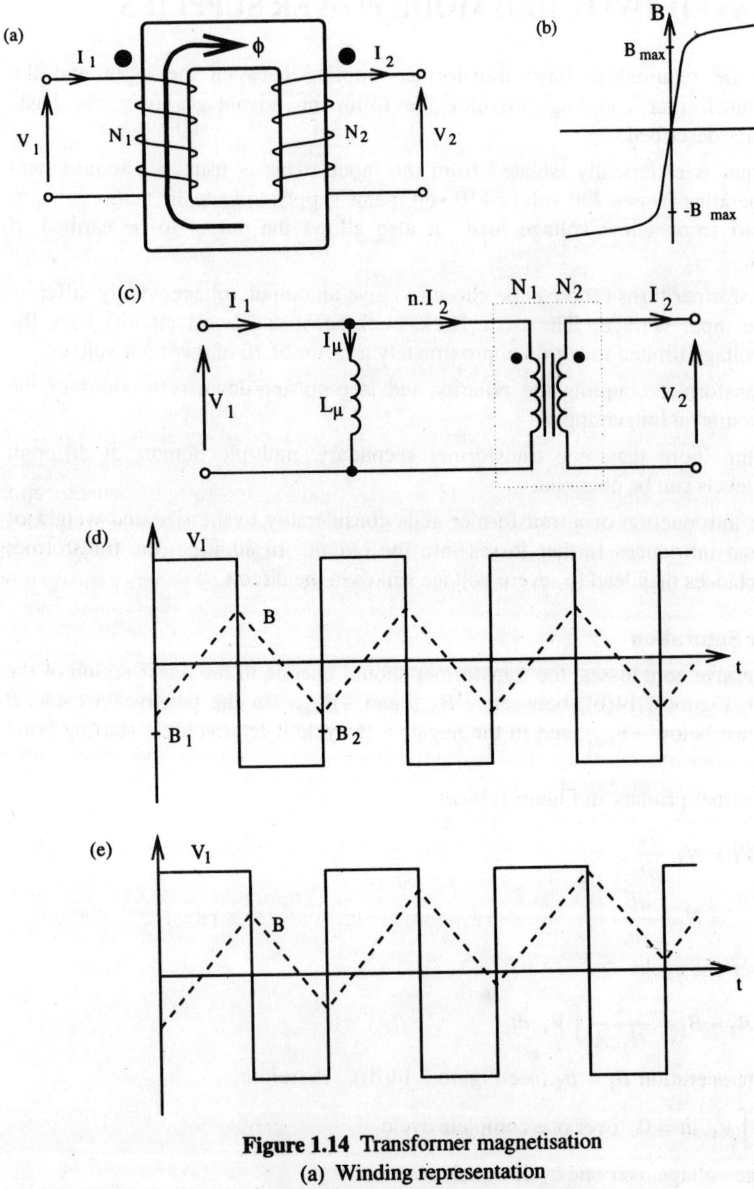

Figure 1.14 Transformer magnetisation

(a) Winding representation

(b) B-H curve for ferrite material

(c) Simplified transformer equivalent circuit

(d) Average primary voltage = 0

(e) Average primary voltage > 0

FLYBACK CONVERTER

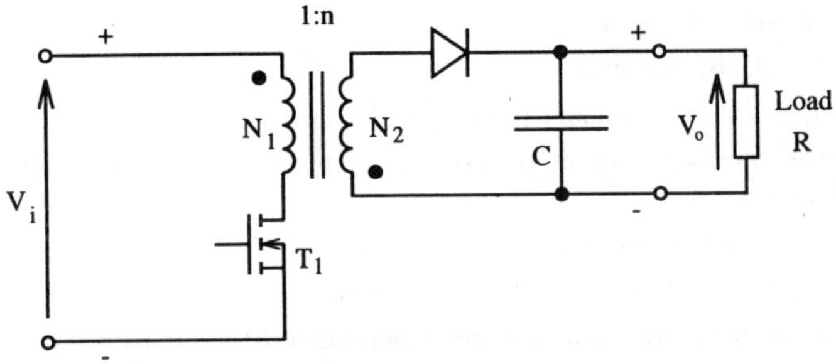

Figure 1.15 Flyback converter

This circuit operates in a very similar manner to the buck-boost regulator, but here the inductor has a secondary winding (or windings). Note that the wound component is an inductor with a secondary winding, combining the functions of both an inductor and a transformer. An inductor is an energy storage device, and so requires an air gap in the magnetic circuit (it is not possible to store significant amounts of energy in the ferromagnetic part of the core). An ideal transformer directly couples energy between the primary circuit and the secondary, and does not store energy. In this circuit an air gap is required, as energy is stored in the device. The equivalent circuit of the coupled inductor is the same as for a transformer: the difference is in the value of the magnetising inductance L_μ. In a transformer, L_μ is designed to be as large as possible (no air gap, and a large number of primary turns), to keep I_μ as small as possible and minimise losses. In the coupled inductor, L_μ is the primary inductance of the inductor, and hence will be designed to be much smaller.

During the transistor on-time, current builds up in a linear manner in the primary circuit ($V_i = L.\ di/dt$), storing energy ($= ½.\ L.\ i^2$) in the inductor. During this period, diode D_1 prevents any current from flowing in the secondary.

During the transistor off-time, the energy stored in the inductor is released to the load.

It can be shown that for continuous mode operation:

$$\frac{V_o}{V_i} = \frac{n.D}{1-D}$$

where: $n = \dfrac{N_2}{N_1}$ = turns ratio

For discontinuous mode operation, the primary inductance should be:

$$L < \frac{R.T.(1-D)^2}{2.n^2}$$

The (primary) current ripple is:

$$\Delta I = D.T.\left(\frac{V_i}{L}\right)$$

as with the buck-boost regulator.

The flyback converter is more commonly used in the discontinuous mode, due to:

(a) smaller inductor required

(b) better closed loop response.

The disadvantages of discontinuous mode operation are:

(a) high peak transistor current (approximately twice that of the continuous mode flyback converter)

(b) large filter capacitor (due to high peak current).

In practice, the flyback converter has two very useful features:

(1) It is able to boost the input voltage (independent of the transformer turns ratio), making it very attractive as a low power EHT supply (eg. in television sets, computer monitors etc.).

(2) Because the wound component is the energy storage inductor, any secondary only requires a diode and a capacitor to produce an independent d.c. supply. Additionally it is possible to include an extra winding for the feedback signal, providing isolation in the feedback circuit, yet without introducing errors due to the volt drop across an output inductor. It is thus an attractive circuit when a number of independent outputs are required.

It should be noted that the peak voltage across the transistor during T_{off} is $V_i + \dfrac{V_o}{n}$

The flyback converter is very common for powers up to about 200 watts.

FORWARD CONVERTER

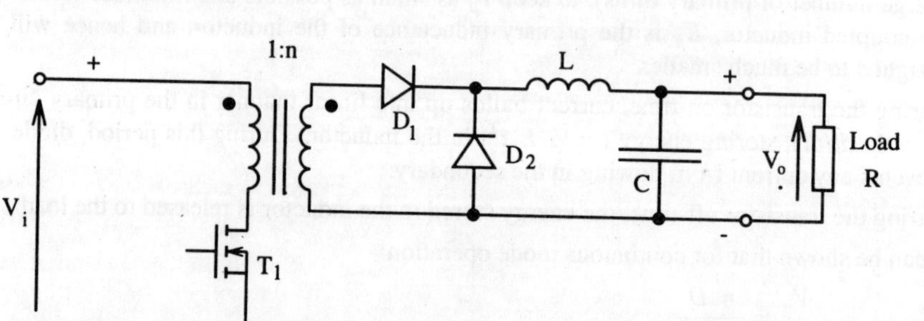

Figure 1.16 Basic forward converter

The forward converter is very similar to the basic buck regulator, but the addition of a transformer provides both isolation and the possibility of a very wide voltage range.

During the transistor on-time, diode D_1 is forward biased, and energy is transferred from the input to the load. During the off-time, D_1 is reverse biased and D_2 is forward biased to maintain continuous current in the output circuit.

In the forward converter shown in Figure 1.16, a serious problem would occur when T_1 is switched off. During the transistor on-time the magnetising current I_μ (Figure 1.15(c)) will have been building up linearly (approximately), storing energy in the transformer core (energy in an inductor = $\frac{1}{2}. L. i^2$). When the transistor is turned off, there must be a path for I_μ to flow, or very high voltages will result ($V = L. \frac{di}{dt}$), which will destroy the transistor.

There are a number of schemes to solve this problem, some of which include extra switching components. A common technique is to include a *tertiary* winding on the transformer core, as shown in Figure 1.17, which conducts during the off-period, providing a path for I_μ.

Transistor on

Current flows through the primary and the secondary (out of the dot end, through D_1). Diode D_3 is reverse biased. The magnetising current I_μ increases.

Transistor off

No current can flow in the primary winding. To prevent the problems described above from occurring, magnetising current must be maintained around the ferrite core. However, it does not matter which coil the current flows in as long as the amp-turns $N.I$ is maintained (Amperes Law states $N.I = \int H.dl$). During t_{on} current was flowing *into* the dot on the primary. With T_1 off, magnetising current cannot flow in the primary, nor can it flow into the dot on the secondary because of D_1, but it can flow into the dot on the tertiary, up through D_3 and back to the supply. This applies V_i to the tertiary, but in the opposite direction (positive away from the dot), thus causing I_μ to reduce.

From Figure 1.14(c):

$$I_1 = I_\mu + n.I_2$$

where: $n = \frac{N_2}{N_1}$

I_1 = total primary current

I_2 = secondary current

If the number primary turns = number tertiary turns, I_μ will rise and fall at the same rate; therefore, the duty cycle D must not exceed 0.5 (50 %) to allow time for I_μ to fall to zero. This results in poor transformer utilisation as energy is being transferred from the primary to the secondary only during the transistor-on period

During the transistor-off period, the tertiary winding induces a voltage of $-V_i$ across the primary, which adds to the input voltage to put $2.V_i$ across the transistor (if the tertiary winding has the same number of turns as the primary).

If the turns ratio of the primary to the tertiary winding is increased (number primary turns > number tertiary turns), the duty ratio may exceed 0.5, but the resulting voltage across the transistor during the off-period will then be greater than $2.V_i$. When operating from a rectified mains voltage (typically 320 volt d.c.), this places a severe duty on the transistor.

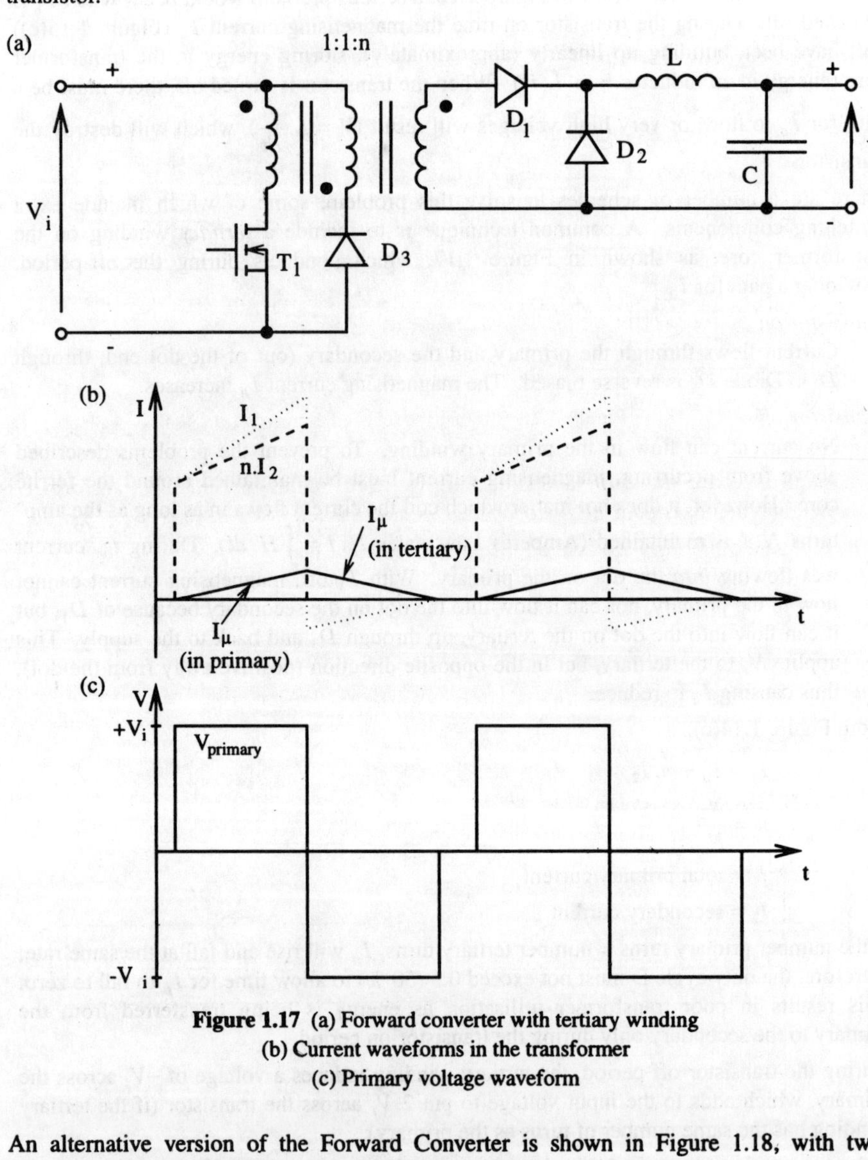

Figure 1.17 (a) Forward converter with tertiary winding
(b) Current waveforms in the transformer
(c) Primary voltage waveform

An alternative version of the Forward Converter is shown in Figure 1.18, with two transistors and two diodes instead of the tertiary winding.

Transistors T_1 and T_2 switch on together, and primary current passes down through the primary winding. When the transistors switch off, the magnetising current continues to flow in the primary, but now through diodes D_3 and D_4, back into the supply. With the diodes conducting, the voltage across the primary is reversed, resetting the core.

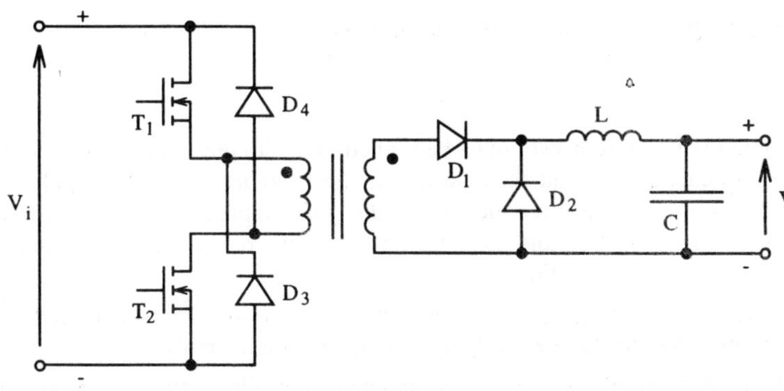

Figure 1.18 2-transistor forward converter

Although an extra transistor and diode are required in this circuit, the transformer is simpler, and the maximum transistor voltage is now limited to V_i, instead of $2 \times V_i$.

The d.c. gain of the forward converter (continuous mode) is:

$$\frac{V_o}{V_i} = n.D$$

The forward converter is normally used in the continuous mode, where the low current ripple does not place a heavy duty on the filter capacitor. At high powers (>500 watts) the poor transformer utilisation results in a bulky design, and other circuits are likely to be preferred.

HALF-BRIDGE CONVERTER

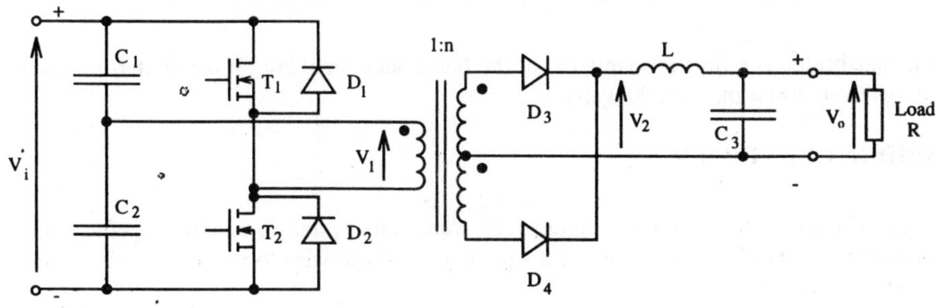

Figure 1.19 Half-bridge converter

In the half-bridge converter, capacitors C_1 and C_2 form a voltage divider for the input voltage V_i, the average voltage at the centre-point being $\frac{1}{2}V_i$. Transistors T_1 and T_2

conduct alternately, switching the primary voltage from $+\frac{1}{2}V_i$ to $-\frac{1}{2}V_i$. Thus the peak transistor voltage is V_i.

The d.c. gain of the half-bridge (continuous mode) is:

$$\frac{V_o}{V_i} = n.D$$

The duty ratio D of each transistor must be limited to 0.5, to prevent both transistors from conducting simultaneously, and thus causing a short circuit across the supply voltage. However, due to the full wave rectification of the centre-tapped transformer rectifier, the effective switching frequency, and the effective duty ratio, of the secondary voltage V_2 is double that of V_1, as shown in Figure 1.20.

Capacitors C_1 and C_2 block any d.c. component to the transformer primary, reducing the risk of core saturation due to unequal transistor conduction intervals.

As T_1 and T_2 are in series, the gate drives cannot be controlled from a common reference voltage. Usually the gate drive circuits have to be transformer coupled, which adds considerably to their complexity.

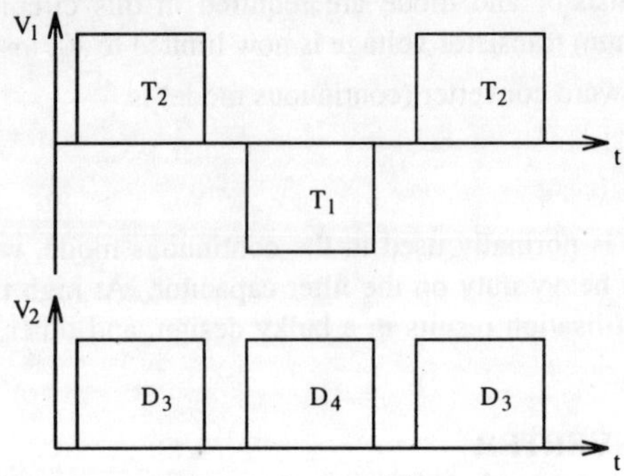

Figure 1.20 Half-bridge primary and secondary voltage waveforms

The half-bridge is a further adaptation of the basic buck regulator. It is popular in power ratings from 300 watts to 1200 watts.

BRIDGE CONVERTER

In the bridge converter shown in Figure 1.21, transistors T_1 and T_4 conduct together, then transistors T_2 and T_3, thus producing a square a.c. voltage waveform equal to $\pm V_i$ on the transformer primary.

The d.c. gain of the bridge converter (continuous mode) is:

$$\frac{V_o}{V_i} = 2.n.D$$

Capacitor C may be included to block any d.c. component arising due to unequal conduction periods on the positive and negative half-cycles, which would lead to saturation of the transformer core. With the capacitor, any imbalance in the conduction periods merely produces a shift in the mean d.c. level of the waveform, so the transformer sees a balanced volt-seconds on the two half-cycles.

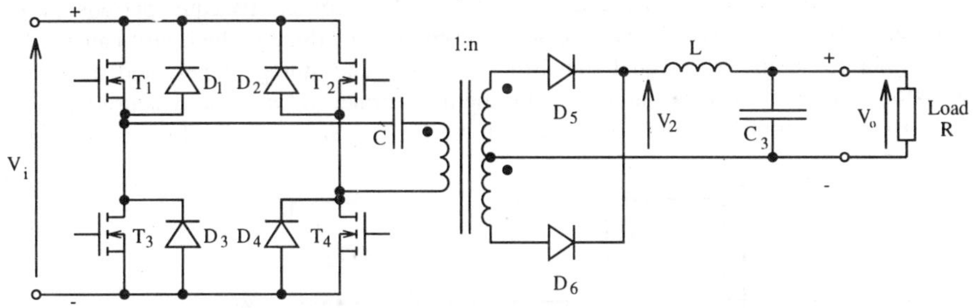

Figure 1.21 The bridge converter

The bridge converter is generally used in high power applications (greater than 750 watts) where the half-bridge capacitors C_1 and C_2 become very large. (With power ratings in excess of 1kW, capacitor C is usually omitted, as it also becomes very large.) The output power from a bridge converter is double that from a half-bridge with equally rated transistors. However, two extra transistors are required, and the gate drive circuits are similarly complex, requiring transformer coupling.

PUSH-PULL CONVERTER

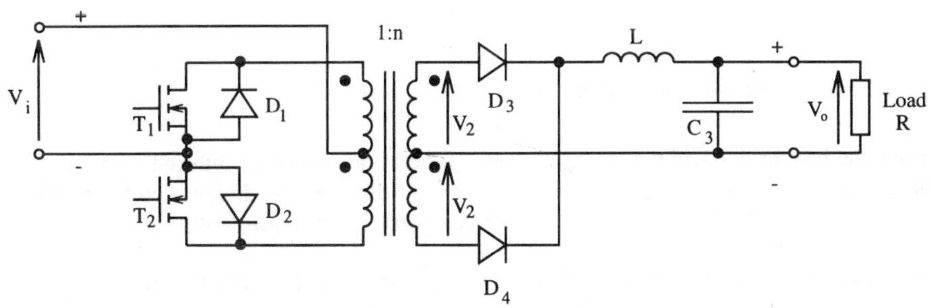

Figure 1.22 The push-pull converter

In the push-pull converter shown in Figure 1.22, another buck-derived circuit, T_1 and T_2 conduct alternately, switching current through the top half and the bottom half of the transformer primary, respectively. This effectively reverses the direction that current is passing through the primary, producing the transformer secondary voltage V_s as shown in Figure 1.23. This is then rectified and filtered to produce a smooth d.c. voltage.

The duty ratio of each transistor must be limited to 0.5 (50 %), to prevent an effective short circuit of the d.c. supply (this will occur if both transistors conduct simultaneously).

Energy is transferred from the primary to the secondary during both halves of the cycle, so the transformer utilisation is much better than in the forward converter.

Care must be taken to ensure that each transistor conducts for exactly equal periods, or a d.c. voltage component will be applied to the transformer primary which will cause the transformer to saturate. Unequal transistor switching and storage times, and unequal transistor saturation voltages, can also cause the transformer to "walk" into saturation. A transformer with an air gap in the core is often used to prevent saturation from occurring.

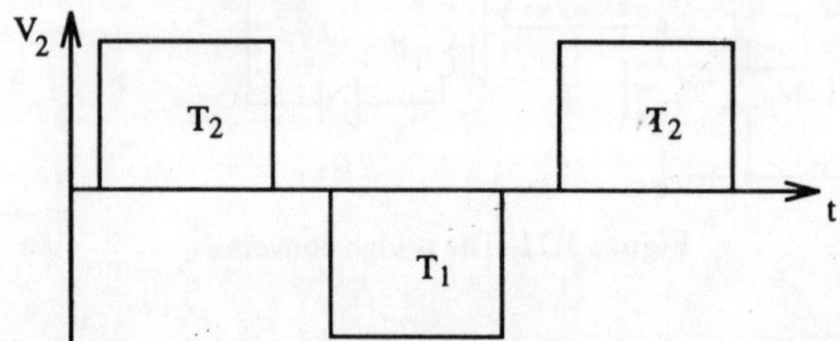

Figure 1.23 Secondary voltage waveform for the push-pull converter

The input voltage V_i is applied across half of the primary winding, so the voltage across the full primary is $2.V_i$. Hence the transistors need to have a voltage rating in excess of $2.V_i$.

The push-pull converter is essentially a buck-type regulator with isolation. The d.c. gain (continuous mode) is:

$$\frac{V_o}{V_i} = 2.n.D$$

where: n = the transformer turns ratio
D = the duty ratio of each transistor.

Unlike the half-bridge and the bridge converters, both transistors are referred to the same voltage (ie. the sources are connected together), so they can be driven directly by the control circuit, without the need for isolating transformers in the gate drive.

SWITCHED MODE POWER SUPPLIES WITH MULTIPLE OUTPUTS

In many applications, more than one output is required, with each output likely to have different voltage and current specifications.

The basic buck, buck-boost and boost regulators are not suitable for multiple output applications. However, multiple outputs can be readily obtained using any of the converters which have an isolating transformer, by employing a separate secondary winding for each output, as shown in the forward converter in Figure 1.24.

In this circuit, each output voltage will be determined by the appropriate turns ratio n_1, n_2 or n_3.

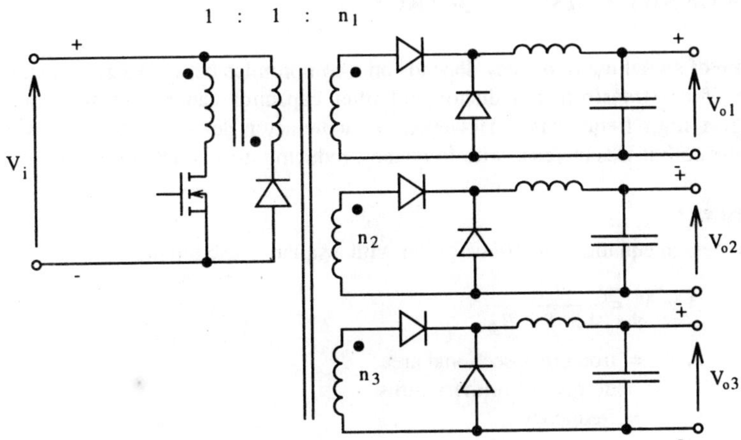

Figure 1.24 Forward converter with three outputs

1.6 CIRCUIT DESIGN CONSIDERATIONS

CHOICE OF SWITCHING FREQUENCY

The choice of switching frequency depends on a compromise between size and efficiency. The size of the transformer, inductor and filter capacitor can be greatly reduced by operating at high frequencies. However, semiconductor device switching losses and transformer core losses increase with frequency, reducing the overall circuit efficiency.

Transformer

The basic design equation for a transformer with a square wave input is:

$$A \times N_1 = \frac{V_1}{4 \times f \times B_M}$$

where: A = iron cross-sectional area
N_1 = number of primary turns
f = frequency
B_M = maximum flux density (avoiding saturation of the core)

For a sinusoidal waveform this becomes:

$$A \times N_1 = \frac{V_1}{4.44 \times f \times B_M}$$

It can be seen from this equation that the size of the transformer is inversely dependent on frequency; therefore operation at high frequency will reduce the transformer size.

Transformer efficiency, however, is reduced as frequency increases, as the eddy current and hysteresis losses both depend on frequency.

Filter Inductor

For the continuous mode buck regulator:

$$L \geq \frac{R.(1-D)}{2.f}$$

Therefore the value of inductance needed decreases at higher frequencies.

Filter Capacitor

The output ripple voltage depends on the value of filter capacitance, the switching frequency and the load.

For the buck regulator:

$$C > \frac{V_o}{\Delta V_o} \cdot \frac{(1-D)}{8.f^2.L}$$

$$> \frac{V_o}{\Delta V_o} \cdot \frac{1}{4.f.R}$$

Thus, by increasing the frequency, the capacitance can be reduced without increasing the ripple voltage.

Switching Transistors

Typical transistor switching waveforms are shown in Figure 1.25, including the power dissipated in the device ($P = v_T . i$).

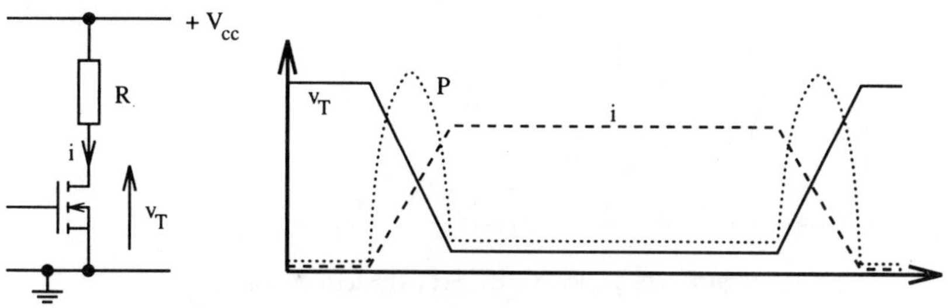

Figure 1.25 Voltage, current and power waveforms of a transistor during switching

Clearly, the semiconductor switching losses will increase with frequency. Switching devices are continually improving, particularly with the use of MOSFETs instead of bipolar transistors, so this limitation on switching frequency is much less important than it was a few years ago.

Electromagnetic Interference

In addition, problems due to EMI increase as the switching frequency increases.

The reduced efficiency of high frequency SMPS creates problems of cooling the switching devices. This may require the use of larger heatsinks and/or the inclusion of fan cooling, which will add to the size and weight of the power supply. Most power supplies are designed to operate with switching frequencies between 40 kHz and 200 kHz, although some designers are experimenting into the Megahertz range.

DESIGN EXAMPLE

Specification

Input voltage	300 volts ±10%
Output voltage	5 volts
Output voltage ripple	< 50 mV peak-to-peak
Output current	3 A to 30 A

Topology

Maximum output power = 150 watts

Therefore, choose a *Forward Converter*

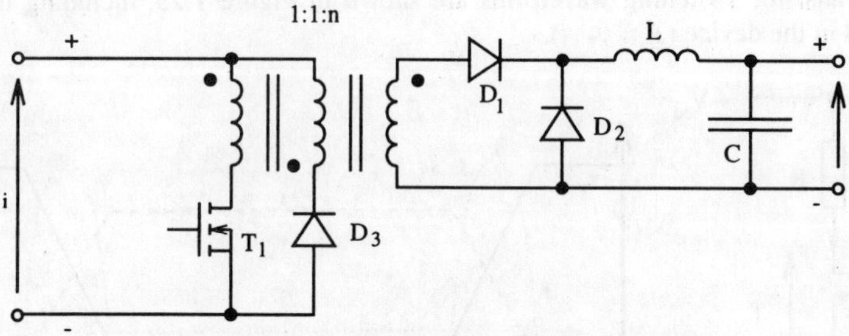

Figure 1.26 Forward converter (with tertiary winding)

Switching Frequency

Switching frequencies are usually in the range 80 kHz to 200 kHz. Choose 100 kHz as a sensible switching frequency.

Transformer Turns Ratio

For a forward converter:

$$V_o = n.D.V_i$$

But: $D < 0.5$, therefore, taking $D_{max} = 0.45$, and allowing for a 0.8 volt drop across the secondary diode and the inductor resistance, the worst case is:

$$5.8 = n \times 0.45 \times (300 - 10\%)$$

Which gives $n = 0.048$

Inductor

For continuous mode operation:

$$L > ½.R_{max}.T.(1 - D_{min})$$

$$R_{max} = \frac{5\ volts}{3\ amperes} = 1.67\ ohms$$

$$D_{min} = \frac{V_o}{n.V_{i(max)}} = 0.37$$

Therefore, $L > 5.3\ \mu H$

Choose $L = 10\ \mu H$

Capacitor

The output ripple voltage is given by:

$$\Delta V_o = \frac{V_o . T^2 . (1 - D)}{8 . L . C}$$

Therefore:

$$C > \frac{V_o}{\Delta V_o} \times \frac{T^2}{8 . L} \times (1 - D_{\min})$$

Gives $C > 79\ \mu F$

Ripple Current

During t_{off} , $V_L = -5\ volts$

$$V_L = L . \frac{di}{dt} = L \times \frac{\Delta I}{t_{off}}$$

Gives:

$$\Delta I = 3.15 \quad amperes$$

Capacitor ESR

$$\Delta V_o = ESR \times \Delta I$$

Gives:

$$ESR < 15.9\ m\Omega$$

Transistor Ratings

$$Peak\ transistor\ voltage = 2 \times V_{i(max)}$$
$$= 660 \quad volts$$

The transistor should be rated to take into account any voltage spikes which may be present; therefore, a voltage rating of 1000 volts would be suitable.

$$Peak\ transistor\ current = n . \left(I_o + \frac{\Delta I}{2} \right)$$
$$= 1.52 \quad amperes$$

In rating the transistor, allowance should also be made for the transformer magnetising current.

CIRCUITS WITH NON-IDEAL COMPONENTS

Diode Forward Volt Drop

The forward volt drop of the rectifying diode(s) on the transformer secondary constitutes a major power loss in the power supply. A 0.7 volt drop in a 5 volt output reduces the overall efficiency by approximately 15%. This can be reduced by the use of Schottky diodes, with their lower on-state volt drop of 0.4-0.5 volts, but the losses are still considerable. This power loss is even more serious with the new requirement for 3.3 volt outputs. In this situation it can be worth replacing the diodes with transistors, used as *synchronous rectifiers*. These operate on the principle that the on-state voltage across a transistor is considerably less than that for a diode.

If a MOSFET is to be used as a synchronous rectifier, care must be taken to ensure that the internal source-drain body diode does not cause problems. As a consequence, it is usual to operate the MOSFET in reverse, with current flowing from the drain to the source (this mode of operation is perfectly satisfactory).

In Figure 1.27, the switching of transistor T_2 is synchronised to T_1, whereas T_3 is on when T_2 is off. The internal body diodes should never conduct (they usually have poor characteristics): a gate pulse should be applied to T_2 just as the diode becomes forward biased, effectively short-circuiting the diode.

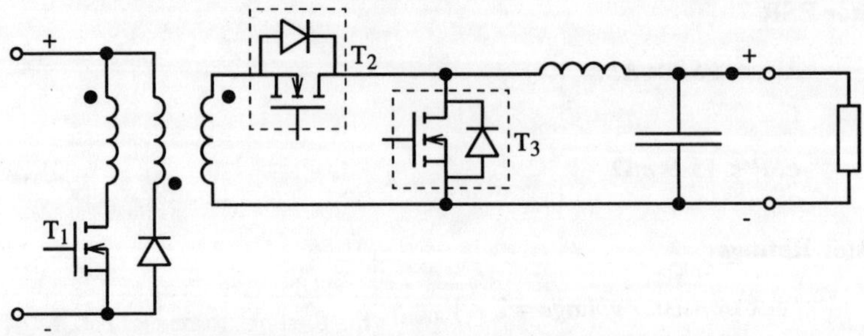

Figure 1.27 Forward converter using synchronous rectifiers

If suitable transistors are chosen with a low on-state resistance, circuit losses can be considerably reduced. However, this has to be balanced with the increased circuit complexity, and also the power requirements to drive the transistors.

The diode volt drop should also be taken into account when selecting the transformer turns ratio (the secondary voltage should be approximately 0.7 volts higher than for the ideal case).

Inductor Resistance

In a Buck regulator (and its derivatives with an isolating transformer), the inductor resistance reduces the output voltage, and also affects the open loop load regulation in the continuous conduction mode. Taking the inductor resistance into account, the output voltage of a buck regulator is given by:

$$\frac{V_o}{V_i} = D.\frac{R}{R+r_L}$$

where:

R = load resistance

r_L = inductor resistance

Transformer Leakage Inductance (Primary)

When the main switching transistor(s) are turned off, it is very important to provide a path for the transformer current to continue to flow, otherwise very high voltages can arise due to suddenly chopping the current through the leakage inductance ($V_L = L_{L1}.\frac{di}{dt}$). This path is normally provided by including diodes in anti-parallel with transistors, so that the stored energy is returned to the supply.

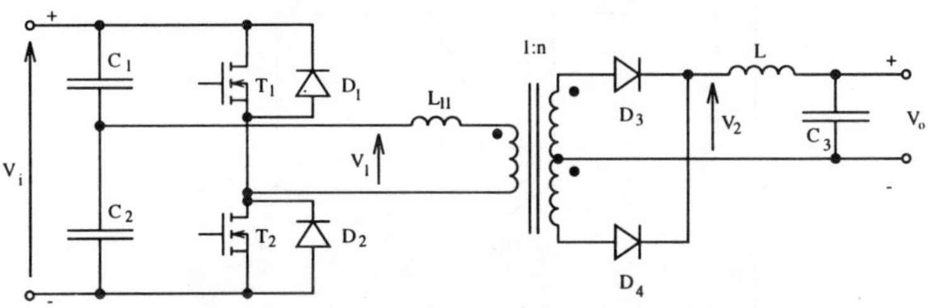

Figure 1.28 Half-bridge converter showing primary leakage inductance

The primary leakage inductance is also a major source of EMI produced by the power supply.

In some cases, the primary leakage inductance can resonate with the transistor internal capacitance, to produce a high frequency ripple. This then has to be damped out with the aid of snubber circuits, increasing circuit losses.

Transormer Leakage Inductance (Secondary)

Just before the switching transistor is turned on, the load current is circulating through the flywheel diode D_2 , and the voltage $V_1 = 0$. When the transistor is turned on, the current through the leakage inductance cannot change instantaneously to the full inductor current, so for a short period Δt current will flow through D_2 and the transformer secondary simultaneously, such that:

$$I_s + I_{D2} = I_L$$

During this period, $V_1 = 0$, and the voltage across L_{L2} is V_s. Hence:

$$V_s = L_{L2}.\frac{di}{dt}$$

$$= L_{L2} \cdot \frac{I_L}{\Delta t}$$

Therefore:

$$\Delta t = \frac{L_{L2} \cdot I_L}{V_s}$$

The above reduces the effective transistor on-time t_{on} by Δt , and hence reduces the effective duty ratio D and the average output voltage by an amount depending on the load current.

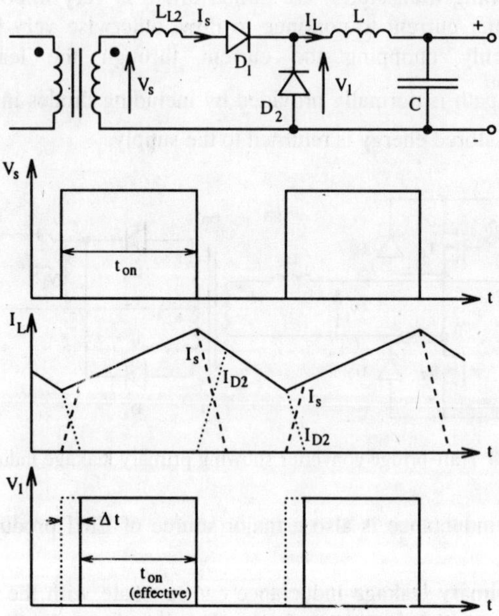

Figure 1.29 Effect of secondary leakage inductance

In a single output closed loop system, the effects of primary and secondary leakage inductances on the output voltage will be compensated for by an appropriate adjustment in the duty ratio D.

In a multiple output converter, the primary leakage inductance is inside the feedback loop; therefore there will be little effect in a closed loop system. However, the secondary leakage inductance of the auxiliary output is outside the feedback loop, and will produce an adverse effect on the load regulation on that output.

The transformer windings should be wound as close as possible to reduce the leakage inductance to a minimum.

Switching Transistors

The transistor "non-ideal" parameters do not usually cause serious problems in medium frequency (80-150 kHz) off-line power supplies. As the transistor is usually on the high-voltage low-current side, the conduction losses are not as severe as with the rectifying diodes. Switching losses normally only become significant if the frequency is greater than 150 kHz.

Capacitor

As mentioned previously, the capacitor ESR is usually the decisive factor in choosing the main filter capacitor.

1.7 OTHER SWITCHING CONVERTERS

CUK CONVERTERS

Much interest has been excited by the characteristics of the Cuk converters, developed by Professor Slobodan Cuk of California Institute of Technology.

The basic Cuk regulator is derived from the boost and the buck regulators, combining the characteristic low input current ripple of the boost regulator with the low output current ripple of the buck regulator.

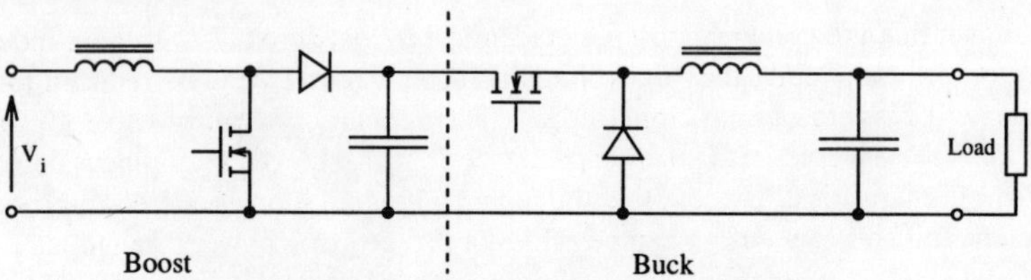

Figure 1.30 A combined boost-buck regulator

The boost-buck circuit above can be simplified to the Cuk regulator shown in Figure 1.31.

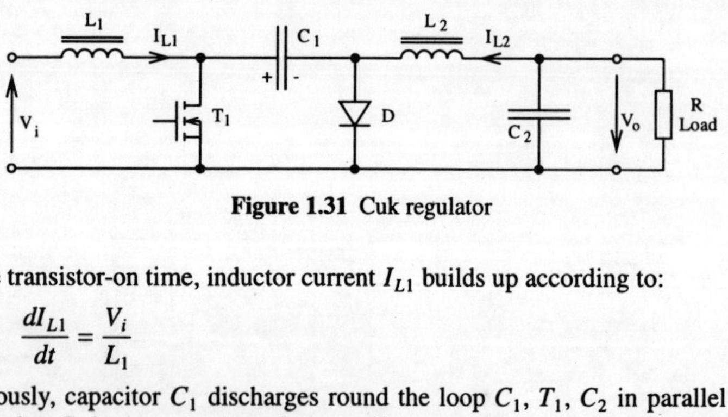

Figure 1.31 Cuk regulator

During the transistor-on time, inductor current I_{L1} builds up according to:

$$\frac{dI_{L1}}{dt} = \frac{V_i}{L_1}$$

Simultaneously, capacitor C_1 discharges round the loop C_1, T_1, C_2 in parallel with load R, L_2, charging C_2 in the opposite polarity to V_i.

When T_1 is switched off, inductor current I_{L1} flows through C_1 and the diode, recharging C_1. Simultaneously, inductor L_2 maintains current round the loop L_2, diode D, C_2 in parallel with load R.

This circuit has a very low output current ripple due to the presence of L_2 in the output circuit, similar to the buck regulator. It also has a very low ripple current in the input circuit due to the presence of L_1, similar to the boost regulator. A further advantage is that only one transistor is required, with no base drive coupling problems as in the bridge and half-bridge circuits.

The d.c. gain of a Cuk regulator is (neglecting losses):

$$\frac{V_o}{V_i} = \frac{D}{1 - D}$$

where V_o is of the opposite polarity to V_i. This is the same as the buck-boost regulator, but without the high input and output current ripple of the buck-boost.

A disadvantage of the Cuk regulator is that the series capacitor is the main energy storage/transfer component, instead of an inductor as in most other circuits. This capacitor, therefore, has to be relatively large, and capable of handling high r.m.s. currents, so a low ESR is essential.

It can be shown that the voltage across L_2 is identical to that across L_1. If these inductors are wound on the same core, then the voltage induced across L_2 can be reduced to zero, hence there will be zero current ripple in L_2. Theoretically, this means that C_2 can be removed; however, in practice a small capacitance is still required to compensate for the effects of circuit parasitics. By coupling the input and output inductors on a single core, a more efficient and compact design can be achieved for the same power throughput.

The Cuk converter with an isolation transformer is shown in Figure 1.32.

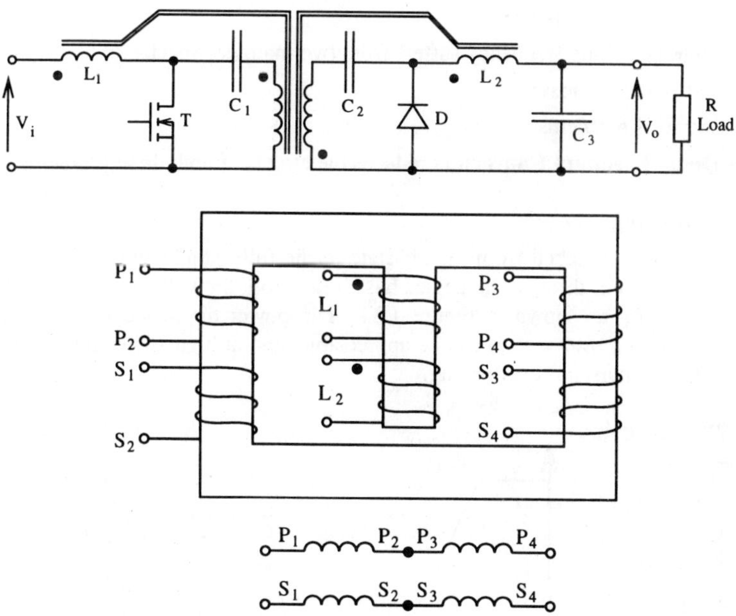

Figure 1.32 Cuk converter with the isolation transformer integrated with the input and output inductors

The transformer primary is P_1 to P_4, and the secondary S_1 to S_4. The coupled inductor is wound on the central limb with the air gap.

The circuit operates in a similar fashion to the basic Cuk regulator, with the coupling capacitor split up either side of the transformer. The presence of a capacitor in series with the primary (and secondary) windings prevents any d.c. components in the transformer, which might lead to the transformer saturating.

If the transformer is magnetically coupled to the two inductors, it is theoretically possible to tune both the input and output current ripples to zero. In practice, very low values can be readily achieved. This attractive feature removes the necessity of a large value, low ESR output capacitor, and greatly reduces the EMI problems on the input and output leads.

RESONANT CONVERTERS

The advantages of operating with a high switching frequency include:

- reduced transformer size,
- reduced inductor size,
- reduced capacitor size,
- improved transient response.

However, a high switching frequency suffers from two main drawbacks:

- increased switching losses,
- increased EMI problems.

The use of **Quasi-Resonant Converters** reduces the effects of both these problems.

Transistor Switching

When a transistor is switched from the off-state to the fully conducting state, there is a period when the current through the device has risen before the voltage across the device has dropped to zero, as shown in Figure 1.33. The power dissipated in the transistor during this interval (*power* = $V \cdot i$) can be appreciable, and at high switching frequencies this can lead to the transistor overheating.

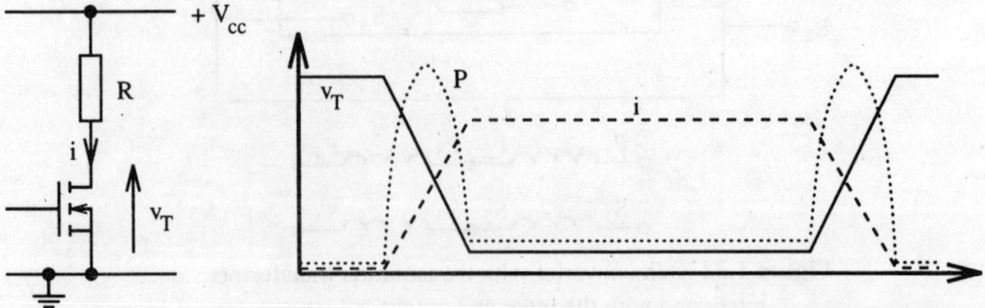

Figure 1.33 Voltage, current and power waveforms of a transistor during switching

The exact shape of these curves depends on the type of transistors used (e.g. MOSFETs or bipolar transistors).

In quasi-resonant power supplies, the main switching waveforms are designed to be sinusoidal rather than square, with transistor switching taking place at either natural current zeros (zero-current switched converters), or natural voltage zeros (zero-voltage switched converters).

Zero-Current Switched (ZCS) Converters

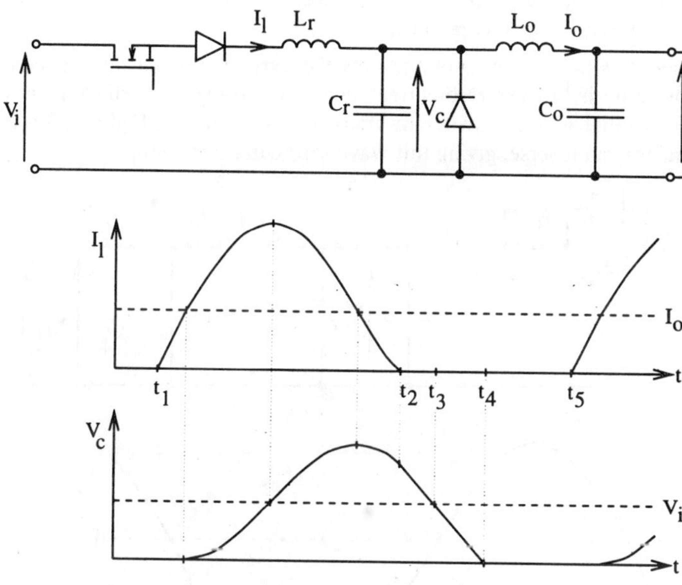

Figure 1.34 Half-wave, zero-current switched buck regulator

The circuit shown in Figure 1.34 is a conventional buck regulator, with a zero-current switch added.

The circuit operates as follows:

t_1 The transistor is switched on. Current i_L cannot increase instantaneously due to the inductor L_r, therefore the load current I_o continues to flywheel through the diode. Voltage v_C is therefore held at zero, so I_L builds up linearly:

$$V_{in} = L.\frac{di_L}{dt}$$

When $i_L = I_o$, current ceases to flywheel through the diode, and excess current $(i_L - I_o)$ charges capacitor C_r.

Both i_L and v_C vary sinusoidally at the resonant frequency until t_2, with v_C peaking when $i_L = I_o$.

t_2 $i_L = 0$, therefore I_o is supplied from C_r, discharging C_r linearly. The transistor will cease conducting at t_2. The transistor base drive should be removed between t_2 and t_3, to prevent it from conducting again at t_3.

t_3 $v_C = 0$, therefore I_o flows through the flywheel diode.

t_4 The transistor is switched on again, and the cycle repeated.

It can be seen from the above that both switch-on and switch-off occur at natural current zeros, greatly reducing the transistor switching losses. In addition, as there are no very fast edges, EMI is also considerably reduced.

The diode in series with the transistor prevents the current through the inductor from reversing, so the result is ½-wave zero-current switching. If the series diode is moved so that it is in anti-parallel with the switching transistor, as shown in Figure 1.35, current through the inductor can reverse, giving full-wave zero-current switching.

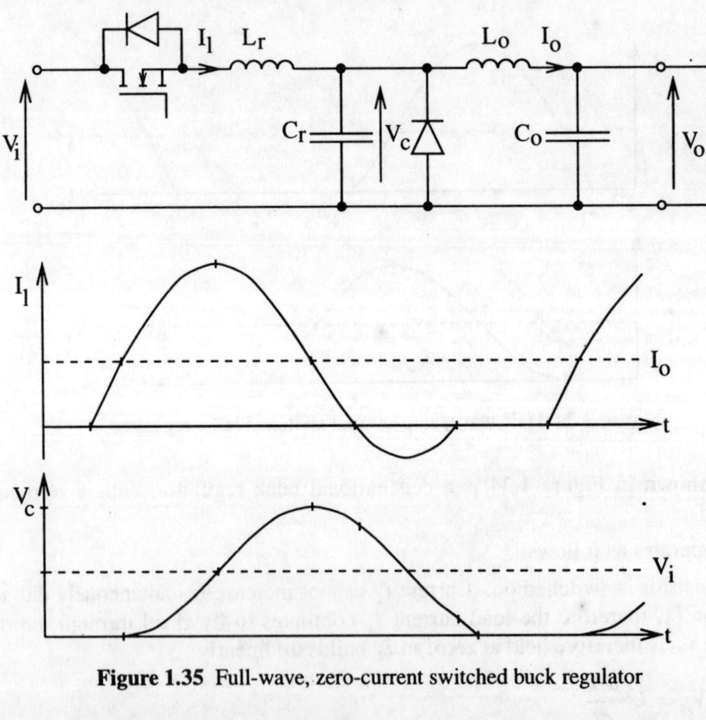

Figure 1.35 Full-wave, zero-current switched buck regulator

An advantage of full-wave ZCS converters over ½-wave ZCS converters is that the output voltage in the former is not dependent on loading, giving very good load regulation. The d.c. gain becomes:

$$\frac{V_o}{V_i} = \frac{f_s}{f_n}$$

where:

f_s = switching frequency

f_n = resonant frequency $= \dfrac{1}{2\pi\sqrt{L_r C_r}}$

Thus, regulation is achieved by *frequency modulation*, rather than by pulse width modulation at constant switching frequency as with more conventional SMPS.

Zero-Voltage Switched (ZVS) Converters

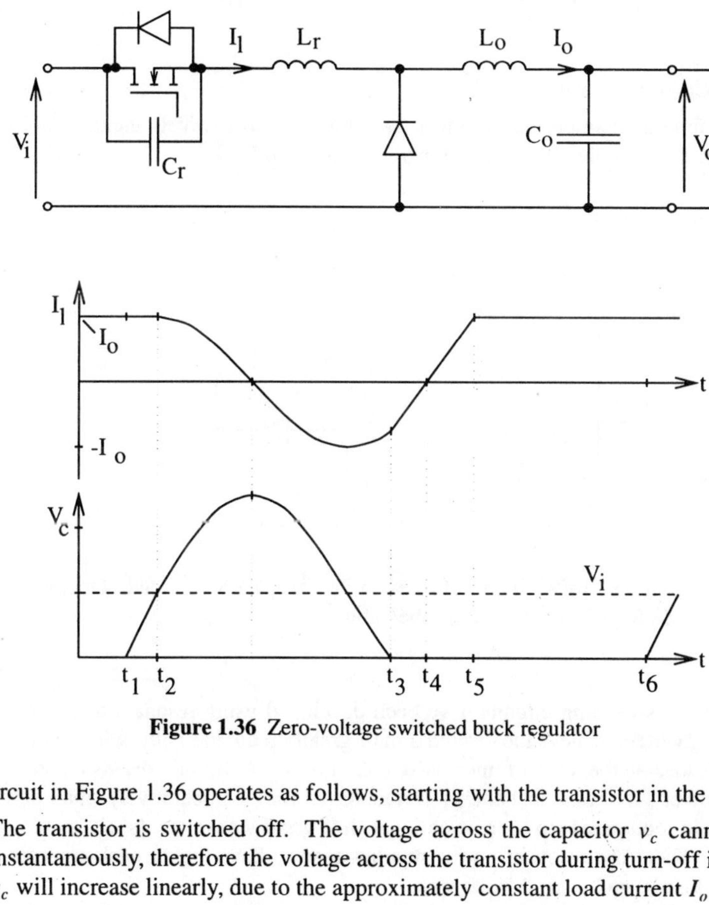

Figure 1.36 Zero-voltage switched buck regulator

The circuit in Figure 1.36 operates as follows, starting with the transistor in the on-state:

t_1 The transistor is switched off. The voltage across the capacitor v_c cannot change instantaneously, therefore the voltage across the transistor during turn-off is zero. v_c will increase linearly, due to the approximately constant load current I_o.

t_2 $v_c = V_i$, therefore the flywheel diode is no longer reverse biased and will start to conduct load current. i_L will therefore start to fall, with C_r and L_r resonating.

t_3 $v_c = 0$, and cannot go negative due to the anti-parallel diode. Current i_L increases linearly.

The base/gate drive to the transistor should be applied during this period (as the anti-parallel diode is conducting, it will not conduct until t_4).

t_4 The transistor starts to conduct again.

t_5 $i_L = I_o$, therefore the flywheel diode is reverse biased.

t_6 The transistor is switched off again, and the cycle repeated.

It can be seen from the above that both transistor turn-on and turn-off occur at natural voltage zeros; therefore switching losses are greatly reduced.

Output voltage control is achieved by controlling the period $(t_6 - t_5)$, ie. by frequency modulation.

Resonant Converters with Isolation

There are a large number of resonant switching circuits which include an isolation transformer, an example of which is shown in Figure 1.37.

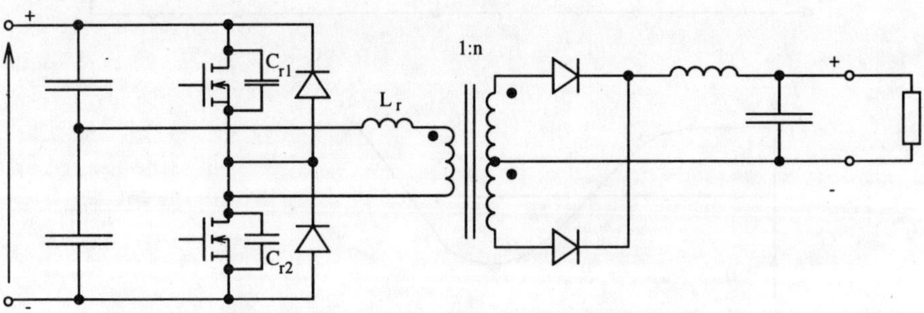

Figure 1.37 Half-wave, zero-voltage, switched half-bridge converter

This is a conventional forward converter, with ½-wave, ZVS included. Operation is very similar to the ZVS buck regulator described above.

Summary

Many different switching circuits have been developed using resonant techniques. ZCS and ZVS converters achieve the desired aim of greatly reducing both switching losses and EMI problems, at the cost of increased complexity. A further disadvantage of most resonant power supplies is that energy is transferred for a comparatively small percentage of the cycle compared to a conventional full-wave converter (such as the bridge converter). Therefore resonant power supplies tend to have higher peak currents (hence higher i^2R losses) and/or peak voltages.

ZVS converters have an advantage over ZCS converters at high frequencies, due to the internal capacitance of the switching transistor. With ZCS, the energy stored in this capacitance is dissipated in the transistor at switch-on, adding to the switching losses. This problem is eliminated with ZVS.

A further advantage of ZVS at high frequencies is that it is possible to use the transistor capacitance as the resonant capacitor, avoiding the use of a discrete device. In addition, circuits with an isolation transformer can use the leakage inductance as the resonant inductor. A very compact, efficient design can thus be achieved.

ZCS converters are typically used up to about 1 MHz; however, ZVS converters have been built which operate in excess of 10 MHz.

1.8 SIMULATION OF SMPS USING SPICE

Conventionally, the process of designing a power supply involves carrying out a paper design (along the lines of the previous sections). A prototype is then constructed, and subjected to rigorous testing. Usually a number of modifications are necessary, which may require the construction of a second prototype, which in turn has to be tested. This design, build, test, re-design loop may have to be followed several times before a final design is reached, and can be very time-consuming and expensive.

Usually, the reasons for failure of the prototype can be assigned to device and/or circuit parasitic elements, which can be very difficult to take account of analytically, the design equations becoming increasingly complex and unwieldy as each parasitic element is added. Computer simulation packages such as SPICE or SABER can be extremely useful in these situations, as the effects of the parasitic elements can readily be tested.

Essentially, the simulation package can be considered as a software breadboard, allowing the designer to test the initial design in software without the requirement for building a hardware version. Modifications can readily be tested, and only when it is considered that the design is robust is it necessary to build a prototype, by which time the designer may have confidence that the design will operate correctly.

The major advantages of using a simulator are decreases in design time (and hence cost), and the ability to try a number of different options without the requirement for building each of them.

SPICE

The most widely used simulator package is SPICE (Simulation Program with Integrated Circuit Emphasis), developed at the University of California, Berkeley, in 1975. Since then there have been tremendous improvements in the simulation algorithms, which are now more robust and powerful. A number of commercial simulation packages have been produced based on SPICE, including MicroSims PSPICE, Intusoft ISSPICE and MetaSoftware HSPICE, all of which are suitable for simulating power electronic circuits.

Circuit Simulation Using SPICE

SPICE is base on nodal analysis, in which unknown voltages and currents are determined using Kirchhoff's current equations. The circuit is described by a Netlist, which lists all the components, their values, and their position in the circuit. Every node in the circuit is numbered, and the position of each component is given by the node to which it is connected.

The Netlist consists of the following:

Title
Analysis control statement
Output control statement
Circuit topology
Energy source
.END statement

An example of a buck regulator and its associated Netlist is shown in Figure 1.38.

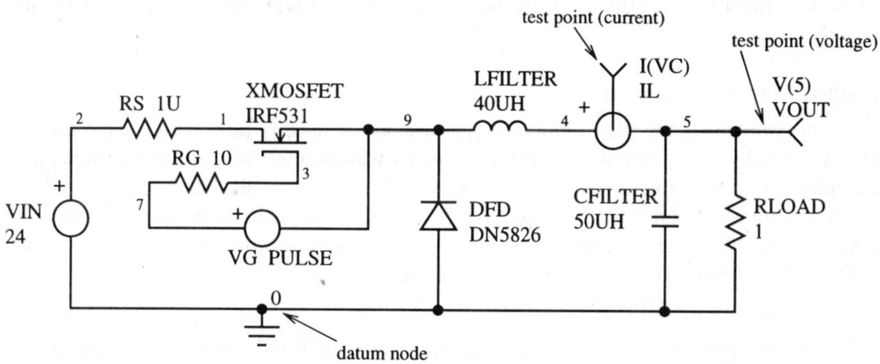

Figure 1.38 Buck regulator drawn using SPICE schematic capture

Netlist	**Explanation**
BUCK SIMULATION	circuit title
*SPICE_NET	comment
*INCLUDE POWMOS.LIB	to include the power MOSFET library
*TIME PERIOD = 10USECS; f = 100 kHz	comment
.TRAN 0.2U 1000U 900U UIC	steady state transient analysis control statement
.OPTIONS METHOD=GEAR RELTOL=0.01	optional cards to increase accuracy
*ALIAS I(VC)=IL	test point to observe current
*ALIAS V(5)=VOUT	test point to observe voltage
.PRINT TRAN I(VC) V(5)	to view the voltage and current waveforms
RS 2 1 1M	resistor included to assist convergence
LFILTER 9 4 40UH IC=5	with initial conditions to study steady state behaviour
CFILTER 5 0 1000UF IC=5	with initial conditions to study steady state behaviour
RLOAD 5 0 1	
RG 3 7 10	
DFD 0 9 DN5826	diode model called from device library
XMOS 1 3 9 IRF531	diode model called from device library
VIN 2 0 24VOLTS	input d.c. voltage
VG 7 9 PULSE 0 10 0.5U 0.1U 0.1U 2.08U 10U	gate pulse
VC 4 5 0	
.END	end of netlist

(Written using Intusoft ISSPICE)

Most simulation packages offer a schematic capture input, in which the user draws the circuit diagram, from which the Netlist is generated automatically.

Title and .END Statement

All Netlists must have a title line at the beginning, and a ".END" statement as the last line of the Netlist.

Analysis Control Statement

Transient Analysis is the most common type of analysis used in power supply circuits; it is used to produce the standard voltage and current waveforms. Voltages and currents are computed as a function of time over a specified time interval. The example below specifies a transient analysis, in steps of 0.2 μs, from 900 μs to 1000 μs. Thus results from the first 900 μs are discarded to allow time for the start-up transients to die away: results from the next 100 μs are fed into the output file.

```
.TRAN 0.2U 1000U 900U
```

SPICE also supports d.c. analysis, a.c. analysis, Fourier analysis, noise analysis, and pole-zero analysis.

OPTIONS statements are used to set various program options; eg.

```
.OPTIONS METHOD=GEAR RELTOL=0.01
```

RELTOL sets the accuracy obtained before stopping the iteration. Reducing this to 0.001 will increase the accuracy, but at the cost of increased computational time.

Output Control Statement

The output is specified through the use of a .PRINT, .PLOT, or .VIEW statement, to generate the output data file. For example, the following prints the transient current through voltage source VC, and the transient voltage at node 5.

```
.PRINT I(VC) V(5)
```

All the standard SPICE packages have a graphical output, to view the output waveforms.

Circuit Topology

Each component in the circuit is described by its reference, the nodes to which it is connected, and a value. The first letter of the element name specifies the type of element. For example:

```
RG 3 7 10
```

describes a resistor called RG, between nodes 3 and 7, of value 10 ohms. A number may be followed by one of the following scaling factors:

$T = 10^{12}$	$G = 10^{9}$	$MEG = 10^{6}$	$K = 10^{3}$	$m = 10^{-3}$
$u = 10^{-6}$	$n = 10^{-9}$	$p = 10^{-12}$	$f = 10^{-15}$	

Letters immediately following a number other than scale factors are ignored. Hence, the "ohm" is ignored in the following statement:

```
RG 3 7 10ohm
```

Initial conditions can be included to speed up the simulation; for example:

CFILTER 5 0 50UF IC=5

describes a 50 μF capacitor with an initial voltage of 5 volts across it, so simulation time does not have to be spent waiting for the capacitor to charge up. In a similar manner, inductors can be given an initial current. The initial conditions are only activated if "UIC" is included in the .TRAN control statement.

Transformers are normally modelled as coupled inductors; for example:

L1 2 0 10M
L2 4 0 0.1M
K12 0.98

L1 is the primary inductance, L2 the secondary inductance, and K12 the coupling coefficient between L1 and L2. This corresponds to the conventional transformer equivalent circuit in Figure 1.39.

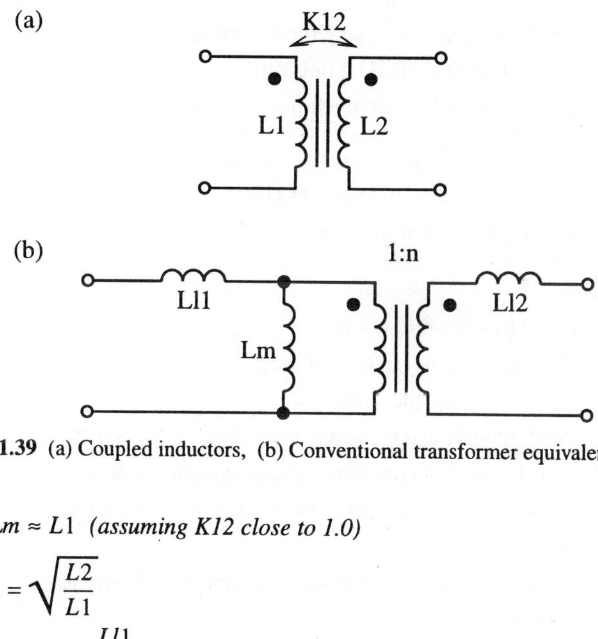

Figure 1.39 (a) Coupled inductors, (b) Conventional transformer equivalent circuit

$$Lm \approx L1 \ \textit{(assuming K12 close to 1.0)}$$

$$n = \sqrt{\frac{L2}{L1}}$$

$$K12 = 1 - \frac{Ll1}{Lm}$$

The above is a linear model of a transformer. It is possible to include non-linearities (to take account of core non-linearities), but this adds considerably to the complexity.

Most popular versions of SPICE have a library of active components (eg. power MOSFETS, diodes etc.) which can be called up. If a suitable model does not exist, it is possible to create one.

There are two rules which must be obeyed:

There are two rules which must be obeyed:

- There must always be a datum node numbered "0" in the circuit.
- The circuit must not contain any loops of only voltage sources and inductors, or only current sources and capacitors.

Energy Source

All SPICE circuits must have an energy source included, the most common being d.c., sinusoidal a.c., and pulse.

A 24 volt d.c. voltage source between nodes 2 and 0 (node 2 positive) is given by:

VIN 2 0 24VOLTS

A 50 Hz sine wave with a peak of 100 volts and zero d.c. offset is given by:

VAC 1 0 SIN 0 100VOLTS 50HZ

A series of pulses can be generated by using the following:

VG 7 9 PULSE 0 10 0.5 0.1U 0.1U 2.08U 10U

This describes a voltage source VG, between nodes 7 (positive) and 9, a series of pulses, initial value 0 volts, pulsed value 10 volts, a delay of 0.5 μs to the first pulse, a fall time of 0.1 μs, a rise time of 0.1 μs, a pulse width (at pulsed voltage) of 2.08 μs, and a period between pulses of 10 μs (ie. a pulse train at 100 kHz).

Current sources are generated in a similar fashion to voltage sources.

Simulation Steps

The standard steps used by the simulator are:

- Find the initial operating point (d.c. solution).
- Choose a first time step (use the default).
- Form approximate models using discrete derivatives (C's and L's).
- Linearise the non-linear elements forming approximate models.
- Form the linear equations associated with the approximate circuit.
- Solve the linear equations.
- Iterate until a solution is reached or reduce the time step and try again.
- Check for accuracy.
- If accurate, continue forward in time, else reduce time step and try again.

Limitations of SPICE

1. SPICE was originally designed for the simulation of integrated circuits. Power converters generally have large time constants due to L-C filters; consequently the simulation can take a long time. There are a number of techniques by which the simulation time can be reduced, such as using initial conditions to pre-charge the capacitors and inductors, and using simplified device models. However, this is now less necessary than before, due to the greatly increased speed of current computers.

2. SPICE does not perform a.c. (frequency domain) analysis of non-linear circuits. This is because the a.c. analysis reduces a circuit to a linear small signal representation about its large signal operating point. Thus it is not possible to model properly the pulse width modulators in power electronic switching circuits. However, this can be achieved using other techniques, such as state space averaging.

SPICE is an extremely useful tool for designing power supply circuits. However, like most computer packages, it has its own idiosyncracies, and its full value is not achieved unless sufficient time is spent mastering them.

SECTION 2

WOUND COMPONENT DESIGN AND PRODUCTION

MAGNETICS: DEFINITIONS AND EQUATIONS

PARAMETER	SYMBOL	UNIT
Magnetic flux density	B	*tesla, (T)*
Magnetic field intensity	H	*ampere* m^{-1}
Permeability	$\mu = \frac{B}{H}$	*henry* m^{-1}, $(H\,m^{-1})$
Permeability (free space)	μ_o	*henry* m^{-1}
Permeability (relative)	μ_r	
Effective magnetic area of core	A_c	m^2
Mean magnetic path length	l_m	*m*
Air gap length	l_g	*m*
Magnetic flux	ϕ	*weber, (Wb)*
Magnetic potential	mmf	*ampere, (A)*
Inductance	L	*henry, (H)*
Inductance index	A_L	*nH* $turn^{-2}$
Wire csa	A	m^2
Number of turns	N	*N*
Mean length of turn	l_t	*m*
Current density	J	*J, ampere* m^{-2}, $(A\,m^{-2})$
Resistivity	ρ	*ohm-m,* (Ωm)
Energy	W	*W, joule, (J)*

REVIEW OF BASIC ELECTROMAGNETICS

Wound components, transformers and inductors (chokes), for use in SMPS, are designed using sets of rules developed by Engineers and characteristics supplied by manufacturers of magnetic cores and of wires. Because of this, it is not usual for designers to make complex theoretical electromagnetic calculations.

The techniques described in this book follow this methodology, and a brief description only is given of the electromagnetic concepts associated with transformer and inductor operation.

Magnetic Fields:

Single Wire

Every electric current has an associated magnetic field: the simplest form is that around a straight wire. The field is said to be *soleniodal* and exists coaxially around the wire. The right-hand screw rule can be used to determine the direction of the flux lines and the field, viz., if it imagined that a corkscrew is moved along the wire in the direction of the current, the magnetic flux will be in the direction of the corkscrew as it turns. The diagram below shows the field near a straight-line conductor carrying N amperes. (The older term, ampere-turns, was probably more help in understanding magnetic fields: N ampere-turns can be set up by one wire carrying N amperes, N wires each carrying 1 ampere, or any combination of number of wires and number of amperes with the product N. The reason for the older term of ampere-turns should now be apparent.)

As with all fields, equipotentials meet flux lines at right angles, so magnetic field equipotential surfaces may be considered as emanating radially from the wire. Magnetic flux lines are always closed loops and are normal to the magnetic field equipotentials. Since inductance is defined in terms of the magnetic flux linked for each ampere flowing in the wire, straight wires have an associated inductance.

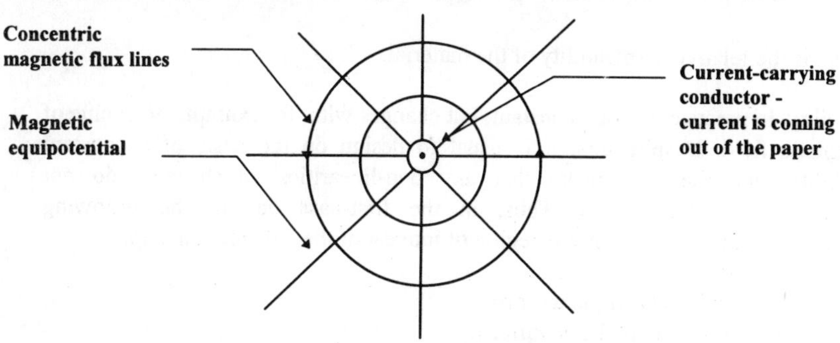

Figure 2.1 Magnetic field around a straight-line conductor

Magnetic Circuits
For any magnetic path, Ampere's Law states that the sum of the different magnetomotive force (m.m.f.) drops around the path is equal to the total magnetic potential

$$\text{m.m.f.} = \oint H.dl \; = \; NI \text{ ampere}$$

The total magnetic field is independent of the path taken around the conductor so we can choose a path which is easily defined. Select a concentric circle (cylinder in three dimensions) in Figure 2.1. The line integral around a contour of radius, r, is $2\pi r$, so Ampere's Law becomes

$$\oint H.dl = 2\pi r H = NI \text{ ampere / metre}$$

$$H = \frac{NI}{2\pi r}$$

B-H Relationship
The flux density, B, is proportional to the magnetic field intensity and a property of the material(s) through which the flux lines pass, viz., the permeability of the material(s):

$$B = \mu H, \text{ tesla}$$

where μ is the permeability of the magnetic medium. Usually, μ is expressed relative to the permeability of free space, μ_o, ie.

$$\mu = \mu_o \mu_r$$

where μ_r is the relative permeability of the material.

Permeability, in practice, is not a constant, but changes with, for example, the value of the magnetic field. Despite this, it is usual to design on the basis of a constant permeability, and then to ensure that any non-linearities which exist do not significantly affect the design. Thus, in the first-pass design, the following assumptions are taken as valid in the region of interest of the B-H relationship:

1. the flux density, B , is uniform
2. the field intensity, H, is uniform
3. the permeability, μ, is constant, ie. linear B-H characteristic

Electromagnetic Induction

For a time-changing magnetic field, there is a voltage inducted in any wire within the field. The magnitude of this voltage is given by Faraday's Law of Induction

$$E = N\frac{d\phi}{dt} = NA_c\frac{dB}{dt} \text{ volt}$$

The Inductor: Energy Storage Within a Magnetic Field

In SMPS, it is the capacity of an inductor to store energy which is generally its most important feature. Energy storage depends directly on the inductance of the device, which can be developed for a long straight coil as follows:

$$L = \frac{N\varphi}{I} = \frac{NBA_c}{I}$$
$$= \frac{N\mu HA_c}{I} = \frac{N\mu NIA_c}{I\, l_e}$$
$$= \frac{\mu N^2 A_c}{l_e} = \frac{\mu_o \mu_r N^2 A_c}{l_e}$$

A_c = cross-sectional area of the inductor core
l_e = effective length of the magnetic path
μ_r = relative permeability of the core material
N = number of turns
μ_o = permeability of air

Note: The inductance is proportional to the square of the number of turns in the inductor (usually in the form of a coil of wire)

Air Gap

If a wire is wound onto a former of magnetic material (ie. a material which has a large value of μ_r, for example, a ferrite) and a small gap, l_g, is made in the core, the flux in the ferrite will be the same as the flux in the air gap. If the air gap is small, the flux will pass across the gap almost in straight lines and the flux density in the gap will be approximately the same as that in the magnetic material. Because of the ratios of relative permeability between the gap (air = 1) and the core (ferrite = 3000, typically) the magnetic field strength in the gap will be much higher than in the ferrite,

$$H = \frac{B}{\mu}$$

With typical values of permeability, to a first approximation, the ferrite can be ignored and all the m.m.f. can be considered to exist in the gap.

Thus, for the gapped inductor: $$H = \frac{NI}{l_g}$$

It is usually the considered that all of the energy in the system is stored in the gap. The energy stored in the field outside the gap causes a few percent error in the calculation of stored energy and inductance but, in practice, it is usually possible to use this assumption.

Notes:

The following points are important

- the inductance is proportional to the square of the number of turns.
- the energy increases if the gap is made smaller with the same ampere-turns in the winding.
- the inductance of such an arrangement increases as the gap becomes smaller.

As noted above, the energy-storage capacity of a wound component is enhanced by the introduction of a gap (air or other non-magnetic material) in series with the magnetic core. Some commercially-available powdered cores actually store energy in a series of microscopic gaps in a magnetically-inert material which holds the particles of core material together. Since this distributed gap cannot actually be measured, the manufacturer measures and specifies the effective permeability of the gap averaged around the length of the core.

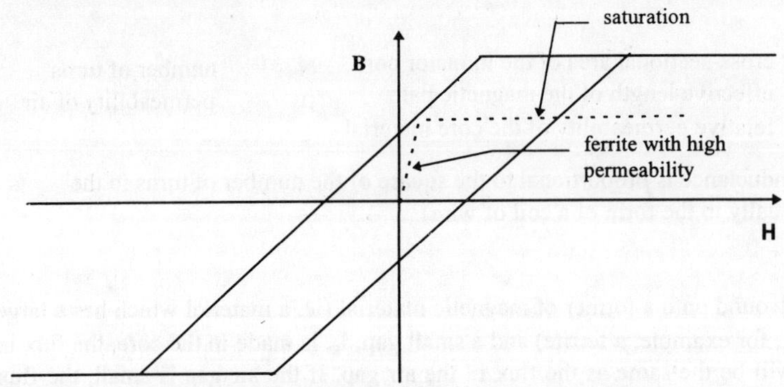

Figure 2.2 B-H characteristic for different permeabilities

Figure 2.2 shows the B-H characteristic of a typical ferrite core with an air gap. The dashed line is the characteristic of the ferrite alone, with high relative permeability and saturation at a relatively low flux density.

The solid line is the effective permeability, ie. that value which would be obtained if the air gap were spread out over the entire length of the magnetic path through the core. For gaps typically encountered, the composite characteristic is dominated by the gap. The energy storage at any operating point is the area to the left of the curve from the origin up to the operating point, equal to the integral HdB, which simplifies to $\frac{BH}{2}$. For ferrites, the area to the left of the characteristic is very small, indicating that it is not possible to store significant energy.

This is ideal for a transformer, where energy storage is undesirable, but not for an inductor, whose main function is to store energy.

The Transformer

Transformers are devices for coupling different parts of a circuit together and for transferring energy with minimum loss. Thus, it contrasts with the inductor, since it is designed **not** to store energy. In practice, the transformer parasitics cause losses and the device is less than 100% efficient.

Figure 2.3 shows a typical transformer for SMPS application. When the primary winding is connected to a supply of power, a small current flows to magnetise the core. This magnetisation develops voltages in the secondary windings providing outputs v_2 and v_3. Since the same magnetic flux couples the primary and secondary windings, the open-circuit voltages induced in the secondaries are proportional to the number of turns on each winding.

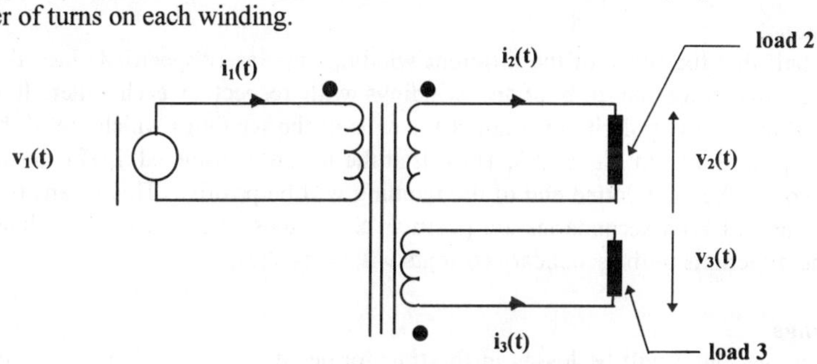

Figure 2.3. Transformer with dot notation

Except for a relatively small magnetising current, the total ampere-turns in all windings add up to zero. The field caused by the ampere-turns of load current in the secondary windings is largely cancelled by the opposing field caused by primary winding current drawn from the power source. These two large opposing currents create a significant field between the two windings. The energy stored in this field represents leakage inductance.

Since the flux is the same for the primary and the secondary, the induced voltages will be proportional to the primary turns N_1 and the secondary turns N_2, respectively. Therefore

$$\frac{V_2}{V_1} = \frac{N_2}{N_1} \quad \text{and} \quad \frac{V_3}{V_1} = \frac{N_3}{N_1}$$

When a load is connected to secondary (2), a current will flow. If we assume ideal (100%) coupling, to maintain an ampere-turn balance in the core, a corresponding primary current will flow, such that:

$$N_1 I_1 = N_2 I_2$$
$$\therefore \frac{I_1}{I_2} = \frac{N_2}{N_1}$$
but
$$\frac{N_2}{N_1} = \frac{V_2}{V_1}$$
$$\therefore \frac{Z_2}{Z_1} = \frac{\frac{V_2}{I_2}}{\frac{V_1}{I_1}} = \frac{I_1}{I_2}\frac{V_2}{V_1} = \frac{N_2^2}{N_1^2}$$

Thus the impedance "seen" by the primary voltage source will be the impedance connected to the secondary multiplied by the turns ratio squared.

Dot Notation

It is important that the sense of the different windings is clearly specified since this dictates the polarity of the ends of the windings with respect to each other. It is conventional to identify polarity by a dot at the ends of the windings which are of the same polarity, as shown in Figure 2.3. Thus, if at the instant considered, $i_1(t)$ is in the direction shown, then the dotted end of the winding will be positive. This means that the dotted ends of both secondaries are positive. Since these are essentially voltage sources, the directions of the secondary currents will be as shown.

Core Ratings

As stated above, there will be losses in the transformer during operation. Cores are rated on their volt-amp capacity, ie. the product of total current and the operating voltage. If we assume an efficiency of η, then the primary volt-amp rating will be

$$VA_1 = \frac{v_2 i_2 + v_3 i_3}{\eta}$$

A typical range for η would be 0.85 - 0.9.

Voltage ratios

Because coupling between primary and secondary is not perfect, a coupling factor must be included when estimating the number of turns on each secondary. Thus, if we assume a coupling factor, c_f:

$$\frac{N_2}{N_1} = \frac{v_2}{v_1 \times c_f}$$

A typical range for c_f would be 0.85 - 0.9.

2.2 WOUND COMPONENT PRODUCTION

A major effort is required for both the design and production of magnetic parts in SMPS. It is important that consideration is given to the wound component requirements of any power supply as ***early*** as possible in the design exercise in order that sufficient space be made available and that any difficulties with respect to weight are identified. As the switching frequency increases, the wound component becomes increasingly difficult to design. If the flux density is restricted to reduce self-heating, most of the common core materials - e.g., ferrite, or powdered iron - are suitable up to, and above, 200 kHz.

Wire

The most commonly used material for windings is copper. When considering wound components, the resistivity of copper is important for two reasons;

- losses (and hence efficiency) of a wound component depends on, among other things, the resistance of the windings, and
- regulation of the output voltage depends on any voltage drop in the resistance of the wound component winding.

While the high-frequency magnetic devices can be wound with standard wire, better copper utilisation is gained with Litz wire or multifilar wire or copper ribbon. These materials reduce skin effects which increase with frequency and, above 100 kHz, may become a problem (difficulties may be experienced at even lower frequencies if the power is high). Grade 2 wire is generally used because it offers a reasonable compromise between a coating of sufficient thickness to avoid shorted turns while being thin enough to allow a practical winding pattern.

Resistance of Copper

The resistivity of copper is dependent on temperature, viz. at 20°C

$$\rho_{copper} = 1.724 \times 10^{-8}\,\Omega\text{m}$$

At temperature t°C:

$$\rho_{copper} = 1.724(1 + 0.0042(t - 20)) \times 10^{-8}\,\Omega\text{m}$$

Current Density in the Windings

The r.m.s. current density in a winding is limited because of the associated temperature rise and a range of values is possible. At higher frequencies, not all the conductor cross section may be used, and care must be taken when selecting wire diameter. A current density of 5 A mm^{-2} (approximately 3000 A in^{-2}) will normally cause about 30°C temperature rise with natural convection cooling for a transformer or inductor installed within an SMPS enclosure. An average value of 7.5 A mm^{-2} may be used, with an upper limit of 12 A mm^{-2}.

With larger cores, the current density for a 30°C rise decreases because the heat-dissipating surface increases less rapidly than the heat-producing volume.

Winding
Difficulties are encountered in winding power transformers for higher frequencies not only in reducing the leakage inductance and capacitance but also in producing symmetrical and predictable voltage in the output windings. Several techniques are available, including interleaving, multifilar, twisted pairs and co-axial transmission lines.

Frequency
Switched mode power supplies are available in the frequency range of a few 10's of kHz to 300 kHz with the lower end typical of the commercial market and the very highest operating frequency more likely to be met in the military field. Designs are now being studied in the 1-3 MHz range but these are not available as standard yet.

Two basic types of wound components must be considered viz., the transformer and the inductor - commonly termed the choke.

PRODUCTION OF TRANSFORMERS

Below is given information on typical transformers used in SMPS. It should be borne in mind that these data are not exhaustive and that many other materials and approaches to design can be adopted. However, effective and reliable designs can be produced if the methodology described in these sections is followed.

Material
For input transformers operating at mains frequency, soft magnetic steel is used. Typical at high-frequency are ferrites and dust cores with a range of compositions.

Operating Frequency
Low frequency - 50 Hz.: High frequency - 20 $\rightarrow$ 300 kHz

Waveform
Usually square

Temperature
Operation is in elevated-temperature ambience, commercially around 60°C, military applications up to 100°C typical.

Current Density
Current densities should be in the range 5-12 A mm^{-2} with 7.5 A mm^{-2} as typical.

Flux Density

This depends very much on the material used and the temperature at which the device will operate, with designs usually restricted to approximately 80% of saturation level. Where an increased safety factor is required, for example, to cope with any change in characteristic with increased temperature or to accommodate the magnetic conditions during overload, operating flux densities may be reduced to as low as 50% of the saturation value. It should be noted that $B_{saturation}$ reduces with increase in temperature. Typical values of $B_{saturation}$ are 400 - 450 mT.

Core Shapes

E-cores

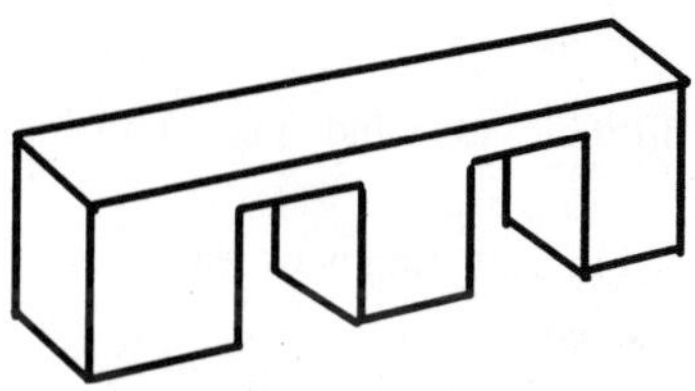

Figure 2.4 E core

These are normally used at mains frequency but may be encountered at high frequency from time to time.

Toroidal

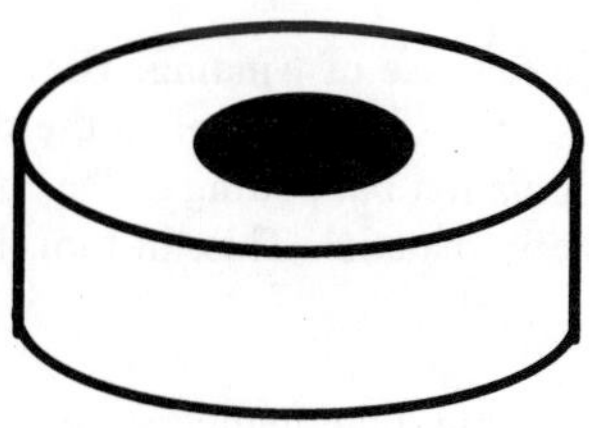

Figure 2.5 Toroid Core

Size

Toroidal cores are available from small beads up to a maximum size of around 4 cm outside diameter.

Advantages

- Toroidal cores are generally used when heavy gauge wire is specified. This avoids the potential problem of shattering the fragile bobbins which are used with pot and RM cores.
- Windings are brought out as flying leads to pins on suitable boards.
- The main advantage of the toroidal shape is that it is available in different aspect ratios - deep with small diameter to shallow with large diameter - and can thus be fitted into unusual spaces. Cores can also be stacked for additional power.
- With toroids, good magnetic coupling can be achieved.
- Cores give minimum reluctance for a given core volume.
- The parasitic capacitance of the wound component can be minimised.

Disadvantages

- Toroids are more difficult to wind than bobbins, especially for multi-layer construction.
- Difficulty is experienced in insulating between layers.
- Toroids are difficult to screen.
- Mechanical fitting to boards can be difficult.
- Impregnation of the unit can give rise to high magnetising currents when ferrite is the core material. This is caused by the varnish or resin shrinking when curing and stressing the ferrite.
- Achieving a suitable termination is more difficult than for the other core configurations.

RM Modular Core

These come with a bobbin for ease of winding. They are generally used because they can be mounted directly onto a p.c.b. It is usual to use double vacuum impregnation of the winding and bobbin configuration but potting of the components can lead to shrinkage and compression of the magnetic material. This, in turn, leads to an increase in magnetising current.

Windings may be made using high temperature materials to withstand the elevated temperatures of manufacture and operation.

Advantages

- Easy to wind, insulate and screen.
- The winding on the bobbin can be impregnated separately from the core, thus avoiding the potential problem of core stressing.
- Terminals are fixed to the bobbin and do not have to be provided by the designer.

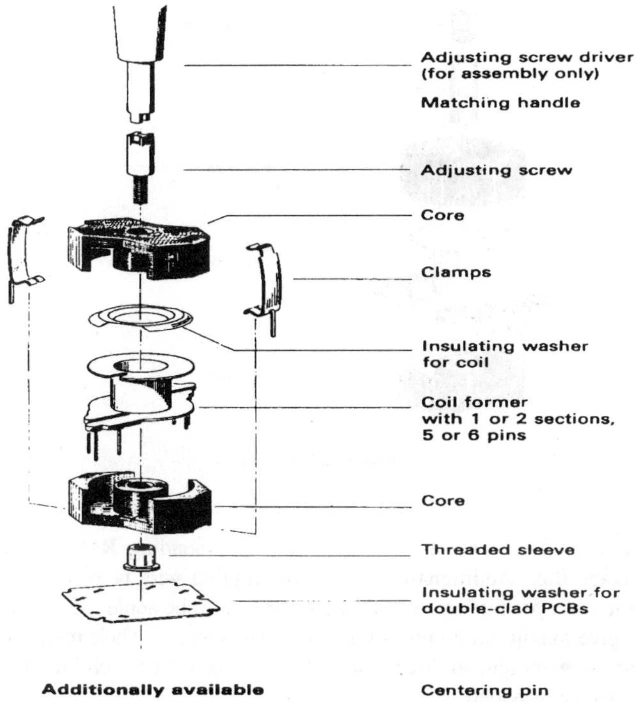

Figure 2.6 RM-modular core

Disadvantages

- Bobbins lack mechanical strength and can be damaged during winding, especially when using heavy gauge wire.
- Bobbins lack mechanical strength to support heavy gauge wire.
- The geometry of the wound component is restricted.

Pot cores

As with the RM core, the pot core provides a convenient method of producing a transformer in that winding is very easy. There is more effective use of the window area because there is no layering effect as with toroids.

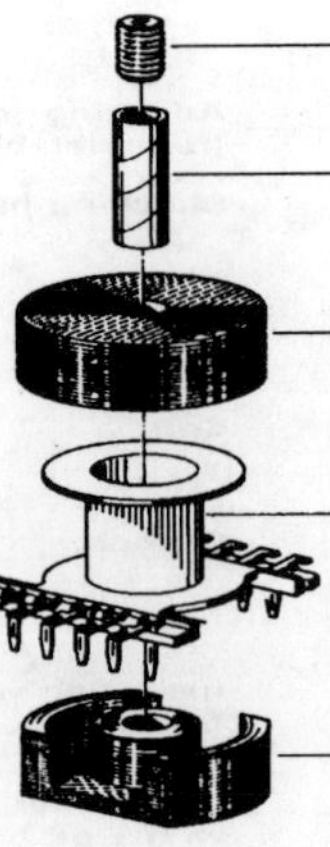

Figure 2.7 Pot core

Pot cores provide slightly more iron than the corresponding RM core and have less associated leakage flux. Additionally, egress for winding wire is available at four points, 90° apart on the core, permitting steps of a quarter turn to be achieved. These factors mean that pot cores give maximum output for a given unit volume. Their major disadvantage is that the bobbins are straight, so direct connection to a printed circuit board is not possible. Flying leads must be provided.

Wire

The universal wiring material is copper, but this is available in different configurations.

Shape

Round cross-section is normally used. Annealed tape wire of thickness 0.2 mm is used when it is important to manufacture with more copper in the same window area. Litz wire, which has a stranded conductor, is used for higher frequencies. Unfortunately, it has a textile covering and so needs more room.

Skin depth

When the skin depth is smaller than the radius of the conductor, it is prudent to explore all the possible options for wire shape so that the most efficient use of the wire is achieved.

$$Skin \quad depth = \left(\frac{6.61}{f^{0.5}}\right) K \text{ cm}$$

where K = 1 for copper.

Coverings
Polyamide is used for specialist applications where high temperatures are expected (180°C and above) but it is tough and must be burnt off, then the wire cleaned with glass paper for termination.

Polyurethane is used for lower temperature applications (up to 150°C) and has the advantage of being self-fluxing which is particularly useful when using thin wires.

Terminations
As stated above, the RM core is provided with bobbin pins which connect direct to the printed circuit board. Standard resin-cored solder is adequate for all applications but, for high voltage devices, the resin must be washed off. When using fine wire, the end of the wire is taken back on itself so that there are three strands. These are twisted into a flex in which only one wire carries current, the other two contributing mechanical strength. Care must be exercised to avoid shorted turns and to solder spikes which may puncture the insulation.

Eyelets are soldered to wire terminations for low frequency (50 and 400 Hz) applications. For toroidal cores, PTFE coated equipment wire is soldered to the winding wire, the joint secured mechanically and the PTFE coated wire brought out to the rest of the circuit.

Winding

Bobbins
Windings on bobbins have a layer of insulation material, normally about 0.012 mm thick for fine wire and 0.025-0.05 mm for heavier gauges, placed between layers of the winding.

For interwinding insulation, a suitable polyester tape may be used for insulation: these have high dielectric and mechanical strength.

Toroidal
Interlayer insulation may be with unimpregnated terylene tape. Interwinding insulation uses the same material.

With high voltage devices, it is good practice to wind the primary on one side of the torus and the secondary on the other, although this reduces coupling efficiency. This technique is also used to minimise capacitive effects at high frequency.

PRODUCTION OF INDUCTORS (CHOKES)

Material
Typical materials are gap ferrites and dust cores with a range of compositions.

Relative Permeability:

Toroidal
μ_r values in the range 10 - 200 are possible depending on the choice of core material.

RM cores
When using RM cores, A_L values of up to 2000 nH turn^{-2} are possible.

Operating Frequency
If low frequency (0 - 15 kHz) is used, choose a core material with high μ_r value, e.g. 200. If a high frequency circuit is to be considered , choose a material with lower μ_r e.g. for frequency of 100 kHz (and above), choose μ_r of 10. This is especially important in bridge circuits where the choke will be subjected to 2 x operation frequency, ie. normally 200 kHz. The variation of μ with frequency is made to optimise the core design by attempting to match the copper and iron losses. Materials with a low μ_r value have high resistivity and thus lower core losses. In addition, such materials result in lower winding-to-winding and winding-to-core capacitance.

Waveform
Normally square, often with d.c. level.

Temperature
As for transformers.

Current Density

5-12 A mm^{-2} with 7.5 A mm^{-2} as typical. With chokes, it is important to take into account the IR voltage drop in the choke (due to output direct current), both for heating effects and for output voltage regulation. A typical value of IR drop is 0.1 - 0.15 V for a 12 V supply.

Flux Density
B_{max} of approximately 0.8 T at low frequency is usual for toroidal cores, with designs lying in the range 0.4 - 0.6 T. At high frequency, $B_{saturation}$ = 0.6-0.7 T, with B_{usual} = 0.3 - 0.4 T at 20°C for the RM core with a suitable gap. Design on the basis of all the m.m.f. being dropped in the air gap and none in the core, ie., the core merely provides a magnetic path for the flux. With all designs take care to avoid core saturation when the design includes polarisation current.

Note: $B_{saturation}$ reduces with increase in temperature.

Core Shapes

E
See transformers.

Toroidal
These are widely used and have an inductance specified in nH per turn^2 (A_L value) to ease design. With respect to the advantages and disadvantages of different sizes of core for choke manufacture, the same comments obtain as for transformers described above.

RM-Modular Core
For choke manufacture, the centre limb has a gap. Otherwise, with respect to the general features of the RM core, the same comments obtain as for their use in transformer manufacture, described above.

Pot Cores
For calculation of inductance, manufacturers tables should be used since the A_L value will vary with the size of gap in the core. Otherwise, with respect to the general features of the pot core, the same comments obtain as for their use in transformer manufacture, described above.

Wire
See transformers.

Winding
See transformers.

Testing:

The following comments pertain to both transformers and chokes. Testing of chokes is done with polarisation current applied.

Voltage Testing
Ionisation testing with up to 12 kV between windings is possible.

Frequency
Up to 300 kHz is used.

Impedance Measurements
- a.c. and d.c. resistance of each winding

- inductance of each winding

- capacitance coupling between windings and between windings and the core insulation resistance between windings (>10 MΩ)

Failure Modes:

Manufacturing-based
- shorted turns

- incorrect number of turns

- short circuits between windings or between winding and core

- dirty terminals causing tracking (this can be avoided by careful cleaning of resin from terminals)

- bad coatings on wires

Operation-based
- overloading

- circuit-generated voltage spikes

2.3 WOUND COMPONENT DESIGN EXAMPLES

TRANSFORMER

The design approach adopted is one of many possible, and it is not claimed that this is the only, or indeed, the best design methodology.

The example uses components from one specific manufacturer, but again, it should be emphasised that many other manufacturers produce components that are equally suitable and have characteristics that meet the specification to which the present designs have been developed.

Specification of the Transformer
The device specification will contain information on which the engineer will base his designs. This list is typical of the information which is supplied. If not supplied by the client, the designer should request it before starting out on the design. If some details are not available, the engineer should choose suitable values, based on personal experience and on discussions with the end-user.

Output VA
Although this may be derived from information given later, it is useful in classifying the design and selecting materials to know the secondary VA.

Frequency and Waveform
The primary switching frequency and the waveform details (eg. duty cycle) are required.

Primary Conditions
Input voltage, both steady state and transient.

Secondary Conditions
Information on the following should be made available:

1. Number of windings.

2. Number of taps per winding - eg. centre tapped.

3. Volts per tap per winding - ie. V per tap plus tolerances. Also, any restrictions on peak output volts should be noted, eg. output not to exceed 75V in worst case.

4. Regulation - Not normally a problem in practice, but requires consideration throughout design. Current per tap per winding - ie. I per tap.

5. Type of load - eg. full wave rectifier bridge or high impedance bridge.
6. Impedance - As for primary, any limitations on impedance must be taken into account.

Mechanical Details
Often it is mainly mechanical restrictions which limit transformer design. The following information is required:

1. Volume, ie. maximum height of component, maximum width of component, maximum length of component.

2. If the component is toroidal, a minimum inner diameter is required.

3. Method of fixing, eg. printed-circuit-board mounted or chassis mounted.

4. Weight limitation.

5. Terminations, eg. flying leads or former terminal pins.

Environmental Details
The working environment must be described in order that component construction, materials, etc. may be designated. The following details are used:

1. Ambient temperature, ie. the temperature envelope including storage temperatures,

   eg. Temperature = -40°C to +60°C.

2. Component finish, eg. dry or varnish impregnated or resin encapsulated.

3. Vibration, frequency and amplitude.

4. Screening, specify electromagnetic and electrostatic screening requirements.

The following worked examples are illustrative of one particular approach, based largely on the methodologies specified by the SEI company. It is emphasised that other approaches using other companies' materials are equally valid.

Design Specification:

$T_{ambient}$	90°C (maximum)	**Input**	140V
Frequency	f= 100 kHz,	**Waveform**	as shown below

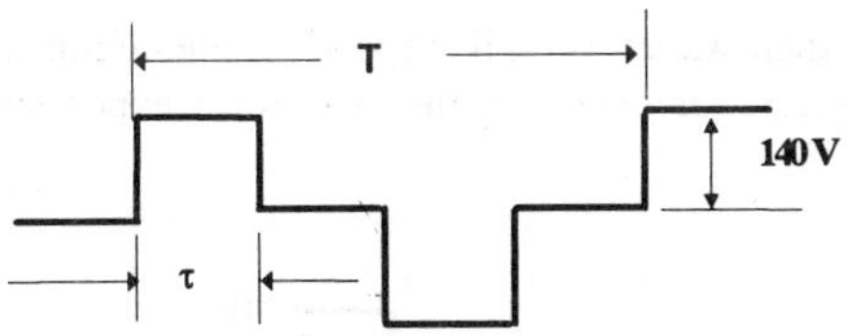

T = 10 μsec and t = 2.5 μsec.

Figure 2.8 Typical voltage waveform

Output

winding A, supplying a centre-tapped transformer rectifier, with an unfiltered output of 32 volt, 2.4 ampere.

winding B, supplying a centre-tapped transformer rectifier, with an unfiltered output of 44 volt, 0.3 A.

winding C, supplying a half-wave rectifier, with an unfiltered output of 24 volt, 4 A.

Figure 2.9 shows how the transformer may be drawn, neglecting any voltage drops across diode.

VA Calculation

The total secondary VA must be calculated. The simultaneous currents in each winding must be multiplied by the appropriate voltage. The centre tapped windings will have only one winding energised at a given time: the single-ended winding feeds a half-wave rectifier.

For the 32 volt output, the waveform, after rectification, but before any smoothing, will be as shown below,

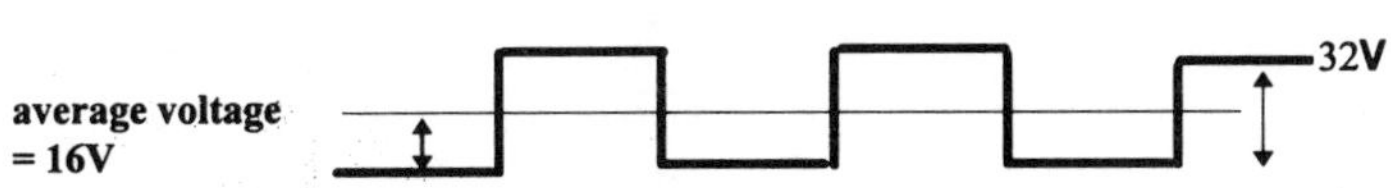

and for the 44 volt output, will be thus

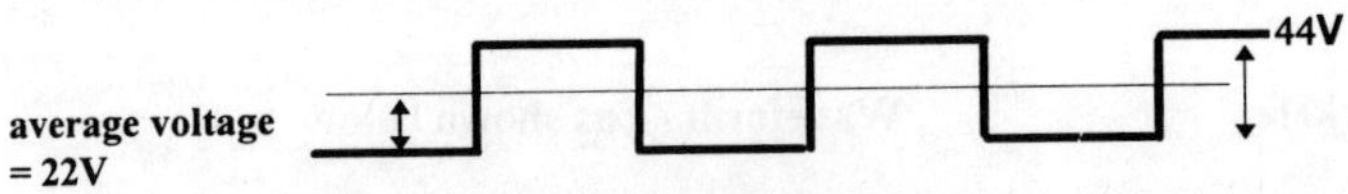

For the single-sided 24 volt supply, then waveform will depend on the circuit to be fed. If the winding feeds a forward converter, for example, the waveform experienced by the winding will be as shown below,

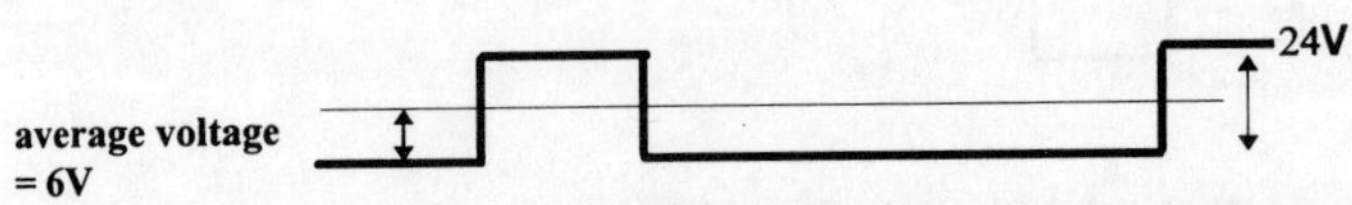

The transformer can now be drawn in schematic form:

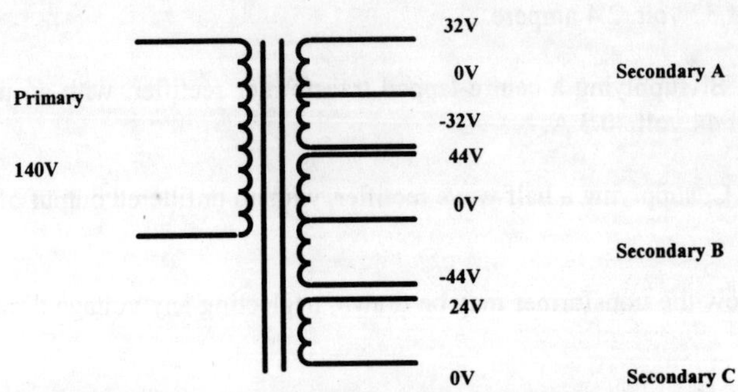

Figure 2.9 Transformer windings

Total secondary VA	=	(16 x 2.4)	SEC (A)
		+ (22 x 0.3)	SEC (B)
		+ (6 x 4)	SEC (C)
	=	(38.4 + 6.6 + 24) = 69	

Assuming efficiency of 90%.

$$\text{Primary VA} = \frac{69}{0.9}$$

$$= 76.7 \quad (I_p \text{ may be derived at this stage})$$

Core Selection
A core from the SEI range of RM ferrites is to be chosen - L2 grade.

L2 grade
This material has characteristics which satisfy anticipated conditions:

1. T_c - Cure temperature losses at 100 kHz not excessive.

2. Mechanical form acceptable ie. printed circuit board mountable.

Choose the suitable RM core from available range. (VA maximum = 77 approximately, given the above conditions - refer to RM selection chart).

RM Core Selection Chart
From the table, an RM8 core will be suitable, ie. RM core SEI M2 808/T/LT.

The selected core has a cross sectional area of 64 mm^2.

Table 2.1 Volt ampere ratings of cores

RM core	Volt amps, VA
RM 4	4-20
RM 6	20-45
RM 8	45-80
RM 10	80-130
RM 14	130-200

Flux Density Selection
From experience, the estimated temperature rise for a typical efficiency η = 90% is 40°C. Hence, estimated operating temperature (worst case) = 130°C.

If $B_{saturation}$ is exceeded at any point of the flux excursion, unacceptable harmonics may be introduced.

From manufacturer's catalogue, the following data on the core are available

$$B_{saturation}(20^\circ C) = 520mT: B_{saturation}(100^\circ C) = 340mT$$

Assuming a linear relationship, extrapolation gives $B_{saturation}(130^\circ C) = 300$ mT

Apply safety factor: typically take $B_{op} = 0.67\, B_{saturation} = 200$ mT

(here, because of the high ambient temperature, we could use bigger safety margin, say 50%, ie. $B_{op} = 150$mT: we will proceed with 200mT).

Turns Per Volt Calculation

The number of turns in each winding may be calculated using Faraday's Law

$$V = N\frac{d\phi}{dt} = N\frac{\Delta\phi}{\Delta t} = NA_c\frac{\Delta B}{\Delta t}$$

N = number of turns on the winding: ϕ = magnetic flux

A_c = cross-sectional area of core: B = flux density in the core

Now for full-wave rectification the excursion is from 0 to + B_{op} in t_{ON} (= DT). Because frequency on secondary side is effectively doubled, $T = \frac{1}{2f}$.

Thus,

$$V = \frac{NA_c\Delta B}{\Delta t} = \frac{NA_c B_{op}}{t_{on}} = \frac{NA_c B_{op}}{DT} = \frac{NA_c B_{op} 2f}{D}$$

Thus, for primary, (V_{in} and$_1$ N),

$$\frac{N_1}{V_{in}} = \frac{D}{2 \cdot B_{op} \cdot A_c \cdot f} = \text{turns per volt}$$

NB. use working value of flux density

Substituting gives turns per volt = 0.195.

Primary Turns Calculation

$$V_{prim} = 140 \text{ V}$$

Therefore, the number of turns on the primary, N_p, may be calculated.

$$N_p = 140 \times 0.195 = 27 \text{ turns, rounding to the nearest whole number,}$$

Secondary Turns Calculation

We must allow for the fact that magnetic coupling between primary and secondary is not 100%. A typical value of 85% will be assumed for magnetic coupling,

SEC(A) V_A = + 32 V 0V -32 V

$$N_{s(A)} = \frac{32 \times .215}{0.85} = \text{approximately } 7 \text{ turns}$$

Note: Because this winding has positive and negative output voltage, we need 7 turns for each 32V output, ie. total number of turns = 7+7 = 14

SEC(B) V_B = + 44 V 0V -44 V

$$N_{s(B)} = \frac{44 \times 0.195}{0.85} = \text{approximately } 10 \text{ turns}$$

Note: Again, because this winding has positive and negative output voltage, we need 10 turns for each 44V output, ie. total number of turns = 10 + 10 = 20

SEC(C) V_C = 24 V

$$N_{s(C)} = \frac{24 \times 0.195}{0.85} = \text{approximately } 5 \text{ turns}$$

Note:

The coupling factor will vary according to several factors - such as core geometry - and, as such, should be user-defined at this stage. For example, using a different coupling factor may yield different numbers of turns which affects ratios and pin-allocations.

Primary Winding Design

Assume the primary winding occupies 53% of the total volume of the former. This is on the basis that the primary and secondary windings should each have half the available volume to allow heat dissipation. Since the primary carries the magnetising current as well as load current, a small extra allowance is made. Details of the dimensions of the former may be obtained from the Manufacturer's catalogue.

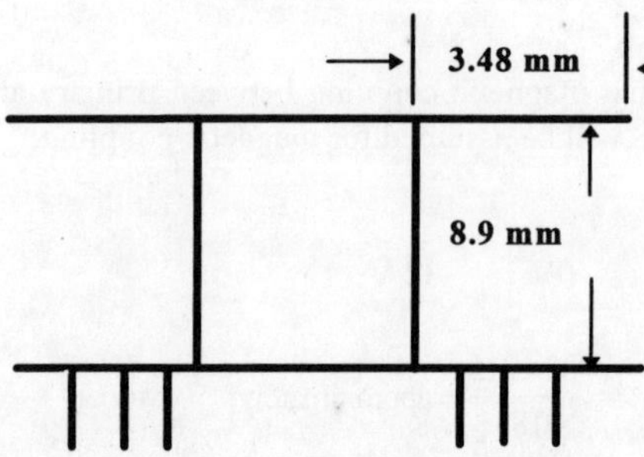

Figure 2.10 Details of winding bobbin

Wire Selection/Build Calculations

For copper conductors operating at a frequency, f kHz, the skin depth is given by

$$\delta = \frac{0.0661}{\sqrt{f}}\,\text{m}$$

for example, for a frequency of 100 kHz, skin depth is around 0.209 mm, so any conductor with a diameter greater than 0.418 mm, ie. 2xδ, will not be utilised fully and will have a non-uniform current density.

A good working value for current density is J = 7.5 A mm^{-2} (see earlier.) If the current density is too high, excessive heating may occur, with possible failure of the insulation around the wires and possible significant change in the magnetic characteristics of the core material.

$$\text{Primary r.m.s. current, } I_p = \frac{VA_{primary}}{V_{pnmary}} = \frac{76.7}{140} = 548\text{mA}$$

To calculate wire size, $J = \frac{I}{\pi \frac{d^2}{4}}$ thus, $d = \sqrt{\frac{4I}{J\pi}}$. Standard wire sizes are available from a range of suppliers, and, from the sizes available we can select the nearest wire size. Here, the nearest diameter of the wire is 0.30 mm.

At this point, the constraints placed upon the designer by the manufacturing process must be considered. An estimate must be made of both the width across, and the depth on the bobbin which are available for placing the winding. The width for winding will not be the full transverse dimension of the bobbin: it is impossible to place turns exactly together and an allowance for "slippage" must be made. This corresponds typically to a 10% reduction in available width.

At the same time, it must be recognised that it is not possible to design on the basis of the full depth of the bobbin. It is not possible to wind exactly onto the bobbin or onto another winding layer without some bulging of the turn of wire. With thick wires this is more of a problem than with thin. We will choose 10% as a reasonable estimate.

For both width and depth, the size of this allowance made will depend on many factors, the most important of which is the experience and skill of the manufacturing workforce.

Details of 0.30 mm Wire

Grade 2 insulation has a maximum diameter including insulation of 0.362 mm. Therefore, the number of turns in 1 layer, including a deduction of 10% for slippage is:

$$\frac{(8\cdot 9-10\%)}{0\cdot 362} = 22\cdot 12 \quad \text{ie.} \quad 22 \quad \text{whole} \quad \text{turns}$$

Hence, if we assume that we can achieve 22 turns across the bobbin, for a primary of 27 turns (see above), this means 2 layers will be required using 0.30 mm Grade 2 copper wire. Including an allowance for bulge, the depth per layer is 0.398 mm (ie. 0.362 x 1.1mm). This gives a winding lay-up with a wire depth of 0.796 mm (ie. 2x0.398.) It will be necessary to spread the windings evenly across the width of the bobbin to give a good winding bed for the next layer.

Primary Cover

To provide a `bed' for the first secondary layer, a reasonable depth of insulation would be an advantage. Here, because of the relatively low voltages, a single layer of No. 56 polyester tape will be enough.

Insulation

If necessary, tape can be placed between layers of a winding to increase insulation strength. There are several proprietary insulating tapes which meets this requirement (eg. 3M No. 56

polyester tape which has a thickness of 0.06 mm.) A Class B system is suitable. Since the maximum temperature (ie. continuous temperature) is expected to be approximately 130°C, a class B system providing a minimum of 500V isolation would be the most appropriate to choose.

Comments on First-Time-Through Design
Full occupation of the available volume will not take place using this wire. The choices are, therefore:

- to increase the wire size until 53% is achieved;
- to elect to use multistrand windings.

It is unwise to increase the single wire size beyond 0.6 mm diameter because thicker wires present an excessive bulk to the former pins and place too much stress on the former. Neither is it desirable to have excessive bulk on pins due to too many wire strands. It is good practice to choose the simplest solution which meets the electrical criteria. For the present design, we will accept the 0.3 mm diameter wire solution. Hence, a winding featuring single strand 0.3 mm diameter Grade 2 copper wire would be suitable.

We can now define the primary winding:

Primary is 27 turns in 2 layers, 0.3 mm Grade 2 copper wire with 1 layer of 3M No. 56 polyester insulating tape between the layers as insulation and one layer over the winding as cover.

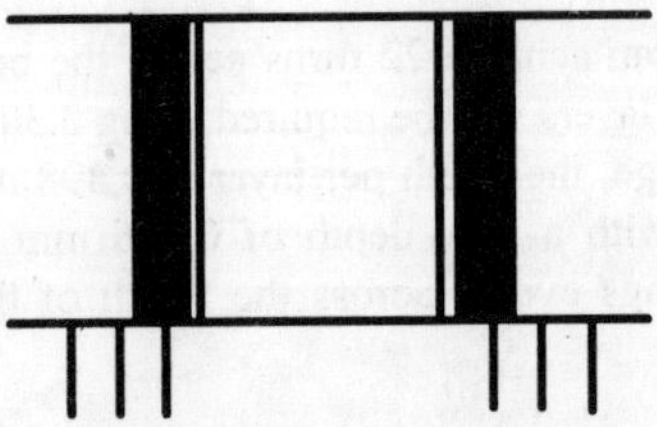

Figure 2.11 Details of primary winding

Total Depth
We must now check on the depth remaining for secondary windings. Primary depth including an allowance for bulge

$$= 0.796 + (2 \times 0.06) \text{ mm} = 0.916 \text{ mm}$$

This is less than the nominal value of 53% of the available depth, ie. 53% of 3.48 = 1.84 mm, so the winding should fit into the permitted volume

$$\text{ie. } \frac{0{\cdot}916}{1{\cdot}84} \times 100 = 50\%$$

Percentage occupation of volume allocated is 50%. We could increase the thickness of wire to achieve a better percentage fill, up to a wire of 0.6 mm diameter copper. However, to illustrate the design process, we will proceed with this configuration.

Secondary Windings

Available depth is 3.48 - 0.916 ie. 2.564 mm. In this transformer there are 3 secondary windings. The winding featuring the largest wire size (ie. largest current-handling requirement) is considered first.

[Normally, heavier gauges are positioned below lighter gauges to reduce the stress on lighter gauges throughout the winding. It is sometimes the case, however, that the opposite is true - for instance, where careful attention to coupling in a particular winding is required.]

32 V Winding

Use J = 7.5 A mm^{-2}. Again, using $d = \sqrt{\frac{4I}{J\pi}}$ the nearest standard wire has been chosen. This wire has a diameter of 0.63 mm. For practical reasons, 0.6 mm diameter wire is the thickest we should use: including insulation this wire has an overall diameter of 0.675 mm. The result of using finer wire is that the current density will be greater than J =7.5 A mm^{-2}, ie. $J = \frac{I}{\pi \frac{d^2}{4}}$ = 8.45 A mm^{-2}, which is within the acceptable range (see above).

The number of turns in 1 layer is $\frac{8{\cdot}9 - 10\%}{0{\cdot}675}$ = approximately 12 turns, and the 32 V winding has 7 + 7, ie. 14 turns, with a centre tap. Again, it is necessary to wind in two layers, with the turns spread evenly across the width of the bobbin to give a good winding bed for the next layer.

Insulation

Because the voltage is low, it is not necessary for insulation purposes to use a layer of tape between the layers of wire. However, to help with "bedding" of the next layer, a layer of tape will be used.

Design is
Secondary(A) : 14 turns, 0.6 mm Grade 2 copper wire (2 layers) with centre tap with one layer of 56 polyester insulating tape between the wire layers as insulation and one tape layer over the winding as cover (with J = 8.45 A mm $^{-2}$ which is OK)

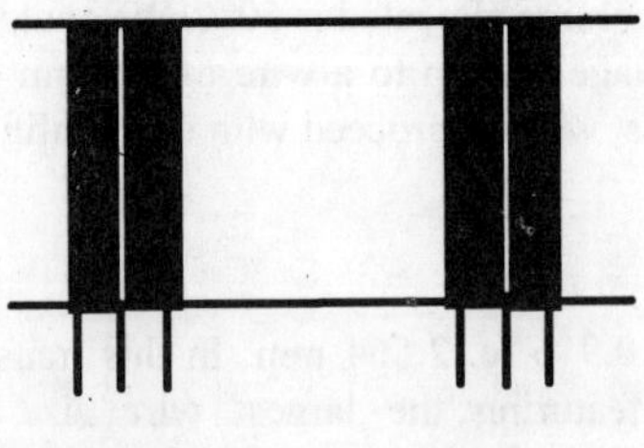

Figure 2.12 Details of secondary A winding

Total Depth
We must now keep a check on the depth remaining.

Primary + cover + secondary(A) + insulation
= (0.916 + (2x0.675) x 1.1 + 2 x 0.06) mm = 2.521 mm

Therefore, depth available for conductors in SEC(B) and (C) is 3.48 - 2.521 = 0.959 mm

44 V Winding
The wire size (for J = 7.5 A mm^{-2}) is 0.22 mm, so 0.2 mm diameter wire may be used. This gives a current density of 9.5 A mm^{-2}, which is acceptable.

$$\text{Hence, number of turns in 1 layer} = \frac{8.9 - 10\%}{0.262} = \text{approximately 30 turns.}$$

The 44 volt winding needs 10 + 10 turns, ie. 20 turns, so 0.22 mm single strand wire is appropriate in a single layer. It is advisable to provide as good a winding lay-up as possible, so the turns should be evenly spread across the width of the former.

The design of the 44V winding is:

Secondary(B)

20 turns, 0.20 mm Grade 2 copper, single layer with centre tap

Insulation
It will be necessary to place a layer of 3M No. 56 polyester tape as a cover (the reasons for selection are as mentioned previously).

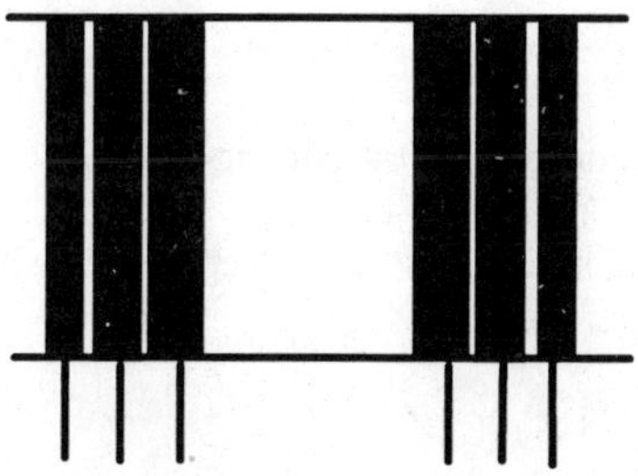

Figure 2.13 Details of secondary B winding

Total Depth

We must now keep a check on the depth remaining.

Primary, secondary(A) and insulation + secondary(B) + cover

= 2.521 + 0.262 x 1.1 mm + 0.06 mm = 2.869 mm

Therefore, remaining depth = 3.48 - 2.869 mm = .61 mm

24 volt winding
Two strand
Using 7.5 Amm^{-2}, a wire diameter of 0.8 mm is suggested. This is greater than that which is practicable to wind. We must consider more than one strand: the simplest is two strands. To obtain the same cross sectional area, the two strands should have diameters related to the original wire by $\sqrt{2}:1$. Because we are restricted in the range of wire sizes available, we can try the heaviest wire available to us, 0.6 mm diameter. Two strands of this implies a current density of around 7.7 Amm^{-2}, which is OK. However, the depth of such a wire will be 0.675x 1.1 ie. 0.743 mm. There is not enough depth available on the former for this so we must try a three-strand solution.

Three strand
Here, the wire diameter reduces to 0.4 mm, the current density rises to 10.6 Amm^{-2}. This is on the high side, but this is the outermost winding, and will be the best cooled. We can therefore proceed with three strands of 0.4 mm diameter wire. This has a thickness of 3x0.462, ie. 1.386. The number of turns per layer is thus

$$\frac{8 \cdot 9 - 10\%}{1.386} = \text{approximately} \quad 6 \text{ turns} \quad \text{per} \quad \text{layer}$$

Since this winding requires 5 turns, it will fit onto one layer.

Total Depth

Primary + secondary(A) + secondary(B) + secondary(C) = 2.869 + 0.462x 1.1 = 3.37

This fits onto the bobbin, which is 3.48 mm deep, even when we make generous allowances for slippage and bulge.

Thus, the design is:

Secondary(C)
5 turns, 0.4 mm three strand Grade 2 copper wire

Insulation & Final Cover

Final cover is placed to prevent mechanical damage and to provide electrical insulation. If space permits, it is prudent to put in place 1 layer 3M No. 56 polyester tape (as previously discussed) plus, as final cover, 1 layer 3M No. 79 woven-glass tape.

Reasons for selection of woven - glass tape:

- meets temperature criteria
- meets electrical criteria
- material allows penetration of varnishing compounds
- material is tough

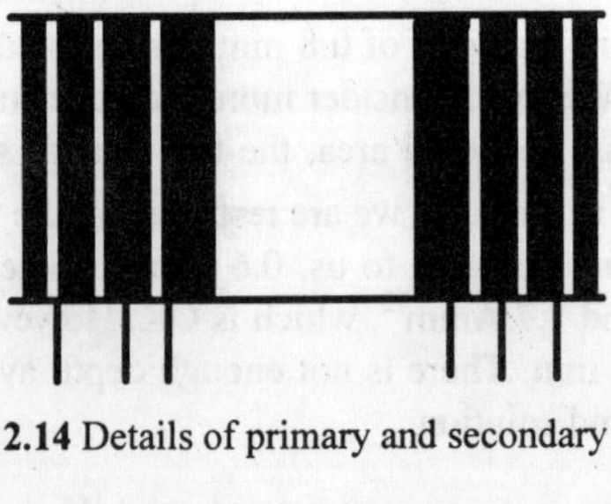

Figure 2.14 Details of primary and secondary windings

Comments on Percentage Fill

The available depth was 3.48 mm and we have used almost all of that. This is a good use of the volume available and would result in a device which is suitable for bulk manufacture and which would be robust in use. Thus the insulation is 1 layer 3M No. 56 polyester tape (as previously discussed) plus, as final cover, 1 layer 3M No. 79 woven-glass tape.

D.C. CHOKE: GAPPED RM FERRITE CORE

Choke Specification

f = 100 kHz ΔI = 12.7%

Direct current = 0.6 A , Inductance, L = 200 μH (minimum),

Maximum voltage drop = 0.1 volt, Output voltage = 5 V r.m.s., $T_{ambient}$ = 40 °C

Core Choice

Select ferrite core with gap for energy storage - for example RM core from SEI Ltd.

Material

We must select a material with characteristics which are suitable for operation at the design frequency (100 kHz) and operating temperature (40°C ambient). SEI L2 material is suitable and we will select it.

Size

I^2 R loss which corresponds to the maximum allowable voltage drop of 0.1V at a current of 0.6A d.c. indicates a resistance, R, of less than 0.167 Ω. Therefore, I^2 R (maximum) = $(0.6)^2$ x 0.167 = 0.06. Therefore, from the curves, an RM6 core is suitable. This is available with A_L = 100 or 160 nH turn^{-2}. Refer to data book curves LI^2 vs $I^2 R$

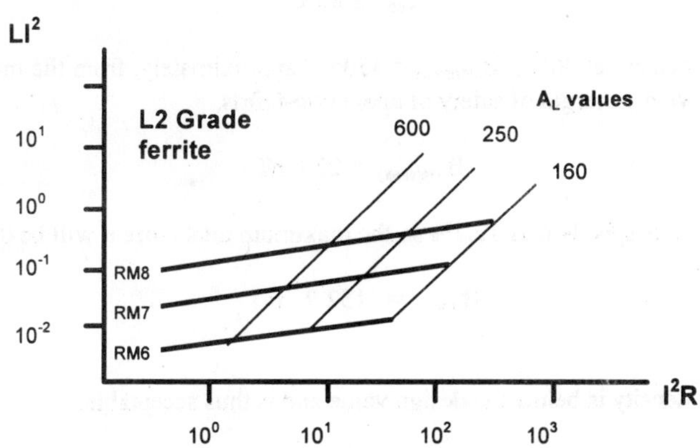

Figure 2.15 Core stored energy versus energy loss

$$LI^2 = 0.2 \times (0.6)^2 \text{ (L in mH, I in amps)} = 0.072$$

Gap Choice
A large gap will support a larger energy storage (ie. LI^2 term) but the magnetising current is larger. Therefore, we will choose a smaller gap initially with $A_L = 160$ nH turn^{-2}. Gap size = 0.20 mm (from catalogue).

Turns Calculation
Using the $A_L = 160$ nH turn^{-2} we can calculate the number of turns required.

$$N = 10^3 \times \sqrt{\frac{L(mH)}{A_L}} = 10^3\sqrt{\frac{0.2.}{160}}$$

= 35.4, rounded to 36 turns.

Flux Density Check

$$B = \mu H \qquad H = \frac{NI}{l_g} \quad \text{where } l_g = \text{gap length}$$

$$\text{Therefore } B = \mu \frac{NI}{l_g}$$

Substituting gives B = 135.7 mT . The maximum permissible flux density depends on the operating temperature, T_{op}. If the ambient temperature, T_a= 40°C, and a temperature rise of 40° is assumed,

$$T_{op} = 80°C$$

Saturation flux density at 80°C, $B_{saturation}$= 350mT approximately, from the manufacturer's catalogue. Allowing a margin of safety of about two-thirds,

$$B_{op(max)} = 230 \text{ mT}$$

The ripple current is specified as 12.7% so the maximum total current will be 0.676 A.

$$B_{max} = 152.9 \text{ mT}$$

Hence, the flux density is below the design value and is thus acceptable.

Variation of Permeability with d.c. bias

The slope of the B-H curve at a given point is the permeability of the core material. The B-H curve is not exactly linear so any d.c. bias from the origin will mean a change in permeability and hence a change in inductance. We must check that change resulting from the present d.c. bias is within acceptable limits. From SEI data book curves RM6,

$$\frac{\Delta L}{L} = I_{DC}(mA)\sqrt{L(mH)} \times 10^{-4}$$

$= 0.0268$. Thus, variation may be neglected.

Winding Design

For a direct current of 0.6 A, and a current density of 5 Amm^{-2}, the wire size = 0.425 mm. If we calculate skin effect at 100 kHz it may be shown that only 0.40 mm of the copper will be used. Therefore, there is nothing to be gained in using a larger wire; consequently we will select 0.40 mm diameter copper wire.

In summary:

Choose grade 2 copper enamelled giving an outside diameter of 0.462 mm.

Former Details

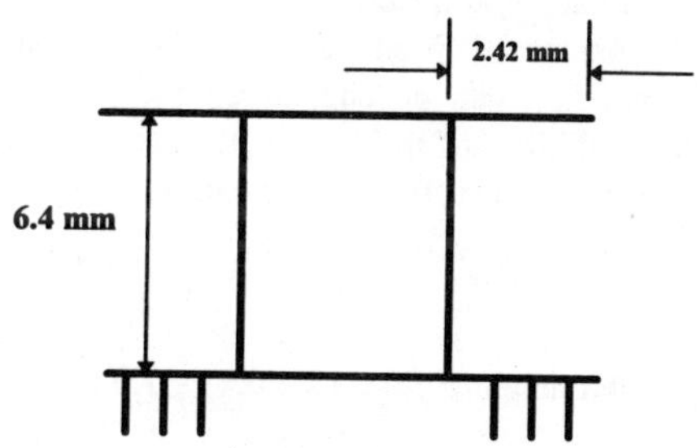

Figure 2.16 Details of winding bobbin for RM6 core

RM6, 4 pin is suitable. This has the following dimensions:

Layer width = 6.4 mm
Layer height = 2.42 mm

Allowances

Not all of the available volume can be used because of the practical limitations of winding. It is good practice to allow about a 20% reduction in the available height because of insulation and bulge.

Therefore, height = 1.9 mm

Similarly, it is good practice to allow about a 10% reduction in the available width because of slippage during winding.

Therefore, width = 5.8 mm

The number of turns which will fit on one layer of winding can now be determined.

$$\text{Turns/layer} = \frac{5.8}{0.462} = 12.5 \quad \text{i.e.} \quad 12 \text{ turns / layer}$$

Thus for the present winding, 36 turns will need 3 layers. This gives a winding height of 1.4 mm. This is within the available height and is acceptable.

Insulation Requirements

The design is for a 5 V inductor and consequently electrical field strengths are not excessive (this is normally expressed in choke design as volts/layer). It follows that the insulation applied to the winding can be considered merely on the basis of providing mechanical strength for the building of the choke. Because of this, 1 layer polyester per layer (with thickness = 0.1 mm) will suffice for insulation.

Therefore

$$\text{Total height} = 1.4 + (2 \times 0.1) = 1.6 \text{ mm}$$

Insulating cover which gives mechanical strength = approximately 0.25 mm.

Resistance Check

Copper wire of 0.04 mm diameter has a resistance of 0.1372 Ω per metre (at 20°C). This is temperature sensitive and allowance must be made for the change in resistance with temperature if the calculated resistance of the winding is close to the maximum specified on the grounds of voltage regulation. The resistance of the winding must be determined; for this we need mean length of turn (m.l.t.)

Turn length (1st layer)

$$= \text{circumference of former}$$

$$= \pi D_f, \quad D_f = 7.45 \text{ mm}$$

$$= 23.4 \text{ mm}$$

Turn length (last layer)

$$2\pi(\frac{D_f}{2} + 0.462 + 0.1 + 0.462 + 0.1)$$

$$= 30.46 \text{ mm}$$

$$\text{mean length per turn} = \frac{30.46 + 23.4}{2} = 26.9 \text{ mm}$$

Therefore length of winding

$$(26.9 \times 36)$$

$$= 969.6 \text{ mm}$$

Therefore

$$R_w = 969.6 \times 0.1372 = 0.133 \ \Omega$$

The initial criterion was $R < 0.167\ \Omega$, so this design is within the limits.

Final Specification

RM6 Gapped Ferrite Core: A_L = 160 nH turn^{-2} Former = 4 pin

Winding 36 turns, 0.40 mm Grade 2 copper wire: Insulation 1 layer polyester tape per layer of winding. Final cover 3 layers polyester

D.C. CHOKE TOROIDAL CORE

Specification

Inductance = 0.15 mH, Operating frequency = 75 kHz, ΔI = 10%, $I_{d.c.}$ = 2.5A

V = 15V $_{r.m.s.}$, Maximum voltage drop = 0.2 V $_{r.m.s.}$, $T_{ambient}$ = 30°C

Core Choice

Toroidal core, iron alloy - e.g. Genalex (SEI)

Important Points about Toroidal Cores

- heavier wire may be applied than on bobbin
- wide range of permeabilities available
- mounting of toroidal chokes is more difficult than bobbin type

From SEI Catalogue

Size of core depends on energy storage requirement and copper loss criteria. The graph given by manufacturer is used

If it is assumed that current density = 7.5 Amm^{-2}, the nearest wire diameter is d = 0.6 mm.

LI^2 = 0.15 x $(2.5)^2$ = 0.937: Ld^4: d = wire diameter in mm

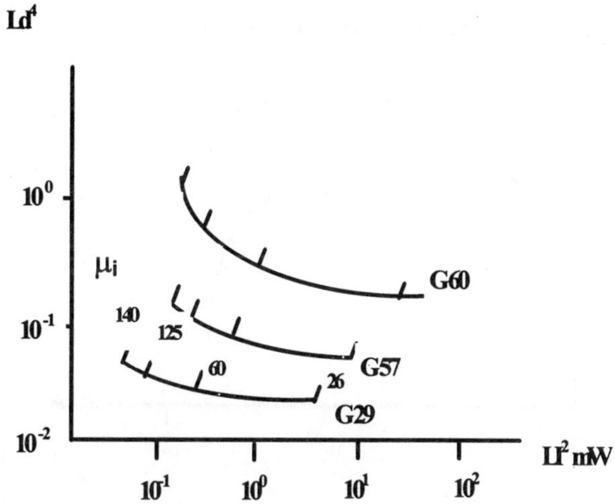

Figure 2.17 Energy storage versus power loss for GENALEX 'H'

Hence, $Ld^4 = 0.15 \times (0.6)^4 = 0.019$. From the graph, a core of G29 size upwards, with $\mu_i = 60$ or under will be suitable.

Choosing a core of higher μ_i will yield more inductance in the same volume. d.c. saturation problems may result, however, and so, normally, a compromise has to be made. In this case, we choose G29 WH.

Details of G29 WH Core

$\mu_i = 50 \pm 5$, $l_m = 5.19\text{cm} = 0.0519\text{m}$, $A_{L(min)} = 24.8 \text{ nH turn}^{-2}$

Turns estimation

$$N = 10^3 \sqrt{\frac{L(mH)}{A_L}} = 10^3 \sqrt{\frac{0.15}{24.8}} = 77.8$$

say 78 turns

Check on the effect of DC bias on the value of permeability

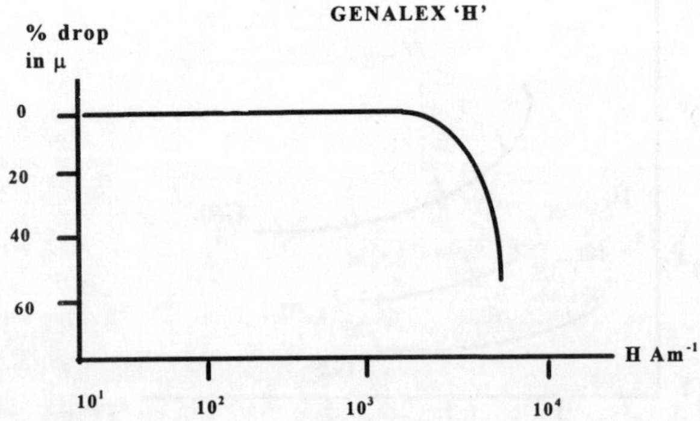

Figure 2.18 Variation in permeability with dc bias for GENALEX 'H'

78 turns with 2.5A d.c. may prove to be excessive for this core,

For conditions specified,

$$H = \frac{NI}{l_m} = \frac{78 \times 2.5}{0.0519} = 3757 Am^{-1}$$

From manufacturer's chart shown below, at 3757 Am^{-1}, the WH grade will experience a drop in μ of approximately 15%. This may imply an unacceptable drop in inductance when d.c. current is applied.

If so, the VH grade may be considered or a larger core size used. For example, choosing the VH grade would result in 106 turns. This increases copper loss (copper loss appears as $I^2 R$ heating) and also increases winding difficulty and cost. A larger core size improves the design but with the penalties of increased weight, volume and, normally, increased material cost.

For this example we will continue with the G29 WH design, ie:

78 turns, G29 WH core, 0.6 mm wire.

Winding on the Core

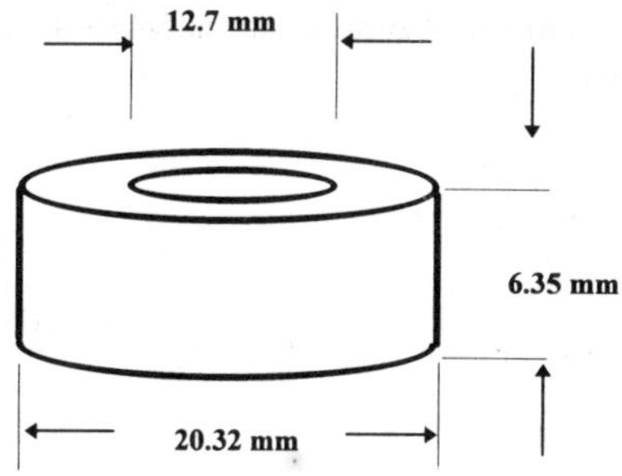

Figure 2.19 Core dimensions

outside diameter = 20.32 mm: **inside diameter = 12.70 mm**
height = 6.35 mm

The number of turns per layer will vary since the inside diameter is decreasing per layer. Hence, it is difficult to be precise about winding resistance etc. - instead, assumptions as to the turns/layer must be made.

Layer 1

Inner circumference = πD = π x 12.7 – 39.9, say 40 mm. Allowing for slippage of conductors of 10%, usable circumference = 36 mm. For 0.6 mm wire, Grade 2, the outside diameter = 0.662 mm. Therefore the number of turns in first layer = 54.3 (which is rounded to 54 turns).

Layer 2

Assume that the first winding presents a uniform surface for layer 2 - ie. the inside diameter is reduced uniformly by twice wire diameter.
The inside diameter now becomes :

$$\pi(12.7 - (2 \times 0.662)) = 35.7$$

usable diameter = 35.7 -10% = approximately 32 mm,

and so,

turns in 2nd layer = 32/0.662 = 48 turns.

Total possible number of turns so far is 54 + 48, ie. 104. We can therefore fit the winding onto two layers.

Resistance Check

$$\text{Length of turn in 1st layer} = (2\times 6.35) + \frac{2\times(20.32-12.7)}{2}$$

$$= 20.32 \text{mm}$$

$$\text{Length of turn in 2nd layer} = 2\times(6.35+2\times 0.662) + \frac{2\times((20.32+2\times 0.662)-(12.7-2\times 0.662))}{2}$$

$$= 25.6 \text{ mm}$$

$$\text{Hence, wire length} = (54\times 20.32)+(24\times 25.6) \text{ mm}$$

$$= 1.711 \text{ m}$$

Resistance per metre = 6.04 x 10^{-2} Ω per metre (at 20°C) giving R = 103 mΩ. Therefore for a current of 2.5A d.c., voltage drop the voltage drop will be 0.258 volts, which is outside the specified value of 0.2 Ω.

Options

The options are to select a core with a higher A_L value, to reduce the number of turns and hence length of wire. Alternatively, we can increase the wire size, since there is plenty room in the toroid window: we will continue the design using 0.8 mm diameter wire.

Layer 1

Inner circumference = πD = π x 12.7 = 39.9, say 40 mm. Allowing for slippage of conductors of 10%, usable circumference = 36 mm. For 0.8 mm wire, Grade 2, the outside diameter = 0.885 mm. Therefore the number of turns in first layer = 40.6 (which is rounded to 40 turns).

Layer 2

Assume that first winding presents a uniform surface for layer 2 - i.e. inside diameter is reduced by twice wire diameter uniformly.
Inside diameter now becomes :

$$\pi(12.7 - (2 \times 0.885)) = \pi \times 10.93$$

$$= 34.3 \text{ mm} - 10\% = 30.8 \text{ or } 31 \text{ mm},$$

and so,

$$\text{turns in 2nd layer} = 31/0.885 = 35 \text{ turns.}$$

Total number of turns so far = 75; this leaves 3 turns to complete the winding. These turns may be arranged to cover the entire core length, or be grouped together as required.

Resistance Check

$$\text{Length of turn in 1st layer} = (2 \times 6.35) + \frac{2 \times (20.32 - 12.7)}{2}$$

$$= 20.32\text{mm}$$

$$\text{Length of turn in 2nd layer} = 2 \times (6.35 + 2 \times 0.855) + \frac{2 \times (20.32 + 2 \times 0.885) - (12.7 - 2 \times 0.885))}{2}$$

$$= 27.4\text{mm}$$

$$\text{Length of turn in 3rd layer} = 2 \times (6.35 + 3 \times 0.885) + \frac{2 \times ((20.32 + 3 \times 0.885) - (12.7 - 3 \times 0.885))}{2}$$

$$= 30.94\text{mm}$$

$$\text{Hence, wire length} = (40 \times 20.32) + (35 \times 27.4) + (3 \times 30.94)\text{mm}$$

$$= 1.864\text{m}$$

Resistance per metre = 3.4 x 10^{-2} Ω per metre (at 20°C) giving R = 63 mΩ. Therefore at 2.5A d.c., voltage drop = 0.1575 volts, which is within specification.

$$I^2 R = 0.39 \text{ watts}$$

Hence, the design meets the specifications. The following is worth pointing out; a larger core size could have been chosen and the addition of 2 or 3 extra turns on the above would increase inductance whilst probably remaining within specification in terms of I^2 R.

Therefore final design is:

G29 WH Toroid

78 turns, 0.80 mm Grade 2 copper wire, wound uniformly and continuously.

2.4 WOUND COMPONENT SAFETY CONSIDERATIONS

(BASED ON IEC 950 AND RELATED DOCUMENTS)

IEC 950 regulates the safety requirements of primary to secondary isolation transformers used in information technology equipment. Isolation transformers for switched mode power supplies are included in this category.

Transformer safety issues are considered under the following:

1. creepage distance
2. clearance distance
3. distance through insulation
4. electric strength withstand
5. temperature
6. insulation system

Items 1, 2, 3 and 4 are all dependent on:

- the mains supply voltage, and
- the highest measured d.c or r.m.s. voltage of the primary circuit; this is usually at the primary winding of the power transformer with respect to safety earth.

Note: For the purposes of voltage measurements, the 0 V of the secondary windings of the transformer is considered to be at earth potential.

Typical voltage ranges of interest for off-line power supplies are 100-127 V_{ac}, and 200-230V_{ac}. Voltages are measured under the following input supply setting and output loading:

- Input mains supply is set to +6% for the lower range, ie. 6% of 127 V_{ac} = 135 V_{ac}, and 10% of the higher range, ie. 10% of 230 V_{ac} = 254 V_{ac} (this was 6% of 240 V_{ac}, until recently, which equals 254 V_{ac}).
- The outputs are loaded to the maximum total power rating.

CREEPAGE DISTANCE

This is defined as the shortest direct path along the surface. The following data on creepage distance are limited to working voltages relevant to off-line power supplies.

Working voltage (Highest Voltage of Primary circuit w.r.t. secondary 0 V or earth V_{dc} or V_{rms}	Primary to Secondary Creepage (Reinforced) for pollution degree 2 material group IIIa and IIIb
151V to 200V (208V permitted)	4.0 mm
209V to 250V	5.0 mm
251V to 300V	6.4 mm
301V to 400V (415V permitted)	8.0 mm
416V to 600V	12.6 mm

Table 2. 2 Creepage Distances

CLEARANCE DISTANCE

This is defined as the shortest direct path through air. When measuring working voltages, the following applies:

⇒ if the working voltage is measured as d.c., the peak value of any superimposed ripple shall be included.

⇒ repetitive switching peaks must be added as per table, (Table 2.4), for such peaks.

⇒ non-repetitive transients shall be disregarded, eg. input line surges.

Working Voltage	Working Voltage	Nominal Mains Supply Voltage 0V to 150V_{rms}	Nominal Mains Supply Voltage 151 V_{rms} to 300 V_{rms}
V_{peak} or V_{dc}	V_{rms}	Pollution Degrees 1 and 2, for reinforced PRI. to SEC.	Pollution Degrees 1 and 2, for reinforced PRI. to SEC.
72V to 210V	51V to 150V	2.0 mm	4.0 mm
211V to 420V	151V to 300V	4.0 mm	4.0 mm
421V to 840V	301V to 600V	6.4 mm	6.4 mm
841V to 1.4kV	601V to 1kV	6.4 mm	6.4 mm

Table 2. 3 Clearance Distances (also see Table 2.4)

Nominal Mains Supply Voltage: 0V to 150 V_{rms} Pollution Degrees 1 and 2	Nominal Mains Supply Voltage: 151 V_{rms} to 300 V_{rms} Pollution Degrees 1 and 2	Additional Clearance Distances Required, mm
Maximum Repetitive Peak Voltage, volt	Maximum Repetitive Peak Voltage, volt	Reinforced Primary to Secondary, mm
210	420	0
298	493	0.2
396	567	0.4
474	640	0.6
562	713	0.8
650	787	1.0
738	860	1.2
826	933	1.4
914	1006	1.6

Table 2. 4 Additional Clearance Distances

DISTANCE THROUGH INSULATION

For thin sheet material insulation, eg. Polyester Tapes, IEC 950 does not define material thickness. However, the minimum number of layers of insulating material and the material electric withstand strength are defined.

For reinforced insulation, the following alternatives are permitted.

1. At least **two layers** of material.

   Each layer to withstand the electrical strength for reinforced insulation for the working voltage applicable.

2. **Three layers** of material.

   All combinations of two layers together to withstand the electric strength test for reinforced insulation for the working voltage applicable. (Note that the Japanese safety regulations require **four** layers of tapes for primary to secondary reinforced insulation).

ELECTRIC STRENGTH TEST

The following tables are abridged versions of the details given in Part 1 and Part 2 published in IEC 950. The abridged tables reflect working voltages applicable to off-line power supplies. For working voltages between the values stated, linear interpolation is permitted to establish the electric strength test voltages required. D.C. equivalent voltages are permitted by multiplying the rms voltage by √2. Note: For type approval tests, the duration of test is 1 minute. For production tests, the duration of test is 1 second.

Working Voltage in Primary Circuit	Electric Strength Test Voltage
0V to 130 V_{rms}	2000 V_{rms} (or 2828 V_{dc})
131V to 250 V_{rms}	3000 V_{rms} (or 4242 V_{dc})
251V to 1000 V_{rms}	3000 V_{rms} (or 4242 V_{dc})

Table 2. 5 Primary to Secondary Windings: Reinforced Insulation

Working Voltage in Primary Circuit	**Electric Strength Test Voltage**
0V to 130 V_{rms}	1000 V_{rms} (or 1414 V_{dc})
131V to 250 V_{rms}	1500 V_{rms} (or 2121 V_{dc})
251V to 257 V_{rms}	1502 V_{rms} (or 2124 V_{dc})
258V to 268 V_{rms}	1531 V_{rms} (or 2165 V_{dc})
269V to 280 V_{rms}	1563 V_{rms} (or 2210 V_{dc})
281V to 292 V_{rms}	1593 V_{rms} (or 2253 V_{dc})
293V to 305 V_{rms}	1626 V_{rms} (or 2300 V_{dc})

Table 2. 6 Primary to Unearthed Body eg. Ferrite Core Basic Insulation

Working Voltage in Primary Circuit	**Electric Strength Test Voltage**
0V to 42.4V_{peak} or 60.0V_{dc}	No test required
31 V_{rms}	536V_{rms} (or 796 V_{dc})
35 V_{rms}	596V_{rms} (or 843 V_{dc})
41 V_{rms}	641V_{rms} (or 906 V_{dc})
45 V_{rms}	669V_{rms} (or 946 V_{dc})
51 V_{rms}	709V_{rms} (or 1003 V_{dc})
61 V_{rms}	771V_{rms} (or 1090 V_{dc})
70 V_{rms}	821V_{rms} (or 1161 V_{dc})
107 V_{rms}	1000V_{rms} (or 1414 V_{dc})
200 V_{rms}	1337V_{rms} (or 1891 V_{dc})
257 V_{rms}	1502V_{rms} (or 2124 V_{dc})

Table 2. 7 Secondary to Unearthed Body (Ferrite Core): (Basic Insulation)

TEMPERATURE

The permissible operating temperature of the isolating transformer is strictly regulated by the Safety Agencies. In general, all wound components comprising the following are temperature regulated by IEC 950, regardless of primary or secondary circuit placement.

Wound component piece-parts:

⇒ plastic bobbins/holders
⇒ magnet wire (copper or aluminium)
⇒ insulating tapes and sleeves
⇒ varnish.

In conjunction with temperature, insulation system regulations will need to be considered. The operating temperature of the isolation transformer in a switched mode power supply is determined under the following test conditions:

1. Input supply voltage is set at -10% of the lowest voltage and +6% of the highest voltage of the nominal rated operating range, (Note: an exception is for 230 V_{ac}, where it is +10%). For example, if the nominal operating range is 100 V -127 V_{ac}, and 200 V - 230 V_{ac}, then tests will be conducted at -10% of 100 V_{ac}, ie. 90 Vac, and +10% of 230 V_{ac}, ie. 253 V_{ac} (rounded up to 254 V_{ac} to be in common with the previous regulation of +6% of 240 V_{ac}).

2. Input supply is set at the highest frequency of the nominal rated values. eg. if the rated operating input frequency is 50/60 Hz, then tests will be conducted with input frequency at 60 Hz.

3. Tests will be conducted at ambient temperature of +25 °C, and the highest operating ambient of the power supply specification.

4. The outputs will be loaded to deliver the maximum rated power.

5. Thermal equilibrium must be established before temperatures are recorded. Time taken to reach thermal equilibrium will depend on factors which include the size, weight, component packing density, etc. of the power supply. To determine thermal equilibrium, temperature measurements should be taken at 15 minute intervals, and if three consecutive sets of temperature readings are within ±1 °C, then thermal equilibrium is established. For the majority of power supplies used in personal computers, one hour is usually required to reach thermal equilibrium.

6. **Temperatures may be measured by:**

a) using "k" type thermo-couples, or

b) using the resistance method.

The Thermo-Couple Method

It is considered sufficient to place the "k" type thermo-couple at the outermost layers of windings of the transformer, to ascertain the temperature of the transformer windings. Two thermo-couples are placed at the "perceived" hottest regions of the transformer windings. The hottest regions are:

- **where the air flow or movement is minimum, and**

- **where neighbouring components of the windings are at high temperatures, creating a local "hot spot".**

A third thermocouple is attached to the core, by using an appropriate glue, to monitor the core temperature. When thermal equilibrium is reached, the temperatures of windings and core, plus the external ambient temperature are recorded.

The Resistance Method

In this method, the following readings are taken:

- **room temperature at the start of the d$_{est}$, designated t_1. (in °C)**
- **resistance of the winding at the start of the test, designated, R_1. (in Ω)**
- **room temperature at the end of the test, designated t_2. (in °C)**
- **resistance of the winding at the end of the test, designated R_2. (in Ω)**

The main primary winding is usually monitored. Temperature rise is calculated using the following.

(a) for copper winding:

$$\text{temperature rise, } \Delta t = \frac{(R_2 - R_1)x(234.5 - t_1)}{R_1} - (t_2 - t_1)$$

(b) for aluminium winding:

$$\text{temperature rise, } \Delta t = \frac{(R_2 - R_1)x(225 - t_1)}{R_1} - (t_2 - t_1)$$

Transformers are classified for maximum permissible operating temperatures. Both methods for temperature measurements are permitted. However, if the thermo-couple method is used, the maximum permissible measured temperature is 10°C **lower** than that using the resistance method. Table 2.7 below shows the classification, and the associated maximum permitted operating temperatures.

Note that the temperature governing materials is to IEC 85, whilst wound components are tested for compliance to IEC 950.

Classification	Maximum Permissible Temperature of Materials to IEC 85	Maximum Permissible Temperature of Wound Component to IEC 950	
		By Resistance Method	By Thermocouple Method
Class A	+ 105 °C	+ 100 °C	+ 90 °C
Class E	+ 120 °C	+ 115 °C	+ 105 °C
Class B	+ 130 °C	+ 120 °C	+ 110 °C
Class F	+ 155 °C	+ 140 °C	+ 130 °C
Class H	+ 180 °C	+ 165 °C	+ 155°C

Table 2. 8 Transformer Classification

IEC 950 also defines the maximum permissible temperature **rise** for the various classes in addition to the **absolute** maximum temperatures of Table 2.7. Table 2.8 shows maximum permissible temperature rise, based on an ambient temperature of +25°C.

Classification	Maximum Permissible Temperature of Transformer	
	By Resistance Method, Δt	By Thermocouple Method, Δt
Class A	+ 75	+ 65
Class E	+ 90	+ 80
Class B	+ 95	+ 85
Class F	+ 115	+ 105
Class H	+ 140	+ 130

Table 2. 9 Maximum Permissible Temperature Rise

The following formula may be used to calculate the maximum permissible temperature rise, Δt, based on the absolute maximum permissible operating temperature, T_{max}, at any ambient temperature.

Let

T_{max} = maximum permissible operating temperature of the transformer

T_{amb}. = actual ambient measured during tests

T_{mra} = manufacturer's specified ambient temperature of operation

Δt = maximum permissible temperature rise

$= T_{measured} - T_{amb}$

Note: The resistance method is assumed

$$\Delta t = T_{measured} - T_{amb} \leq T_{max} - T_{mra}.$$

Worked example:

A manufacturer specifies that the maximum operating ambient, T_{mra}, of the PSU is +50°C. The transformer is to be designed to comply with Class B limit, ie. T_{max}= +120°C. What is the permitted temperature rise, Δt, of the transformer? Assume the ambient temperature, T_{amb} , measured during testing is +35°C.

Applying the formula gives:

$$\Delta t = 120 - 50 = 70°C$$

and

$$T_{measured} = T_{amb} + \Delta t = 35 + 70 = 105°C.$$

CLASSIFICATION OF INSULATION SYSTEMS

Indiscriminate combinations of hydrocarbon based and similar man-made materials can result in chemical reactions when subjected to elevated temperatures. These chemical reactions will degrade the properties of the individual materials of the combination, and may cause emission of toxic fumes, fire hazards, and loss of insulation properties amongst other effects. As insulation systems are generally a combination of such materials, and are subjected to elevated temperatures in use, a classification system has been developed to permit the combinations, and minimise hazardous chemical reactions.

The isolation transformer is one in which such a combination of materials is used, and operation is usually at high temperatures.

Most isolation transformers comprise the following:

bobbin/former	plastic, setting plastic, thermo setting plastic, etc.
insulation tapes	polyester, woven glass fabrics, impregnated paper, etc.
insulation sleeves	PVC, polyolefin, etc.
magnet wires	copper (or aluminium) with polyester basecoat and polyamide topcoat, etc.
varnish	polyester resin, etc.

The previous discussion on transformer temperature limits made reference to this Classification System, ie. Class A, E, B, F and H.

Class A Insulation System
An important point to note is that if the maximum temperature of the transformer does not exceed +100°C, Class A Insulation System may be used. This gives the greatest flexibility for manufacture, because in Class A system, any mix of material is permitted, provided each item is rated as Class A material. Also, these materials are generally lower in cost.

Classes E, B, F, and H Insulation Systems
For Classes E, B, F, and H, the combinations of materials are restricted by having to register with a Safety Agency a specified list of manufacturers and their material types. The

combinations of these material types will be tested by the Safety Agency to ensure that no chemical reactions occur to cause hazardous conditions.

This registration of the file of manufacturers and materials is referred to as an electrical insulation system, and is allocated an official safety file number.

Manufacturers and materials not mentioned in this file may not be used, regardless of superior temperature and other properties of the materials.

A typical Class B registered file would be as follows:

Company code number, class 130(b) electrical insulation system.
Safety agency file number: 123456

Typical manufacturers and materials from this file are:

Bobbin/Holder	-	name/s of manufacturer/s and trade name/s of material/s
Insulation tapes	-	name/s of manufacturer/s and trade name/s of tape/s
Varnish	-	trade name/s of varnish/es
Magnet wire	-	any recognised component in category obmw2, single build or greater, copper or aluminium. Polyester basecoat with polyamide topcoat, ansi mw76. polyurethane basecoat with Polyamide topcoat, ansi mw28.

SECTION 3

SEMICONDUCTOR COMPONENTS AND SMPS CONTROL

3.1 SEMICONDUCTOR DEVICES

In the past, three types of semiconductor devices dominated SMPS technology - the bipolar junction transistor (BJT), the metal oxide semiconductor field effect transistor (MOSFET) and the diode. In recent years, the use of the bipolar transistor has largely been abandoned, except in a few specialist applications. At the same time, MOSFETs have become available in a much larger range of ratings, both voltage and power.

The range of available diodes has also increased and much faster devices are now widely used in circuits operating at increased frequency.

SEMICONDUCTOR DIODE

The simplest type of semiconductor device is the junction diode, shown schematically in Figure 3.1; the arrow symbol used for the anode represents the direction of conventional current flow.

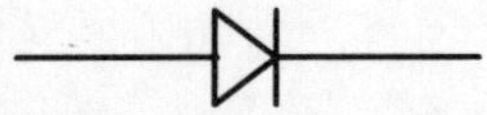

Figure 3.1 Schematic symbol for a semiconductor diode

Silicon diodes are available in a wide range of current capabilities, ranging from tenths of an ampere to several hundred amperes or more, and are capable of operation at voltages as high as 1000 volts or more. Parallel and series arrangements of silicon diodes permit even further extension of current and voltage limits. Silicon diodes can be operated at ambient temperatures up to 200°C

Because of their high forward-to-reverse current ratios, silicon diodes can achieve rectification efficiencies greater than 99%. They are very small and lightweight, and can be made highly resistant to shock and other severe environmental conditions. In addition, they have excellent life characteristics which are not affected by ageing, moisture, or temperature.

Important Characteristics
Of the various diode characteristics for which data are given, for SMPS applications, the most important are thermal impedance, forward-voltage drop, reverse (leakage) current, and reverse recovery time. These four characteristics help determine the performance and environmental capabilities and limitations of diodes.

Thermal Impedance
Although silicon diodes can operate at high temperatures, the actual pellet of silicon which performs the rectification is quite small and has a very low thermal capacity.

During normal operation, the diode p-n junction dissipates approximately 1 watt of power for each ampere of forward current. For safe operation the temperature of the junction should not rise above 200°C. For this reason, the silicon pellet is mounted between heavy copper parts in a symmetrical direct-soldered arrangement that results in uniform distribution of thermal stresses, minimum thermal fluctuations, and low thermal resistance.

Figure 3.2 shows a cross-sectional diagram of a typical silicon power diode.

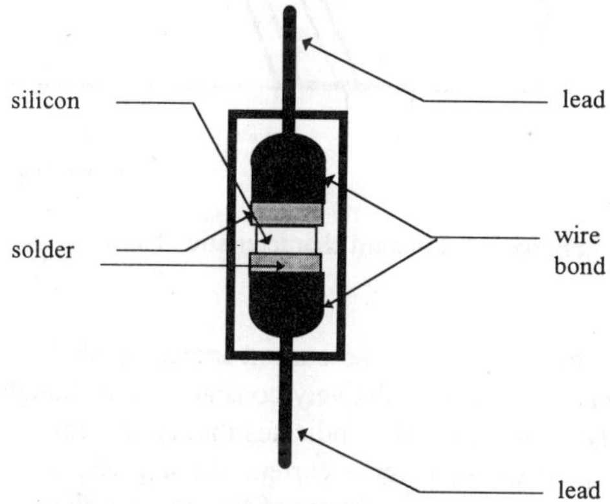

Figure 3.2 Typical Silicon Power Diode

Manufacturers' specifications on silicon diode thermal resistance are expressed in °C per watt. When multiplied by the power dissipated by the diode, the rise in junction temperature above the case temperature is obtained.

Forward-Voltage Drop

The major source of power loss in a silicon diode arises from the forward-conduction voltage drop, usually around 0.4 to 0.8 volt. The slope of the voltage-current characteristic at voltages above this threshold value represents the dynamic resistance of the diode. Figure 3.3 shows how the forward biased characteristic is affected by the operating temperature of the device.

The approximate expression for power losses P in a silicon diode, given by the following equation, can be used to explain how this type of operation is possible

$$P(\text{watts}) = (V_{dc}\, I_{dc}) = (I_{r.m.s}^{\;2}\, R_{dyn})$$

where the voltage V_{dc} is 0.4 to 0.9 volt depending upon the junction temperature, and R_{dyn} is the dynamic resistance of the diode over the current range considered.

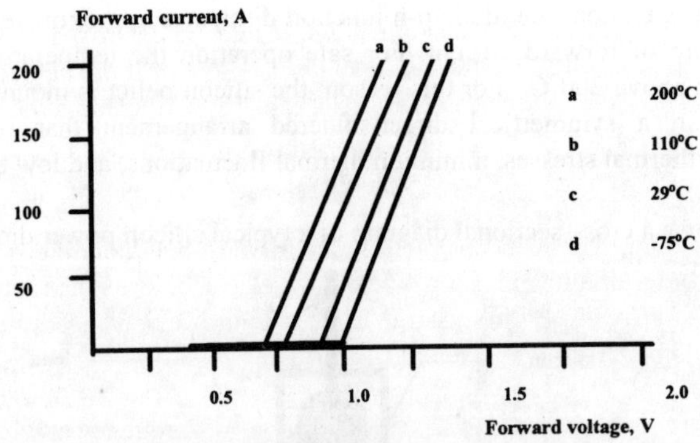

Figure 3.3 Forward characteristic of silicon diode

Reverse Current

Initially, as shown in Figure 3.4, reverse current increases slightly as the reverse voltage increases, but then tends to remain relatively constant, even though the reverse voltage is increased significantly. The figure also indicates that an increase in operating temperature causes a substantial increase in reverse current for a given reverse voltage. Reverse-blocking thermal runaway may occur because of this characteristic if the reverse dissipation becomes so large that, as the junction temperature rises, the losses increase faster than the rate of cooling.

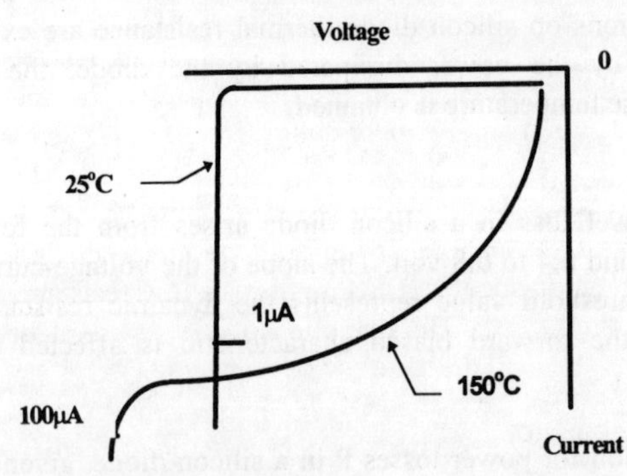

Figure 3.4 Reverse characteristic of silicon diode.

If the reverse voltage is continuously increased, it eventually reaches a value (which varies for different types of silicon diodes) at which a very sharp increase in reverse current occurs. This voltage is called the breakdown or avalanche (or Zener) voltage. Although a diode can operate safely at the avalanche point, it may be destroyed as a result of thermal runaway if the reverse voltage increases beyond this point or if the device temperature rises sufficiently (e.g., a rise in temperature from 25°C to 150°C increases the current by a factor of several hundred).

Reverse-Recovery Time
After a silicon diode has been operated under forward-bias conditions, some finite time interval (in the order of a few microseconds) must elapse before it can return to the reverse-bias condition. During this period, charge carriers in the device constitute a reverse current known as the reverse-recovery current.

The reverse-recovery time imposes an upper limit on the frequency at which a silicon diode may be used. Any attempt to operate the diode at frequencies above this limit results in a significant decrease in rectification efficiency and may also cause severe overheating and resultant destruction of the diode because of power losses during the recovery period.

Ratings
Ratings for silicon diodes are determined by the manufacturer on the basis of extensive testing. These ratings express the manufacturer's judgement of the maximum stress levels to which the diodes may be subjected without endangering the operating capability of the unit. These include: peak reverse voltage, forward current, operating and storage temperatures, amperes squared-seconds, and mounting torque.

Schottky Diodes
As operating frequencies of SMPS increase, the duty on the diodes has resulted in designers using diodes with better high-frequency performance. The Schottky diode is one of those devices found increasingly in SMPS circuits.

Structure
A Schottky diode is formed by placing a thin film of metal in direct contact with a semiconductor. The metal-semiconductor structure forms a low-resistance ohmic contact to semiconductor materials of all types. The operation of the device depends on quantum-mechanical effects which are beyond the scope of this book.

The arrangement has a rectifying v-i characteristic very similar to that of a pn junction diode. The major difference is that at any given forward current, the voltage across the Schottky diode is smaller than that across a pn junction. The difference amounts to roughly 0.3 V, which means that Schottky devices are less lossy than conducting pn junction diodes. Thus, the Schottky diode may be preferable for use in some power applications.

In the reverse direction, the Schottky diode has a reverse leakage current that is larger than that of a comparable silicon pn junction diode. With present fabrication techniques, the breakdown voltage of a Schottky diode cannot reliably be made much larger than 100 volts.

Switching Characteristics

A Schottky diode turns on and off faster than a comparable pn junction diode. The basic reason is that Schottky diodes are majority carrier devices and have no stored minority carriers that must be injected into the device during turn-on and removed during turn-off.

The lack of any significant stored charge changes the shape of observed switching waveforms in important ways. During turn-off, there will be no reverse current associated with removal of stored charge. However, reverse current, associated with the growth of the depletion layer charge in reverse bias, will flow.

Schottky diodes have much less voltage overshoot during device turn-on than comparable pn junction diodes. The basic reason is that the ohmic resistance of the drift regions in a Schottky diode must be made much less than that of a pn junction diode in order to carry the same forward current because there is no excess carrier injection to short out high-resistivity drift regions. Some voltage overshoot associated with parasitic inductance will be observed if di/dt is large.

METAL-OXIDE-SEMICONDUCTOR FIELD EFFECT TRANSISTORS (MOSFETs)

The circuit symbol of an n -channel MOSFET is as shown in Figure 3.5.

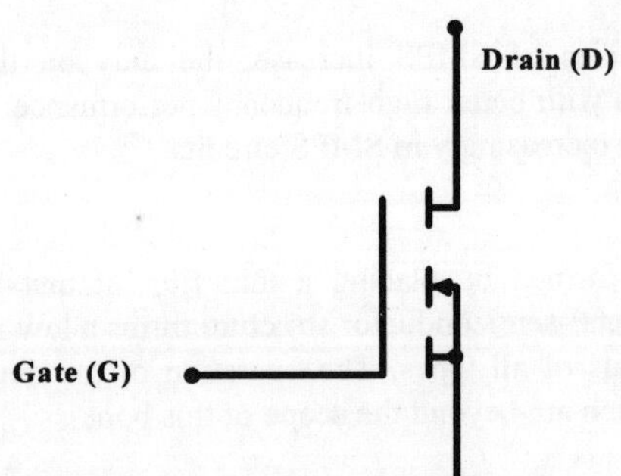

Figure 3.5 Circuit symbol of an n-channel MOSFET

The power MOS Field Effect Transistor (MOSFET) is a device that evolved from MOS integrated circuit technology. The motivation for the development of these devices arose from the large base drive current required by power bipolar transistors and their limited switching speed capability.

Neglecting all the variation in structure and theory, there is one difference between a conventional bipolar transistor and a metal oxide field effect transistor that greatly affects their performance in an operating environment. That is: the bipolar device is *current* driven, while the MOSFET is *voltage* driven. The major reason for this is that the gate of the MOSFET is electrically isolated from the source by a layer of oxide, giving a very high input resistance.

Current-Voltage Relationship for a MOSFET

Again, we are interested in the switching performance of the transistor. For the MOS transistor in saturation, we can define:

$$g_m = \frac{1}{R_{DS(ON)}}$$

$$I_D = \frac{g_m}{2(V_{GS} - V_T)}$$

where $R_{DS\ (ON)}$ is the device on-resistance in the linear region. The voltage-current relationship of a conventional MOSFET is as shown in Figure 3.6.

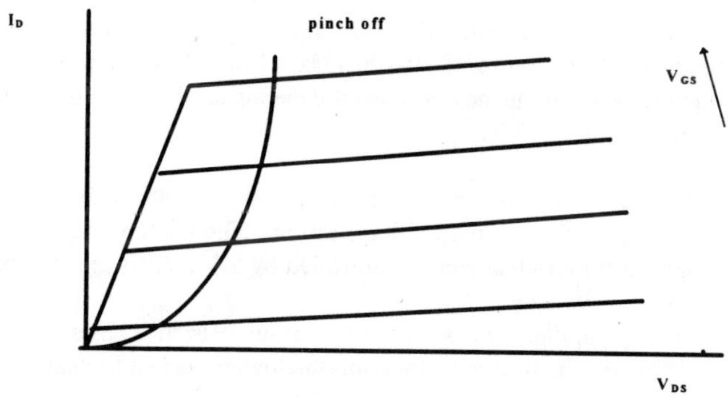

Figure 3.6 V-I relationship for a conventional MOSFET

Gate control is achieved by applying a positive voltage slightly in excess of the gate-to-source threshold voltage, $V_{GS(th)}$. Because of the relatively low drive voltage requirement and its high input impedance, the device is well suited for the control of high power directly from low-level logic circuits such as CMOS and TTL, provided adequate charge is supplied to charge up the input capacitance.

When a sufficiently large the gate-source voltage is applied, the device turns fully on and approximates a closed switch. The MOSFET is off when the gate-source voltage is below the threshold value, $V_{GS\,(th)}$.

MOSFETs require the continuous application of a gate-source voltage of appropriate magnitude in order to be in the on-state. No gate current flows except during the transitions from on to off or vice versa when the gate capacitance is being charged or discharged. The switching times are very short, being in the range of a few tens of nanoseconds to a few hundred nanoseconds depending on the device type.

The on-state resistance $r_{DS\,(on)}$ of the MOSFET between the drain and source increases rapidly with the device reverse voltage rating. On a per unit area basis, the on-state resistance as a function of reverse voltage rating BV_{DSS} can be expressed as

$$r_{DS\,(on)} = k\,BV_{DSS}^{\;2.5 \text{ to } 2.7}$$

where k is a constant that depends on the device geometry. Because of this, only devices with small voltage ratings are available that have low on-state resistance and hence small conduction losses.

However, because of their fast switching speed, the switching losses can be small. From a total power loss standpoint, 300-400-V MOSFETs compete with BJTs only if the switching frequency is in excess of 30-100 kHz. However, no definite statement can be made about the crossover frequency because it depends on the operating voltages, with low voltages favouring the MOSFET.

MOSFETs are available in voltage ratings in excess of 1000 V but with small current ratings and with up to 100 A at small voltage ratings. The maximum gate-source voltage is ± 20 V, although MOSFETs that can be controlled by 5-V signals are available.

MOSFETs are easily paralleled because their on-state resistance has a positive temperature coefficient. This causes the device conducting the higher current to heat up and thus forces it to equitably share its current with the other MOSFETs in parallel.

Switching MOSFETs

BJTs, when driven by low output transducers or logic circuits (such as SMPS control circuits), require an interface buffer, whereas a power MOSFET may not. While there are other differences that make one or the other transistor preferable in specific applications, these other differences are often of second-order importance.

MOSFET Capacitances

The physical structure of a MOSFET results in capacitance between the terminals. The metal oxide gate structure determines the capacitance from gate to source (C_{GS}) and gate-to-drain (C_{GD}): C_{GD} is enhanced by the Miller effect into an equivalent input capacitance which is given by

$$C_M = (1+g_m R_L) C_{GD}$$

The total input capacitance is formed by the combination of gate-source and Miller capacitances. The pn junction formed during fabrication results in a junction capacitance from drain to source (C_{ds}).

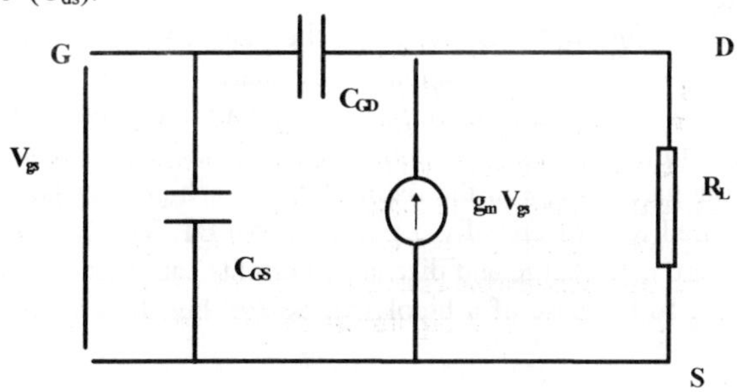

Figure 3.7 MOSFET capacitances

These capacitances, shown in Figure 3.7, are characterised as input, output and reverse transfer capacitances on data sheets. In driving a MOSFET, the input capacitance is an important consideration. On a transient basis, gate current will flow to charge up this capacitance in order to gain gate voltage control. The generator, or driving impedance, and the input capacitance affect the switching capabilities of the MOSFET: the lower the generator resistance (R_{gen}), the faster the switching speed. Temperature variations have very little effect on the capacitor values.

Claims of infinite current gain for the power MOSFETs are valid only at low frequency. As the switching frequency rises, the gate drive circuit needs to be able to source and sink the pulse currents required to charge and discharge the high input capacitance of these devices. This is particularly frustrating, since it is at high frequency where the power MOSFET is particularly valuable due to its inherently high switching speed.

MOSFET CHARACTERISTICS

The use of bipolar transistors (BJT) for SMPS has largely been discarded, we will deal only with MOSFETs. Where possible, the MOSFET will be contrasted with the BJT in order to clarify the reasons for its almost universal adoption.

Ideally, a transistor used as a switch will have the following characteristics:

- a high input impedance
- a low switching resistance

- a low on-resistance
- a high off-resistance
- an ability to withstand high overvoltages
- ruggedness.

Drive requirements

In a MOSFET, the oxide layer that separates the gate from the channel region gives an input impedance of 10^9 to 10^{11} ohms as compared to 10^3 to 10^5 for the bipolar transistor. A MOSFET requires little current to maintain a constant voltage on its gate but current is required to change the gate voltage. Sufficient drive current must be sourced or sunk to change the gate voltage in the required time. A higher voltage (approximately 10 volt) is also required to turn on fully a power MOSFET. The combination of high gate voltage and non-zero gate charge and discharge currents can often be met more easily than providing the drive to the base of a bipolar transistor, but these drive requirements must still be met.

Switching Time

The switching speed is directly related to delays within the structure and to capacitances which must be charged and discharged. The distance that carriers must travel from the emitter to the collector in a bipolar transistor is comparable to the source-to-drain distance in the MOSFET structure. Accordingly, any delays associated with carrier transit are similar to those of a BJT. The switching time in a power MOSFET is determined by the gate capacitance and the current available from the drive circuitry.

Voltage Drop in the On State

Power MOSFETs have been portrayed as being capable of fast switching speeds, but having a relatively large forward drop in the on state. The same resistance value is present in the collector of the bipolar transistor and the drain of the MOSFET. The power loss resulting from both switching and resistive losses means that the bipolar transistor has less total power loss at low frequencies while the power MOSFET is superior at high frequencies.

Device Off Resistance

The techniques used in the manufacture of power MOSFETs result in transistors with suitably low leakage currents at room temperature. However, at elevated temperatures, the leakage current increases due to the thermal generation of carriers. This unwanted junction "leakage" sets one limit on the maximum transistor operating temperature. Leakage currents do not affect the operation of power MOSFET devices significantly, and power MOSFETs with a rated junction operating temperature of 200°C are typical. There is no reason that this temperature rating cannot be achieved on all hermetic power MOSFET devices.

Transistor Breakdown Voltage

No electronics component is capable of withstanding an infinite voltage. The higher the voltage a device will withstand, the higher the voltage drop at a given current. It is most efficient to use a transistor with a voltage rating matched to the application. Investigation of the high voltage limits of power MOSFETs shows that there is a significant advantage in voltage withstand for the MOSFET over the BJT under all operating conditions. The bipolar transistor collector region thickness and resistivity must both be increased if the sustaining voltage of the bipolar transistor is to equal the breakdown voltage of the power MOSFET. This change in the collector material reduces the voltage drop advantage that a bipolar transistor has over a power MOSFET.

Ruggedness

The allowable limits for simultaneous voltage and current levels during a transistor operating cycle, including switching, are defined by the Safe Operating Area (SOAR) characteristic. The manufacture gives this for a range of operating conditions, from steady d.c. to short pulses.

The power MOSFET transistor has a superior temperature characteristic to the bipolar transistors because it has a negative temperature coefficient. The MOSFET is rugged at high currents. The negative temperature coefficient of the MOSFET reduces the current through localised regions, allowing the transistor to sustain a considerably higher current over the entire chip.

With reference to the MOSFET SOAR characteristic shown in Figure 3.8, the constraints are provided in three regions:

- The maximum allowable drain current. This is determined by thermal considerations for the mechanical parts of the device, that is leads, solder etc.
- The maximum allowable internal power dissipation in the silicon wafer. The resulting temperature rise will not cause chemical changes and damage.
- The upper operating voltage limit. Operation above this voltage is only possible under restricted conditions.

The SOAR for switching is different and more extended than the SOAR for linear operation. In fact, during switching, the operating point has two stable low dissipation states and only transitionally traverses the zones of high dissipation, that is to say during a very short period of time compared to the thermal time constant of the transistor.

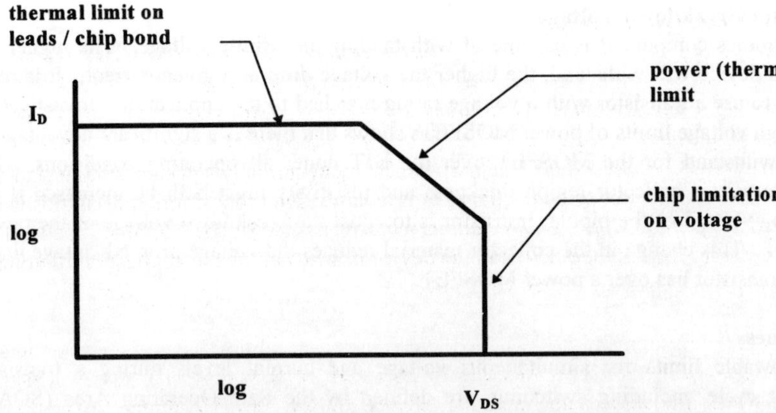

Figure 3.8 Safe operating areas of power MOSFET devices.

The maximum junction temperature is the limiting temperature that the silicon device can tolerate. This temperature must never be exceeded, since the device could then be damaged or destroyed. Lower operating temperatures improve transistor reliability. When the above recommendations are respected, even under worst case conditions, the switching transistors are a very reliable device.

Economics

For the same die size, MOSFETs cost the around same as the equivalent bipolar transistors and, in lower power devices, MOSFETs are cheaper. The prevailing trend in costs is downwards for both types of device, as can be seen in Figure 3.9.

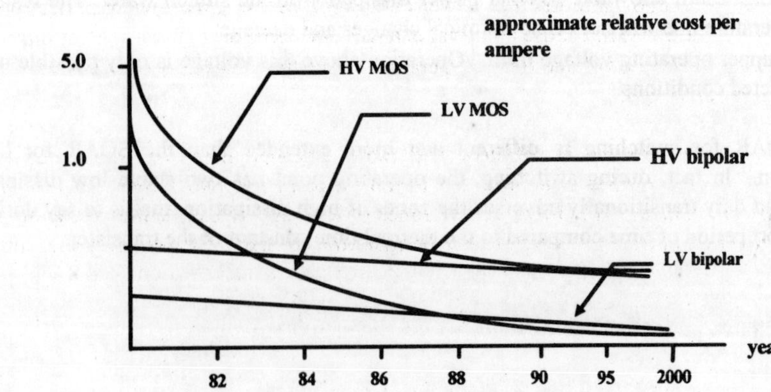

Figure 3.9 Cost trends of power semiconductors.

3.2 DRIVE CIRCUITS

GATE DRIVE FOR POWER MOSFETs

The circuitry to drive MOSFETs in a switched mode initially appears simple and the application of such devices to power supplies is an attractive proposition. Indeed, this is the case at low frequency, where the very high input resistance of the MOSFET means that very low current levels are required and the device is switched by the application of voltage alone.

However, the development of switched mode power supplies has involved a steady movement to higher switching frequencies because of the increased power densities possible. At such frequencies, the input capacitance of the MOSFET becomes the dominant feature of the input impedance, and driver circuits must be designed to have the current source and sink capability to charge and discharge, respectively, the effective gate-to-source capacitance.

Some integrated circuits, including those specifically designed for switched mode power supply control purposes, can provide up to 100 mA of sink and source output capability; and when directly coupled, a MOSFET can switch reasonably efficiently at 20 kHz. However, to switch efficiently at higher frequencies, several amperes of drive may be required.

Drive Requirements

A MOSFET responds instantaneously to changes in gate voltage and will begin to conduct when the threshold is reached (V_{GS} = 2 to 4 V) and be fully on when V_{GS} = 7 to 8 V. Gate waveforms will show a step at a point just above the threshold voltage which varies in duration, depending on the amount of drive current available. The drive current determines both the rise and fall times for the drain current. The drive current can be estimated as follows:

$$I_m = C_{DG}\ dV/dt$$
$$I_G = C_{GS}\ dv/dt$$

where I_m is the current required by the Miller effect to charge the drain-to-gate capacitance at the rate it is desired to move the drain voltage, and I_G is the current required to charge the gate-to-source capacitance through the linear region (2 to 8 V).

As an example, if 30 ns switching times are desired at 300 V, where

$$C_{DG} = 100\text{ pF and } C_{GS} = 500\text{ pF},$$

then,

$$I_m = 100 \text{ pF x } 300 \text{ V/30 ns} = 1.0 \text{ A}$$

$$I_G = 500 \text{ pF x } 6 \text{ V/30 ns} = 0.1 \text{ A}$$

This example shows that speed is directly tied to drive current,that C_{DG} will have the greatest effect on switching speed and that C_{GS} is important only in estimating turn-on and turn-off delays.

Drive Circuits

The drive requirements of the power MOSFET result in simple drive circuits, whether isolated or non-isolated.

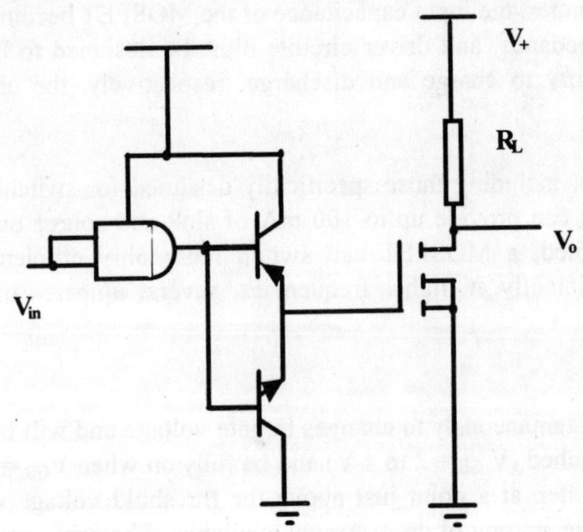

Figure 3.10 MOSFET drive circuit

The circuit shown in Figure 3.10 derives a basic low-power switching waveform from CMOS logic and achieves the required drive current capability from a bipolar transistor pair. If voltage isolation is required this can be achieved with a transformer.

There are applications where higher drive capability must be provided. The circuit shown in Figure 3.11 is an improvement on the CMOS drive circuit above. Here, current gain is again provided by bipolar transistors with the final drive stage being fed from a higher voltage supply, with corresponding increased drive capability, especially where high-power MOSFETs are used.

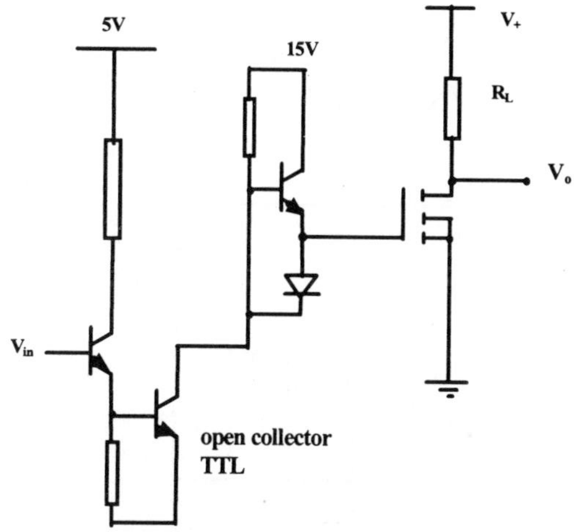

Figure 3.11 Improved MOSFET drive circuit

SNUBBERS

High frequency power conversion circuits subject power transistors to high instantaneous power dissipation during switching, both turn-on and turn-off. Additionally, as semiconductor manufacturers continually make their devices faster, the safe areas of operation must be carefully considered to prevent device failure. Consequently the circuit designers must pay particular attention to the turn-on and turn-off load lines to ascertain that they lie within the appropriate safe regions of the operation area. If the SOAR limits are being exceeded, load line shaping by the use of turn-on and turn-off snubbers must be employed.

Snubbers are passive switching aid circuits composed of diodes, resistors and impedances (capacitors or inductors) which reduce the severity of electrical effects on the transistor while switching. Of particular interest are:

- the rate of increase of voltage dV/dt while the transistor is being turned off.
- the rate of growth of the current dI/dt while transistor is being turned on.

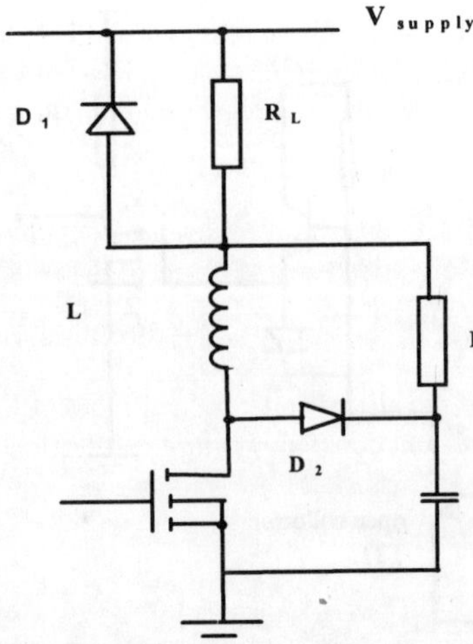

Figure 3.12 Unified snubber circuit

Figure 3.12 shows a unified snubber circuit: this has two principal functions, viz.

- it reduces the rate of growth dV/dt of the voltage on the transistor for the turn-off time, and consequently allows the use of a transistor having a smaller safe operating area.
- it allows considerable reduction of losses in the transistor. It could be said that, approximately, the switching losses are transferred from the transistor to the resistor R.

For other types of application, other advantages become apparent; parallel connection of transistors is made easier, reduction of EMI/RFI, etc.

The reduction of losses in the transistor gives the advantages of better reliability and faster switching times, both of which benefit from a fall in junction temperature.

In most switched mode power supply circuits the switching transistor load lines are inductive during turn-on because the short circuit created by output diode reverse recovery times is isolated by leakage inductance in the transformer. The inductance effectively snubs the turn-on load lines so that the diode recovery (or short circuit) current and the input voltage are not applied simultaneously to the transistor.

For most of the circuits (mainly non-isolated converters) where simultaneous high-voltage, high-current transients are applied to the transistors, the need for device protection will not be required, owing to the fact that the high speed switch is far more capable of absorbing this energy pulse in the forward biased mode than during turn-off. Nevertheless, the presence of such a power pulse will lead to higher average junction temperatures by way of dissipation in the switch.

When parasitic inductance is small and turn-on losses are considered excessive, a lumped series inductance is often purposely added in the form of a series turn-on snubber. The snubber reduces the rate of growth of the current $\frac{dI_D}{dt}$ for the turn-on time. It allows the reduction of turn-on losses in the transistor, and can lead indirectly to improved efficiency by allowing for a lower average junction temperature. Additionally, it may serve as a protective device in those situations where the forward biased safe operating area may be jeopardised by an extremely severe turn-on load line.

Severe and very often damaging, turn-on load lines can occur in half- and full-bridge PWM converter circuits fitted with the simple RCD turn-off switching aid network as described.

Protection Against Spike Voltages

The main purpose of the switching aid network at turn-off is to reduce the rate of rise of the re-applied voltage. Its effect as a spike voltage limiter is small.

If the presence of wiring inductance or leakage inductance of the transformer results in the generation of high spike voltages (fly back and push pull circuits in particular), it is possible to reduce these by using a component (eg. Zener diode) or a clamping circuit.

Parasitic Oscillations in MOSFETs

Power MOSFETs are very fast devices with appreciable gain at frequencies into the megahertz range. This high frequency gain, coupled with the internal and external circuit parasitic capacitances and inductances, particularly the loop inductance between discrete power MOSFETs, can cause unwanted parasitic oscillations to appear. The frequency of oscillation can range from 1 to 300 MHz.

The oscillations occur while the device is in the active mode where the transconductance is large. This means that in a switching application, the oscillations will occur on a transient basis during the turn-on and turn-off transitions. Parasitic oscillations cannot normally be tolerated and must therefore be eliminated. A small (1-5 ohm) non-inductive resistor in series with the gate lead of each device can reduce the problem to manageable proportions. A ferrite bead around individual gate leads is also sometimes used to good effect.

3.3 CONTROL REQUIREMENTS AND TECHNIQUES

A power supply should be designed to:

- have good line regulation, such that the output remains constant if the input voltage varies;
- have good load regulation, such that the output remains constant if the load changes;
- have good transient response to system disturbances, such as sudden changes to the input voltage, or to the load;
- remain stable under all operating conditions.

The above requirements are met by designing a feedback control system, which will control the duty ratio, D, of the transistor to keep the output constant at all times.

A sudden increase in load (ie. a reduction in R) will produce one of the effects on the output voltage V_o shown in Figure 3.13.

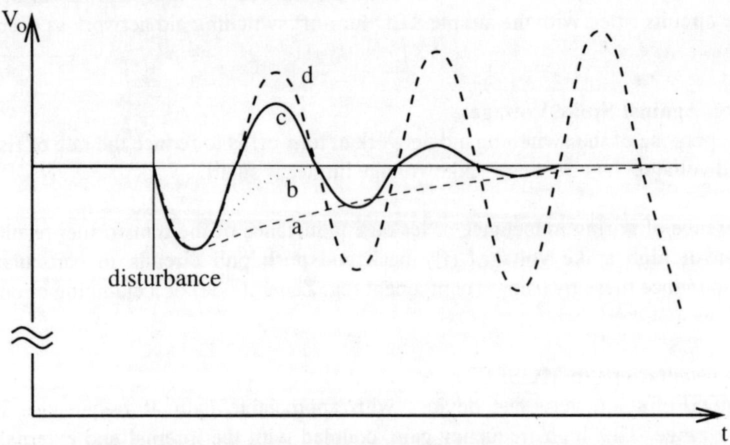

Figure 3.13 Output voltage response to an increase in load
(a) over-damped (poor response)
(b) critically damped (optimum)
(c) under-damped (oscillatory)
(d) unstable

A good power supply will return to the nominal output voltage very quickly, with minimal oscillations.

A simple buck regulator with feedback control is shown in Figure 3.14(a), and is redrawn in Figure 3.14(b) as a control block diagram. In designing the feedback loop, the transfer function of each block must be determined, and the loop transfer function optimised.

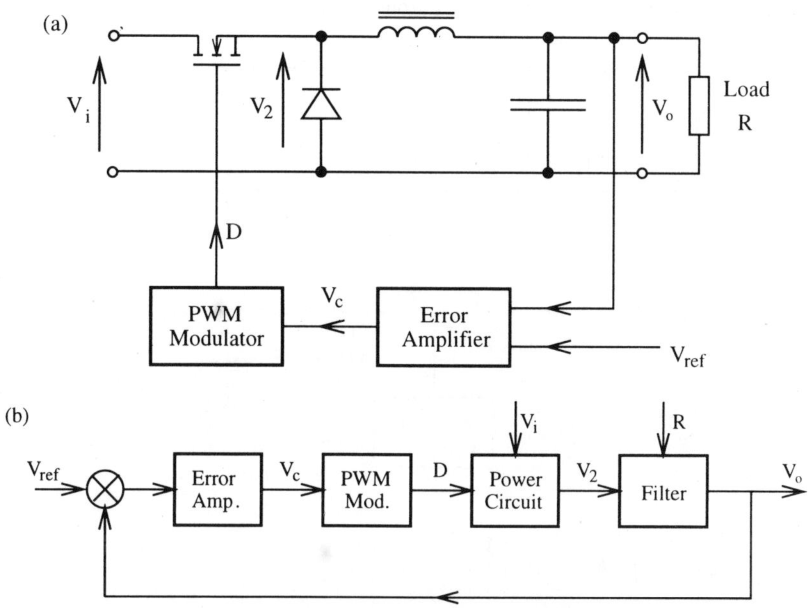

Figure 3.14 (a) Buck regulator with feedback control
(b) Power supply control block diagram

PWM CONTROLLERS

Direct Duty Control

In most SMPS, the output voltage V_o is controlled by comparing the output voltage with a reference voltage, and using the resulting error to adjust the duty ratio D.

In direct duty control, D is obtained by comparing the control voltage V_c with a fixed frequency sawtooth voltage, as illustrated in Figure 3.15. It can be seen that if the control voltage is increased, the duty ratio D is also increased. Thus:

$$D = \frac{t_{on}}{T} = \frac{V_c}{V_s}$$

In this technique, the sawtooth waveform has a fixed amplitude as well as fixed frequency, and the duty ratio D is adjusted only by a change in the output voltage altering the control voltage V_c .

This technique used to be very popular as it is very simple, but it does have drawbacks. The open loop line regulation is poor; ie. if the feedback loop is broken, a change in V_i will cause a significant change in the output voltage V_o. Direct duty control also has a poor closed loop transient response to changes in V_i, as a change in V_i will result in a compensating change in D delayed by the output L-C filter.

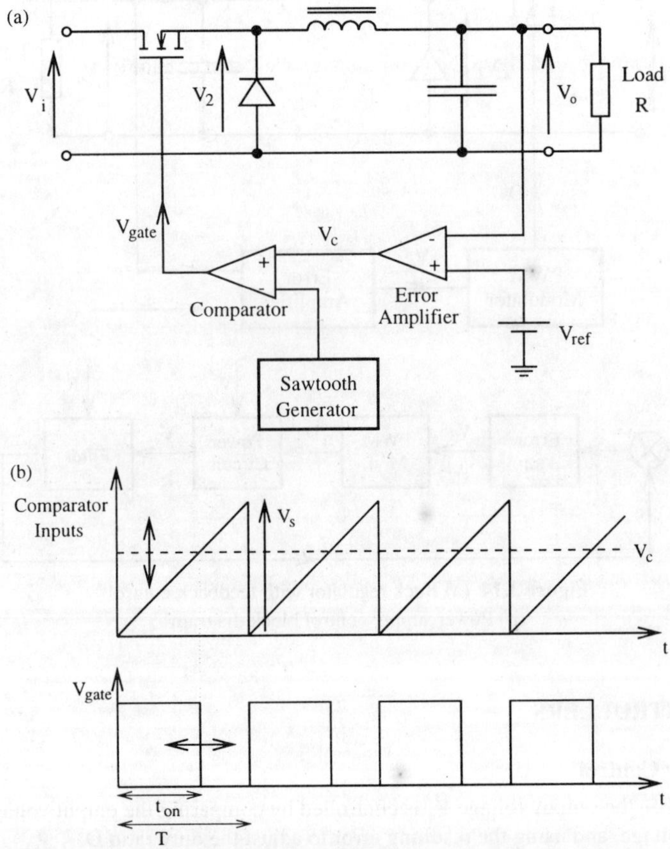

Figure 3.15 (a) Power supply with PWM control
(b) Control circuit waveforms

Voltage Feedforward Control

This is very similar to direct duty control, except that the magnitude of the sawtooth waveform, V_s , is proportional to the input voltage V_i. Therefore:

$$V_s = \frac{V_i}{K}$$

where K is a constant.

But:

$$D = \frac{V_c}{V_s}$$

Therefore:

$$D = K.\frac{V_c}{V_i}$$

In a buck regulator operating in the continuous mode, the d.c. gain is:

$$\frac{V_o}{V_i} = D$$

$$= \frac{K.V_c}{V_i}$$

Therefore:

$$V_o = K.V_c$$

Thus the output is no longer dependent on the input voltage; ie. the system has excellent open loop line regulation.

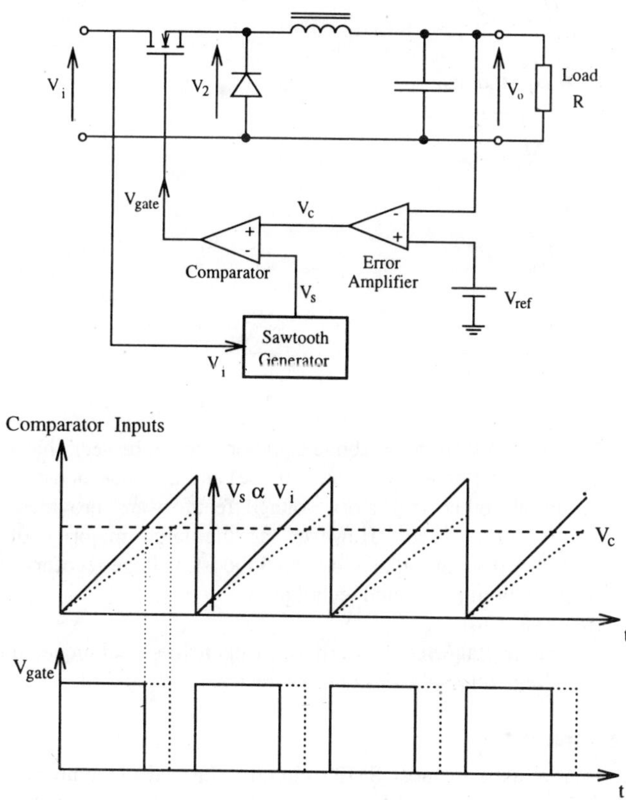

Figure 3.16 Buck regulator with voltage feedforward control

The closed loop transient response to input voltage changes is also excellent, as the delay caused by the L-C filter is not in the feedforward control line. Thus the compensating change in D is instantaneous and precise.

The d.c. gain for the 3 basic regulators in both modes of operation is shown below:

(a) Buck, Continuous.

$$\frac{V_o}{V_i} = D$$

(b) Buck, Discontinuous.

$$\frac{V_o}{V_i} = \frac{2D}{D + \sqrt{D^2 + (8L/RT)}}$$

(c) Buck-Boost, Continuous.

$$\frac{V_o}{V_i} = \frac{D}{1 - D}$$

(d) Buck-Boost, Discontinuous.

$$\frac{V_o}{V_i} = D.\sqrt{\frac{RT}{2L}}$$

(e) Boost, Continuous.

$$\frac{V_o}{V_i} = \frac{1}{1 - D}$$

(f) Boost, Discontinuous.

$$\frac{V_o}{V_i} = \frac{1 + \sqrt{1 + 2D^2TR/L}}{2}$$

By substituting $D = (K.V_c)/V_i$ into the above equations, it can be seen that V_i disappears from the d.c. gain in only the buck (continuous mode) and the buck-boost (discontinuous mode) regulators. In all other regulators voltage feedforward provides only partial compensation, and is rarely used. However, as the large majority of SMPS are continuous mode buck or discontinuous mode buck-boost, voltage feedforward control is a very important and easily implemented technique.

It should be noted that voltage feedforward is an open loop technique; therefore it is important that the scaling factors are designed correctly.

Current Mode Control

This technique is now used in most SMPS circuits. Instead of comparing the control voltage to an independently generated sawtooth voltage, the V_c is compared to a voltage derived from the inductor current, forming a second, inner control loop.

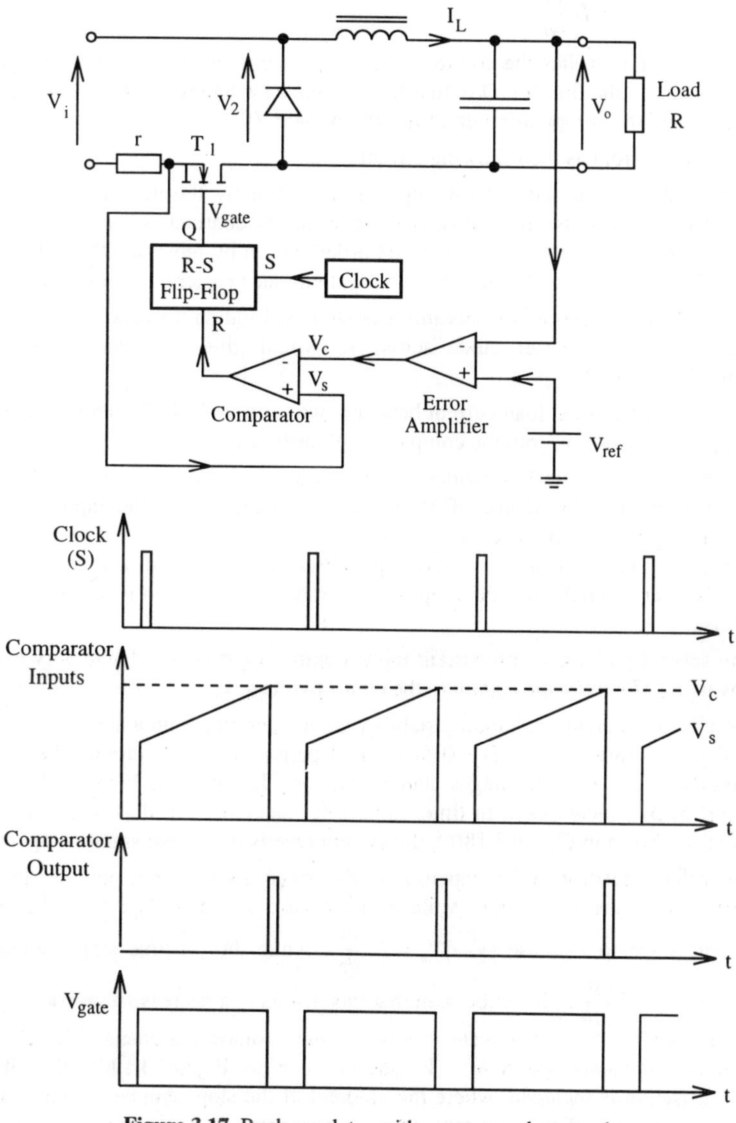

Figure 3.17 Buck regulator with current mode control

In the buck regulator shown in Figure 3.17, the clock sends a pulse to the R-S flip-flop which sets the Q output to logic "1", thus switching on the main transistor. The inductor current will then build up in a linear fashion:

$$V_i - V_o = L.\frac{dI_L}{dt}$$

When V_s (= I_L.r) reaches the control voltage V_c , the comparator output changes to a logic "1", resetting the flip-flop Q output to "0", hence switching off T_1. V_s immediately goes to zero, and the comparator output reverts to logic "0".

Current mode control has the following advantages:

- Because the inductor current is being controlled directly, the effect of the inductor in the feedback loop is eliminated, making what (in continuous mode circuits) is a second order control system into a first order system by removing the inductor pole from the loop. This makes the resulting system much easier to stabilise.
- Current limit protection is easily implemented, by limiting the maximum value of V_c and hence I_L (a Zener diode across V_c would give an effective, though not adjustable, clamp).
- Precise sharing of the load current between two (or more) SMPS can be achieved by feeding a common V_c into the comparator of each SMPS.
- Current mode control provides a measure of voltage feedforward control, eliminating the dependence of V_o on input voltage V_i. If the input voltage V_i increases, then the inductor voltage (V_i - V_o) increases, and the gradient dI_L/dt increases. Thus V_s reaches V_c more quickly, reducing t_{on} and hence the duty ratio D. There are no delays in the loop, so duty ratio compensation is instantaneous and precise.

There are several problems with current mode control, most of which can very easily be solved by using *Slope Compensation* to the control voltage V_c.

- There is an inherent open loop instability when operating with a duty ratio $D > 0.5$. In Figure 3.18(a), where $D < 0.5$, a small perturbation ΔI_L rapidly dies away in subsequent cycles, indicating a stable situation. However, in Figure 3.18(b), with $D > 0.5$, ΔI_L increases with time, indicating instability. If slope compensation is added as shown in Figure 3.18(c), the system reverts to a stable situation again.
- The voltage feedforward compensation described above is not perfect. In Figure 3.19(a), an increase in input voltage (from case 1$\rightarrow$ case 2) causes the on-time current slope to increase ($V_i - V_o = L.\frac{di}{dt}$), while the off-time slope remains the same ($-V_o = L.\frac{di}{dt}$). It can be seen that this results in a decrease in average inductor current, which should not occur if only the input voltage has changed (assuming the load has remained constant). It can be seen in Figure 3.19(b) that if slope compensation is included, where the gradient of the slope compensation is half the gradient of the off-time current slope, the average inductor current remains the same, indicating effective voltage feedforward compensation.
- A further problem with current mode control is that there can be a sub-harmonic oscillation at half the switching frequency. This also is improved by including slope compensation.

Slope compensation can be applied either by adding the sawtooth waveform to the current signal, or by subtracting from the control voltage.

The main disadvantage of current mode control is that control is dependent on the load current - a higher value of V_c and hence steady state error is apparent at high load currents.

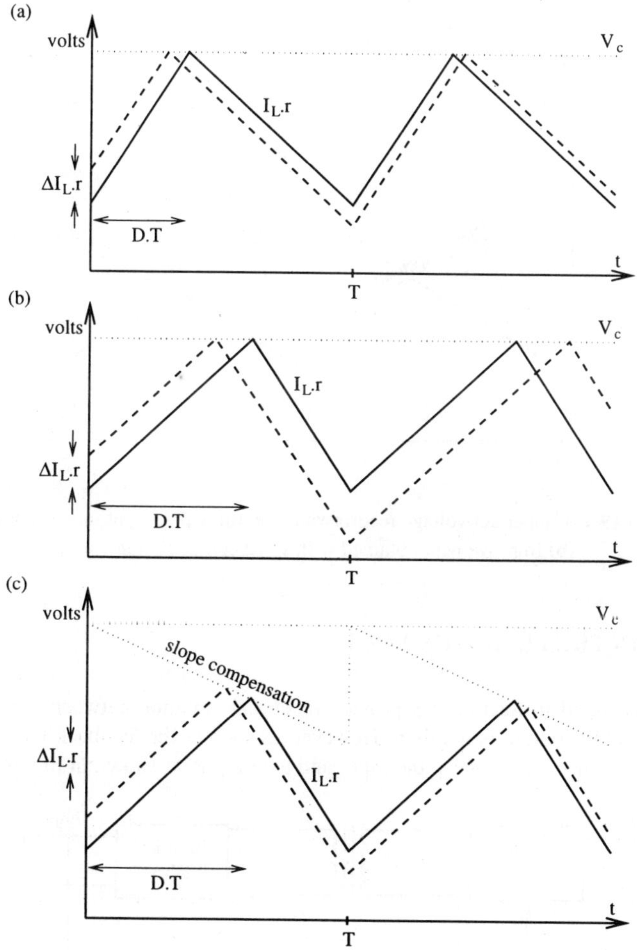

Figure 3.18 Effect of small perturbations with current mode control
(a) Stable system with D<0.5
(b) Unstable system with D>0.5
(c) Stable system with D>0.5 with slope compensation included

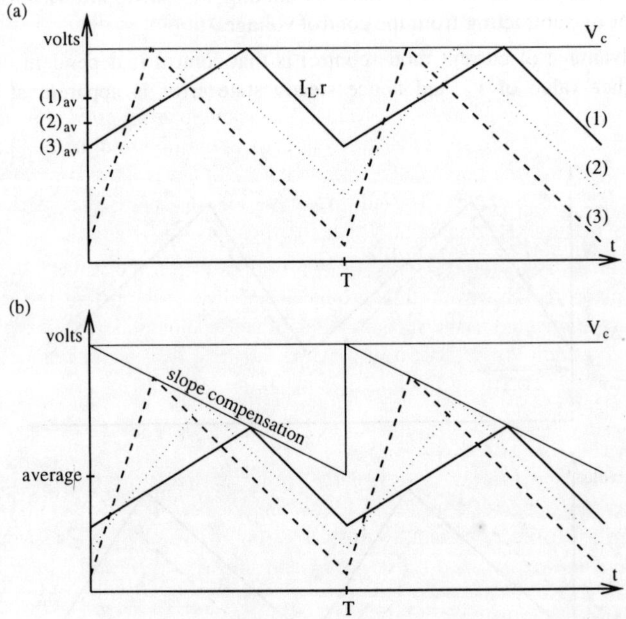

Figure 3.19 (a) Imperfect voltage feedforward control with current mode control
(b) Improvement obtained with slope compensation

ISOLATION IN THE FEEDBACK LOOP

The circuits discussed in Section 1.3 provide electrical isolation between the input and the output, so that the output is floating. However, as soon as the feedback loop is closed, there is another connection between the input and the output, as shown in Figure 3.20.

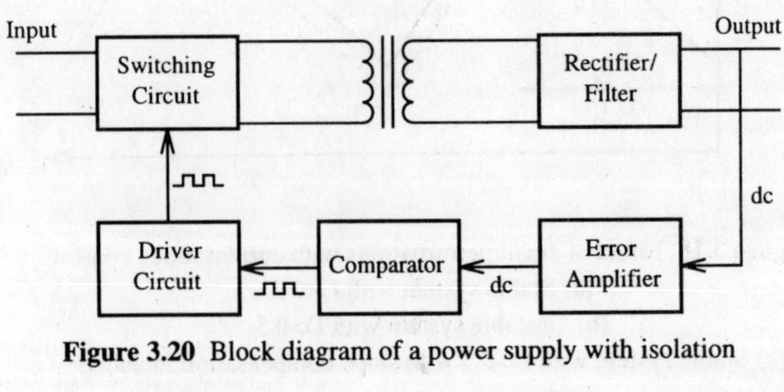

Figure 3.20 Block diagram of a power supply with isolation

For the output to be floating, some form of isolation is necessary in the feedback loop. This can be provided by magnetic coupling, using a transformer, or opto-coupling.

Magnetic Coupling

Transformers only work with a.c., so a transformer cannot be inserted directly between the output and the error amplifier, or between the error amplifier and the comparator. If a transformer is to be inserted here, a high frequency a.c. carrier waveform would have to be generated, and the d.c. signal used to amplitude modulate the carrier. This is sometimes done, but it adds considerably to the complexity of the circuit.

Much more common is to insert a pulse transformer between the driver circuit and the switching transistor(s). However, this produces another problem, as the control and driver circuits are connected to the secondary, and therefore must derive their power from the secondary. This can create start-up problems, as there will be no secondary voltage until the transistors have started switching.

Opto-Coupling

Another alternative is to use an opto-isolator, either between the output and the error amplifier, or between the error amplifier and the comparator. This means that the control and driver circuits can be powered from the d.c. input (which may cause problems if operating from a high d.c. voltage). However, opto-isolators tend to be very non-linear, and extra biasing circuitry may be necessary to produce a reasonably linear transfer function. This is not a major problem if the opto-isolator is placed after the error amplifier, as any non-linearities are compensated for by the feedback loop.

In circuits where regulation is not particularly tightly specified, the feedback signal can be taken from an extra winding on the transformer. This is the simplest technique, but no feedback compensation will be made for any volt drops on the secondary circuit, such as across the rectifying diodes or the filter inductor.

POWER SUPPLIES WITH MULTIPLE OUTPUTS

In many applications, there is more than one output, each fed from a separate transformer secondary. The output voltage feedback signal, which is fed into the control circuit to set the transistor duty ratio D, can only be taken from one output. Hence the value of D will be set at a level which will keep that particular output at the required voltage, regardless of the voltage at the other outputs.

In the case of the forward converter shown in Figure 3.21 operating in the continuous mode, the d.c. gain is:

$$\frac{V_o}{V_i} = 2.n.D.\frac{R}{R + r_L} \quad \text{including the effect of inductor resistance, } r_L$$

From the above, it can be seen that a change in the input voltage V_i would affect each output in the same proportion, so the feedback signal from output 1 would produce an adjustment in the duty ratio D which would correct each output. Hence the *line* regulation for the auxiliary outputs would be approximately the same as for the main output.

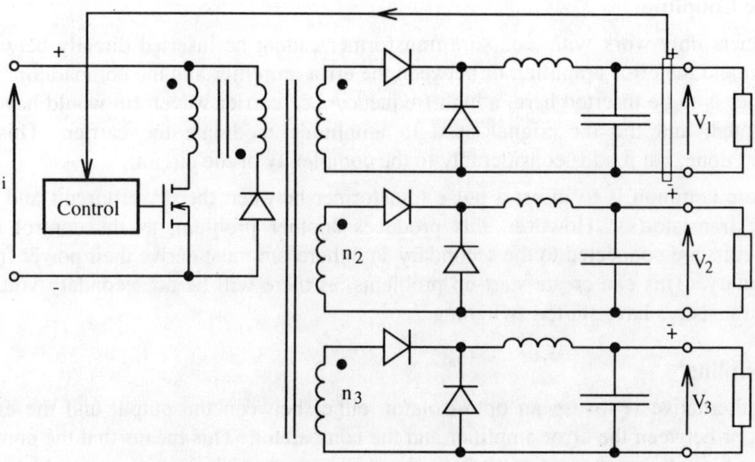

Figure 3.21 Forward converter with three outputs

In a practical converter where $r_L \neq 0$, a change in load resistance R will produce a change in the output voltage. In the case of the main output, the feedback signal will produce a compensating adjustment in D. However, a change in load in any of the auxiliary outputs will not substantially affect the main output voltage; therefore there will be no compensating adjustment in D. Thus the *load* regulation of the auxiliary outputs will not be as good as for the main output. This will be accentuated if discontinuous mode operation is used, as the output voltage inherently depends on the load R.

Typically, a multiple output SMPS may have 0.5% load regulation on the main output, but only 3% on each of the auxiliary outputs.

If close regulation on an auxiliary output is required, then a post-regulator must be used. This is normally either a linear regulator or a basic buck regulator, which will add considerably to the size and weight of the total power supply. Magnetic amplifiers are also making a comeback as post-regulators, due to the development of new core materials and custom magnetic amplifier control integrated circuits.

Dynamic cross-regulation between the regulated output and the unregulated outputs tends to be poor, as it takes a long time for the control circuit to see the effect on the regulated output of a load change on an unregulated output. A useful technique for improving the dynamic cross-regulation is to wind the output inductors on the same core, so that a change in an unregulated output is immediately coupled to the regulated output, which can be then corrected by the feedback circuit. However, this can make it more difficult to stabilise the power supply.

3.4 BODE DIAGRAMS

Bode's technique of plotting the system gain and phase response against frequency for a sinusoidal disturbance provides a very useful graphical method of analysing the system, and calculating the necessary compensation components to ensure both stability and a fast transient response.

R-C Low-pass Network

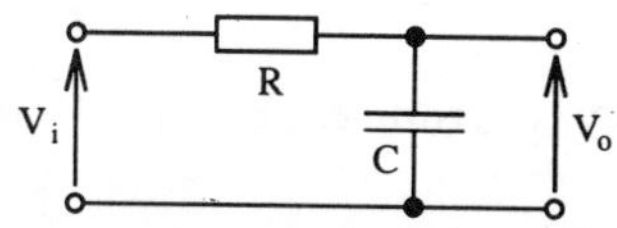

$X_C = \frac{1}{j\omega C}$

Figure 3.22 R-C low-pass network

In the circuit in Figure 3.22, for a sinusoidal input V_i at frequency ω $(= 2\pi f)$:

$$V_o = V_i \times \left[\frac{\frac{1}{j\omega C}}{R + \frac{1}{j\omega C}} \right]$$

Therefore:

$$\frac{V_o}{V_i} = \frac{1}{1 + j.RC.\omega}$$

$$= \frac{1}{1 + j.\frac{\omega}{\omega_p}}$$

where:

$$\omega_p = \frac{1}{RC}$$

If $\omega \ll \omega_p$

$$Gain = \frac{V_o}{V_i} = 1$$

or, expressed in decibels:

$$Gain = 20 \log_{10}\left(\frac{V_o}{V_i}\right)$$

$$= 20 \log_{10}(1)$$

$$= 0\ dB$$

The phase difference between V_i and V_o is 0°.

If $\omega \gg \omega_p$:

$$\frac{V_o}{V_i} = \frac{\omega_p}{\omega}$$

Therefore, the gain in decibels is:

$$Gain = 20 \log_{10}\left(\frac{\omega_p}{\omega}\right)$$

$$= 20 \log_{10} \omega_p - 20 \log_{10} \omega$$

$$(= 0 \ dB \qquad at \ \omega = \omega_p \ )$$

The slope of gain (dB) against frequency is -20 dB/decade. Also, V_o lags V_i by 90°.
At $\omega = \omega_p$, V_o lags V_i by 45°.
The circuit gain and phase can be plotted against frequency on log-linear scales as shown in Figure 3.23.

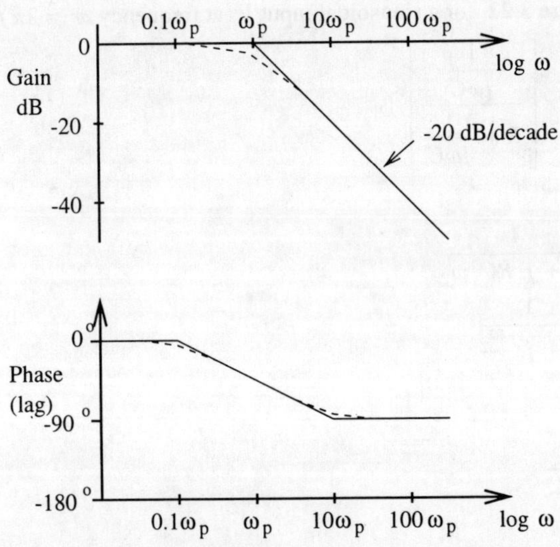

Figure 3.23 Gain and phase response of R-C low-pass network

If s = jω then:

$$\frac{V_o}{V_i} = F(s) = \frac{1}{1 + j\dfrac{s}{\omega_p}}$$

The denominator = 0 when s = -jω_p
ie. a *pole* exists at ω_p $(F(s) \rightarrow \infty)$

A network with opposite gain and phase responses is said to introduce a zero into a system. The Bode diagram in Figure 3.24 shows the gain and phase responses of a network with a single zero. The gain response increases at 20dB per decade, from ω_z, while the phase response has a 90° lead centred on ω_z. Such a network can be useful to compensate the response of a system with several poles.

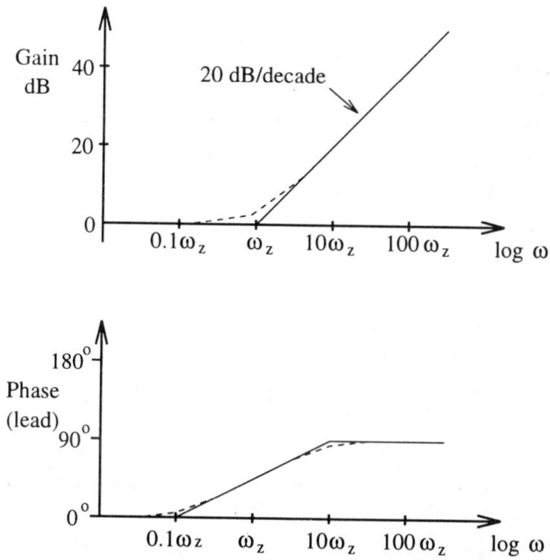

Figure 3.24 The gain and phase response associated with a zero

To summarise: a pole has a phase lag and a down-turned frequency response plot, while a zero has a phase lead and an up-turned frequency response plot associated with it.

L-C Network

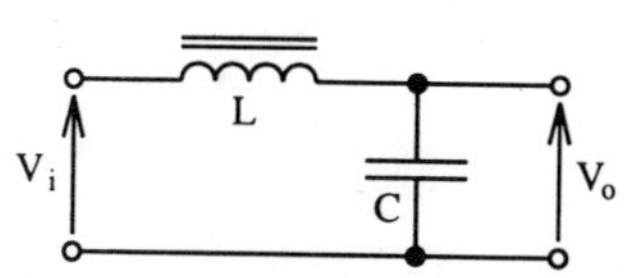

$X_L = j\omega L$

$X_C = \frac{1}{j\omega C}$

Figure 3.25 An L-C network

Ideally, for a lossless circuit:

$$\frac{V_o}{V_i} = \frac{\left(\frac{1}{j\omega C}\right)}{j\omega L + \left(\frac{1}{j\omega C}\right)}$$

$$= \frac{1}{1 + (j\omega)^2 LC}$$

$$= \frac{1}{1 + \dfrac{(j\omega)^2}{(\omega_p)^2}}$$

where:

$$\omega_p = \frac{1}{\sqrt{LC}}$$

In the above ideal, lossless, circuit, (V_o/V_i) tends to infinity at $\omega = \omega_p$.

The effective circuit resistance R_s limits the gain at $\omega = \omega_p$ to a finite value, depending on the circuit Q factor, where:

$$Q = \frac{\omega L}{R_s}$$

The gain becomes:

$$\frac{V_o}{V_i} = F(s) = \frac{1}{1 + \left(\dfrac{s}{\omega_p} \cdot \dfrac{1}{Q}\right) + \left(\dfrac{s}{\omega_p}\right)^2}$$

which has a double pole at $\omega = \omega_p$.

The gain and phase plots against frequency are shown in Figure 3.26 for different Q values.

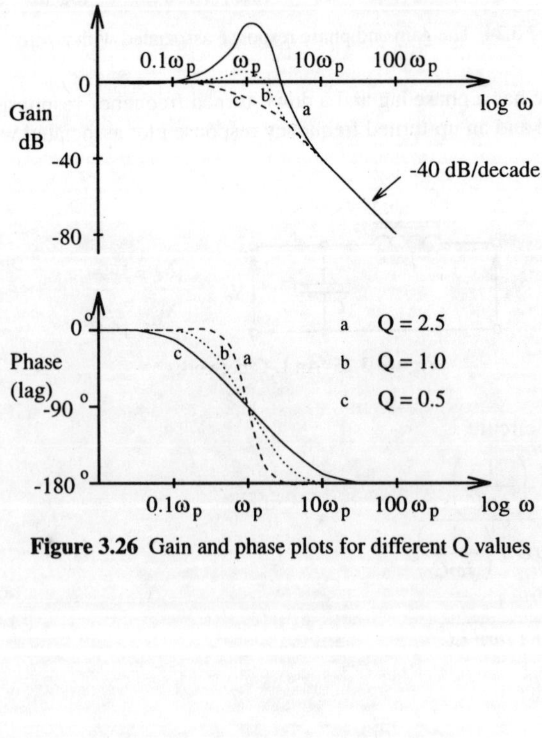

Figure 3.26 Gain and phase plots for different Q values

Blocks In Cascade

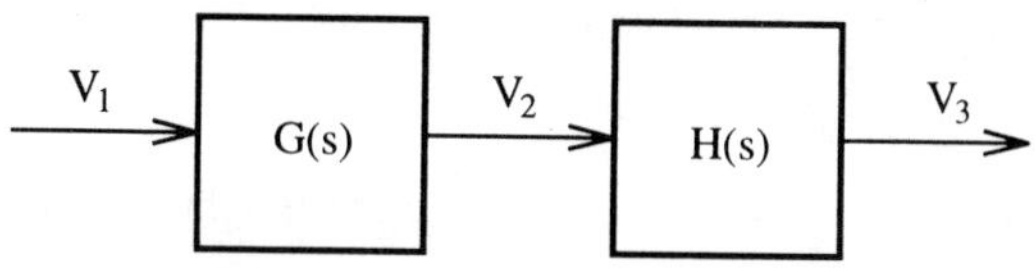

Figure 3.27 Two cascaded networks

In Figure 3.27:

$$V_2(s) = G(s).\, V_1(s)$$

$$V_3(s) = H(s).\, V_2(s)$$

Therefore:

$$\frac{V_3(s)}{V_1(s)} = G(s).\, H(s)$$

ie. The gains of cascaded blocks multiply.

Plotting Functions With Several Poles And Zeros

Example:

$$G(s) = \frac{10\, .\, (1 + 0.\,1s)}{s\, .\, (1 + 0.\,5s)}$$

(a) Constant gain term, (10):

In decibels, $= 20 \log_{10} 10 = 20\ dB$

No effect on phase.

(b) First pole term, $\left(\frac{1}{s}\right)$:

In decibels, $= 20 \log_{10} \left(\frac{1}{s}\right)$

This is a straight line of gradient -20 dB/decade, passing through 0 dB at $\omega = 1$ rad/s.

It will produce a 90° phase lag at all frequencies.

(c) Second pole term, $\left(\frac{1}{1 + 0.\,5s}\right)$:

In decibels, $=20 \log_{10}\left(\frac{1}{1+\frac{s}{2}}\right) = -20 \log_{10}\left(1+\frac{s}{2}\right) dB$

This will be 0 dB from 0 to s=2 rad/s, thereafter a straight line of gradient -20 dB/decade.

There will be 0° phase lag from 0 to 0.2 rad/s,
a 90° lag from 20 rad/s upwards, and
a straight line from 0.2 rad/s to 20 rad/s, passing through 45° at 2 rad/s.

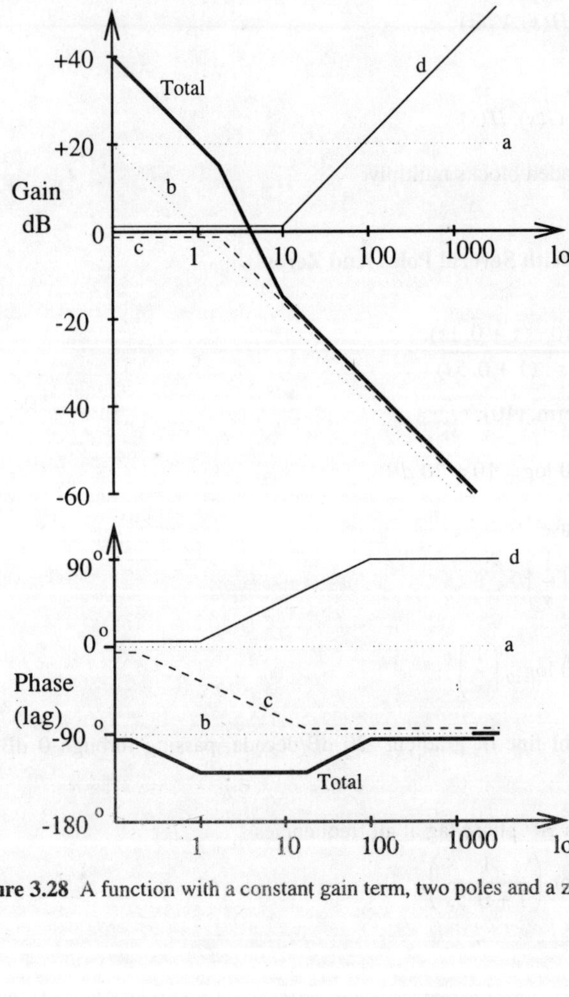

Figure 3.28 A function with a constant gain term, two poles and a zero

(d) Zero term, $(1 + 0.1s)$:

In decibels, $= 20 \log_{10}\left(1 + \frac{s}{10}\right)$ dB

This will be 0 dB from 0 to 10 rad/s, thereafter a straight line of gradient +20 dB/decade.

There will be 0° phase lag up to 1 rad/s,
a 90° phase *lead* from 100 rad/s,
a straight line from 1 rad/s to 100 rad/s, passing through a 45° lead at 10 rad/s.

STABILITY ANALYSIS

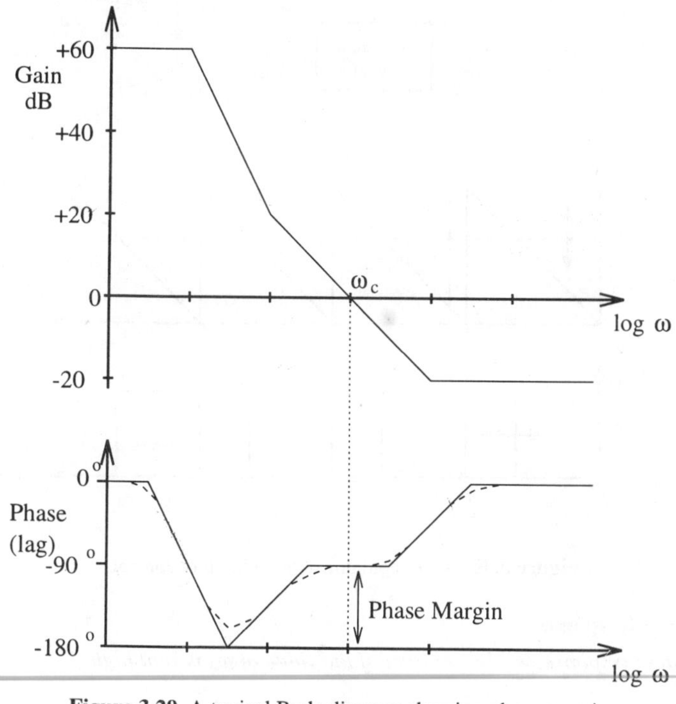

Figure 3.29 A typical Bode diagram showing phase margin

(a) Regulation

From Figure 3.30:

$$V_c = (amplifier\ gain) \times (error\ voltage)$$

$$= \frac{R_f}{R_i} \times (V_o - V_{ref})$$

ie. a large amplifier gain results in a small error voltage.

Good line and load regulation will be achieved if the d.c. gain (the gain at ω =0) is high.

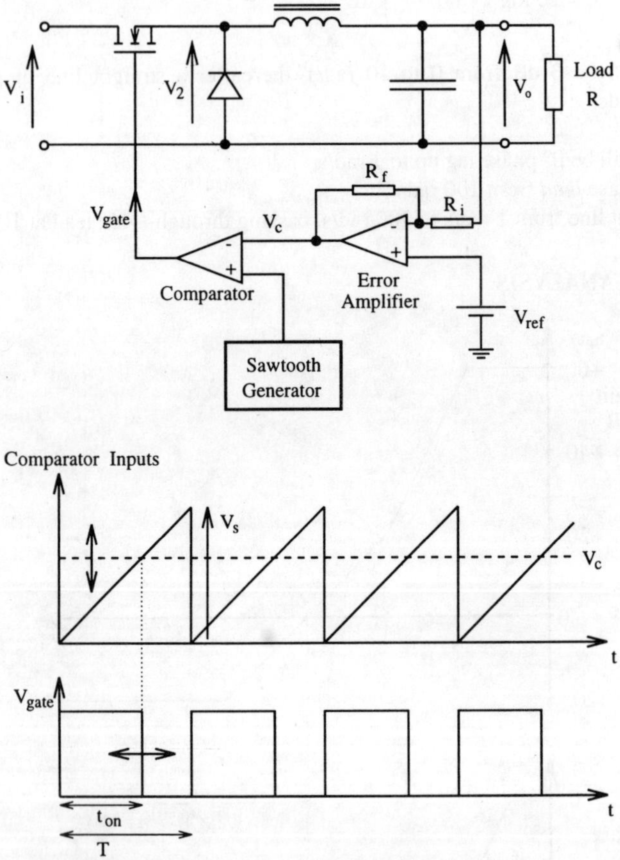

Figure 3.30 Buck regulator with direct duty control

(b) Transient Response

A fast transient response will be achieved if the value of ω_c is kept high.

(c) Stability

For a stable system, the phase lag at ω_c must be less than 180°.

If the Phase Margin is small, the system will be very oscillatory.

A phase margin of 45°→60° generally gives a good response.

3.5 ERROR AMPLIFIER COMPENSATION TECHNIQUES

The block diagram of a switched mode power supply as a control system is shown in Figure 3.31.

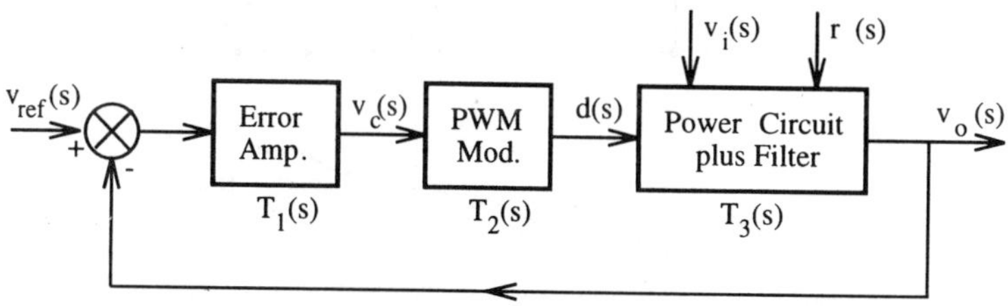

Open loop gain = $T_1(s) \, . \, T_2(s) \, . \, T_3(s)$

Figure 3.31 Power supply control block diagram

Possible system disturbances are:

- change in input voltage, V_i ,
- change in load resistance, R,
- change in V_{ref} (never likely to occur).

As discussed in section 3.3, the effects of a change in V_i can be largely eliminated by the use of either voltage feedforward control or current mode control in continuous mode buck and discontinuous mode flyback regulators.

The transfer function of the power stage and filter, $T_3(s)$, depends on the circuit topology chosen, and whether it is operating in the continuous or discontinuous current mode. $T_2(s)$ depends on the type of controller used: normally direct duty, voltage feedforward, or current mode. There is little flexibility to alter either T_2 or T_3; however, a potentially unstable loop can be stabilised by adding suitable compensation components to optimise the transfer function of the error amplifier, T_1.

POWER CIRCUIT AND FILTER

Power supplies operating in the continuous current mode have a dominant 2 pole characteristic associated with the capacitor and the inductor, plus a (high frequency) zero from the capacitor ESR.

The inductor current when load is suddenly applied to a buck converter operating in the continuous current mode is shown in Figure 3.32.

It takes several cycles for the inductor current to build up to the new load current, due to the large value of inductance necessary to maintain continuous current. During this period the capacitor has to supply the extra load current, causing the output voltage to fall temporarily.

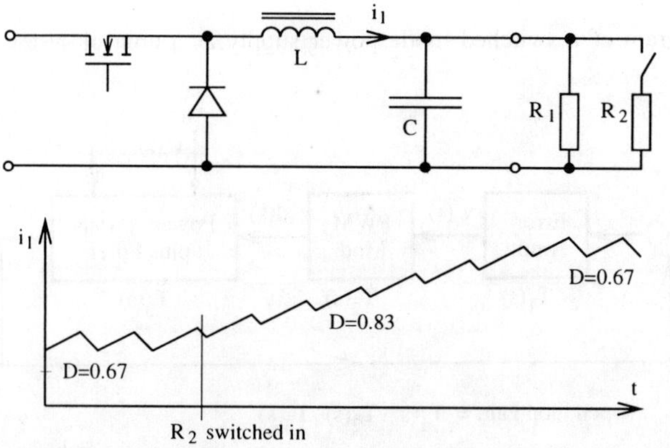

Figure 3.32 Inductor current in a continuous mode buck regulator as load is applied

If, however, the circuit is designed to operate in the discontinuous current mode, then the inductance has to be small enough for the current to be able to build up to any value within a cycle, as shown in Figure 3.33.

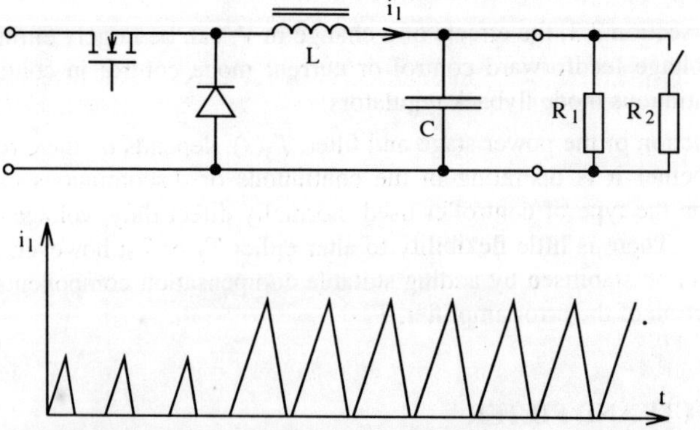

Figure 3.33 Inductor current in a discontinuous mode buck regulator as load is applied

As changes in the duty ratio D can only be made once per cycle, the inductor disappears from the feedback loop, leaving a single pole characteristic associated with the filter capacitor, which is much easier to stabilise.

The d.c. gain of the buck-boost regulator operating in the continuous current mode is:

$$\frac{V_o}{V_i} = \frac{D}{(1 - D)}$$

and for the boost regulator operating in the continuous current mode:

$$\frac{V_o}{V_i} = \frac{1}{(1-D)}$$

The term $(1 - D)$ in the denominator has a dramatic effect on the response of the circuits to sudden load changes.

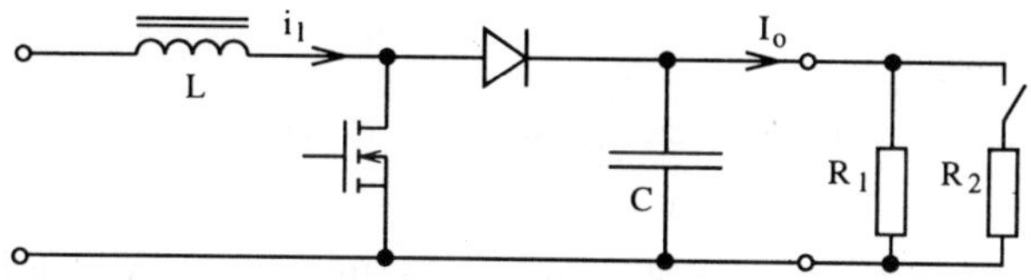

Figure 3.34 Boost converter

In the boost converter in Figure 3.34, the output voltage will drop if load R_2 is switched on. The feedback circuit will compensate by increasing D to bring V_o back to its rated value. The inductor has a large value in continuous mode circuits, so i_L cannot quickly increase to the new load current, so the *immediate* effect of increasing D is only to reduce the time current is flowing through the diode, so *reducing* the energy transferred, causing the output voltage to *reduce* still further.

The term $1/(1 - D)$ leads to a *right half plane zero* in the open loop transfer function. The effect of an RHP zero is, like a normal LHP zero, to reduce the gain slope by -20 dB/decade, but it *increases* the phase lag by 90°. This makes continuous mode buck-boost and boost circuits very difficult to stabilise, and for this reason buck-boost and boost regulators are usually operated in the discontinuous current mode.

The two most common circuit topologies used are continuous mode buck converters and discontinuous mode buck-boost converters.

Continuous Mode Buck Converters

The d.c. gain of a continuous mode buck converter is:

$$\frac{V_o}{D} = V_i$$

Under small signal a.c. conditions with either direct duty or voltage feedforward the transfer function is:

$$T_3(s) = \frac{v_o(s)}{d(s)} = V_i . H_e(s)$$

where:

$$H_e(s) = \frac{\left(1 + \frac{s}{\omega_z}\right)}{1 + \left(\frac{s}{\omega_p} \cdot \frac{1}{Q}\right) + \left(\frac{s^2}{\omega_p^2}\right)}$$

with:

$$\omega_z = \left(\frac{1}{R_c.C}\right)$$

$$\omega_p = \frac{1}{\sqrt{L.C}}$$

$$Q = \left(\frac{R}{\omega_p.L}\right)$$

R_c = capacitor effective series resistance (ESR)

R = load

The asymptotic plot of the gain and phase of $T_3(s)$ against frequency is shown in Figure 3.35. It should be noted that the Q-factor of the combined filter and load can cause peaking at the double pole, which may result in the response differing markedly from the asymptotic plot around this double pole.

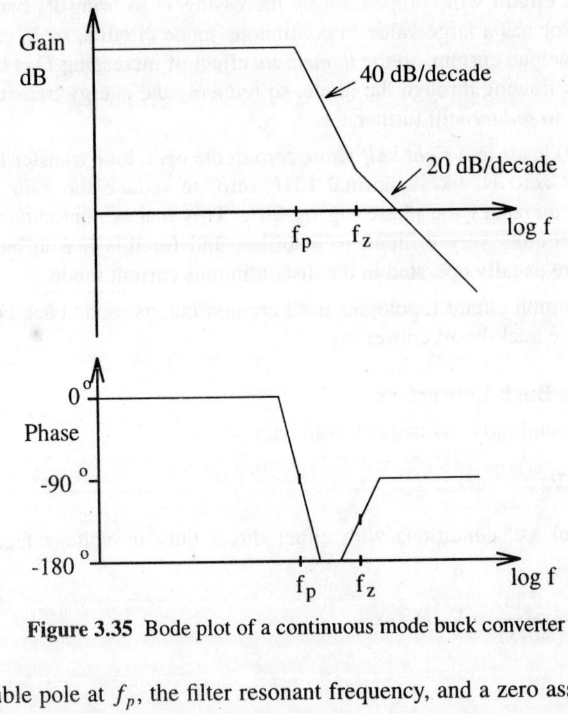

Figure 3.35 Bode plot of a continuous mode buck converter

There is a double pole at f_p, the filter resonant frequency, and a zero associated with the capacitor ESR.

Discontinuous Mode Flyback Converters

The d.c. gain of a buck-boost converter is:

$$\frac{V_o}{D} = V_i \cdot \sqrt{\frac{R}{2.L.f}}$$

Under small signal a.c. conditions:

$$T_3(s) = \frac{v_o(s)}{d(s)} = V_i \,.\, \sqrt{\frac{R}{2.\,L.\,f}} \,.\, H_e(s)$$

where:

$$H_e(s) = \frac{\left(1 + \frac{s}{\omega_z}\right)}{\left(1 + \frac{s}{\omega_p}\right)}$$

$$\omega_z = \left(\frac{1}{R_c.\,C}\right)$$

$$\omega_p = \left(\frac{2}{R.\,C}\right)$$

The gain and phase of $T_3(s)$ are plotted against frequency in Figure 3.36.

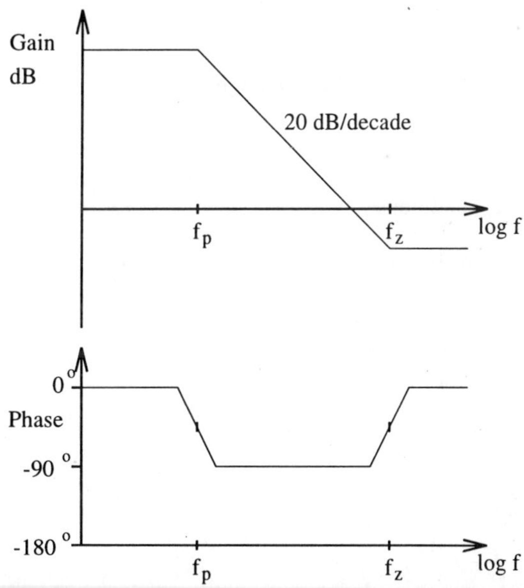

Figure 3.36 Bode plot of a discontinuous mode buck-boost converter

There is a single pole associated with the capacitor and the load, and a high frequency zero associated with the capacitor ESR.

PWM CONTROLLER

(a) Direct Duty

$$T_2(s) = \frac{d(s)}{v_c(s)} = \frac{1}{V_s}$$

where V_s is the peak sawtooth voltage.

(b) Voltage Feedforward

$$T_2(s) = \frac{d(s)}{v_c(s)} = \frac{K}{V_i}$$

(c) Current Mode

Current mode control removes the inductor pole from the power stage and filter transfer function, so it is easier to consider the combined transfer function $T_2(s).\,T_3(s)$. In current mode control:

$$I_L = K.\,V_c$$

In buck regulators, $I_L = I_o$, so under d.c. conditions:

$$V_o = I_o.\,R$$
$$= K.\,V_c.\,R$$

Under small signal a.c. conditions:

$$\frac{v_o(s)}{v_c(s)} = K.\,R.\,H_e(s)$$

where:

$$H_e(s) = \frac{1 + \dfrac{s}{\omega_z}}{1 + \dfrac{s}{\omega_p}}$$

with:

$$\omega_p = \frac{1}{R.\,C}$$
$$\omega_z = \frac{1}{R_c.\,C}$$

In discontinuous mode buck-boost circuits:

$$I_o = I_L\,.\,D_1$$

where:

$$D_1 = \text{duty ratio of the series diode}$$
$$= \sqrt{\frac{2L}{RT}}$$

So:

$$V_o = I_o . R$$
$$= K . V_c . \sqrt{\frac{2LR}{T}}$$

using $I_L = K . V_c$.

The small signal transfer function is:

$$\frac{v_o(s)}{v_c(s)} = K . V_c . \sqrt{\frac{2LR}{T}} . H_e(s)$$

where:

$$H_e(s) = \frac{1 + \dfrac{s}{\omega_z}}{1 + \dfrac{s}{\omega_p}}$$

with:

$$\omega_p = \frac{2}{R . C}$$
$$\omega_z = \frac{1}{R_c . C}$$

ERROR AMPLIFIER

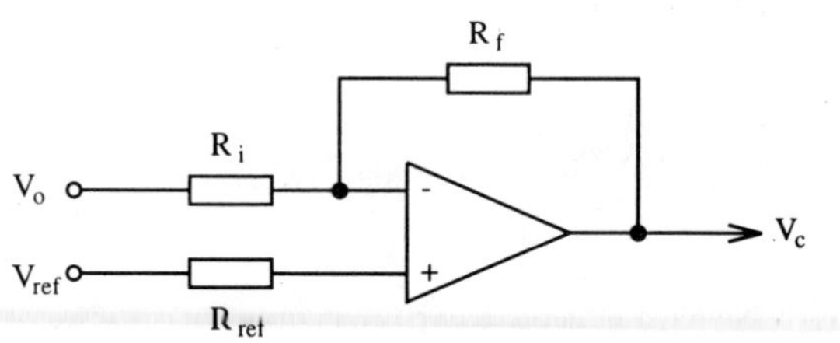

Figure 3.37 Error amplifier with proportional feedback control

In the error amplifier shown in the system in Figure 3.37:

$$V_c = -\frac{R_f}{R_i} . (V_o - V_{ref}) + V_{ref}$$

Therefore the gain of the amplifier is (R_f/R_i), or in decibels 20 $\log_{10}(R_f/R_i)$. This is a constant value, independent of frequency, producing zero phase shift.

By adding suitable compensating resistors and capacitors around the error amplifier, its gain and phase frequency response can be shaped to ensure stability under all conditions, whilst retaining good output voltage regulation and a fast transient response.

There are a number of standard compensation circuits, each with well documented characteristics. Two of these, which between them are suitable for the majority of SMPS circuits, are given below.

(a) Single Pole Compensation

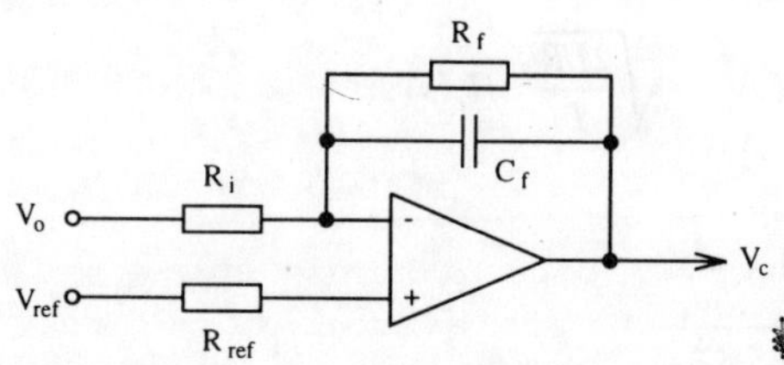

Figure 3.38 Error amplifier with single pole compensation

The low frequency gain $\left(R_f \ll \dfrac{1}{\omega C_f}\right)$ is the same as in the uncompensated circuit shown previously, (R_f/R_i) ; or, in decibels:

$$Gain = 20 \log_{10}\left(\frac{R_f}{R_i}\right) \quad dB$$

The phase lag here is 0°.

For $R_f >> \dfrac{1}{\omega C_f}$, the gain becomes:

$$Gain = 20 \log_{10}\left[\frac{\left(\dfrac{1}{\omega C}\right)}{R_i}\right] = -\,20 \log_{10} (K.\omega)$$

ie. a slope of -20 dB/decade.

The phase lag is now 90° .

The single pole (break point) is at $\omega = \omega_p = \dfrac{1}{R_f . C_f}$

R_{ref} should be equal to R_i to cancel out the amplifier input voltage offset caused by the amplifier input bias current.

(b) Two Pole Compensation

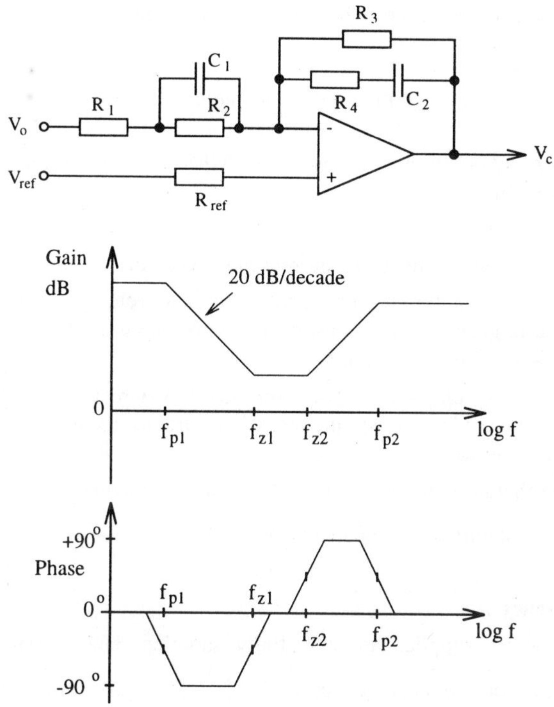

Figure 3.39 Error amplifier with two pole compensation

In the circuit in Figure 3.39:

$$d.c.\ gain = \left(\frac{R_3}{R_1 + R_2} \right)$$

The poles occur at:

$$\omega_{p1} = \frac{1}{(R_3 + R_4).\,C_2}$$

which tends to zero if R_3 is omitted (as it sometimes is).

$$\omega_{p2} = \left(\frac{R_1 + R_2}{R_1.\,R_2.\,C_1} \right)$$

The zeros occur at:

$$\omega_{z1} = \frac{1}{R_4.\,C_2}$$

$$\omega_{z2} = \frac{1}{R_2.C_1}$$

Usually the two zeros are designed to be at the same frequency; ie.

$$\omega_{zi} = \omega_{z2}$$

This circuit does not have a good response to large disturbances, due to saturation of capacitor C_1.

Single Pole Compensation circuits are used for SMPS where the filter has a single pole characteristic. These are:

1. all discontinuous mode circuits;
2. all continuous mode circuits using current mode control.

In all these circuits the inductor current is controlled on a cycle-by-cycle basis (it does not depend on the current in the previous cycle), and therefore the inductor does not constitute a delay in the feedback circuit.

Two Pole Compensation circuits are used for SMPS where the filter has a two pole characteristic. This includes all continuous mode circuits using either direct duty or voltage feedforward control.

It should be noted that continuous mode buck-boost and continuous mode boost circuits usually require extra stabilising components due to the term $\left(\frac{1}{1-D}\right)$ in the gain.

Crossover Frequency

Switched mode power supplies are essentially sampled data systems; therefore the maximum theoretical crossover frequency is $f_c = \left(\frac{f_s}{2}\right)$ (Nyquist sampling theorem). It is usual to design the feedback loop with a crossover frequency between $\left(\frac{f_s}{10}\right)$ and $\left(\frac{f_s}{5}\right)$, which should ensure stability, while still providing a fast transient response.

f_s = switching frequency

$$f_c = \left(\frac{\omega_c}{2\pi}\right)$$

EXAMPLE CALCULATION 1

SMPS Specification

Buck-Boost regulator, discontinuous mode, direct duty control.
Frequency = 100 kHz (ie. T = 10 microseconds).
Input: 10 to 15 volts.
Output: -15 volts, 1 amp to 5 amps.
L = 3 μH

C = 10,000 μF
R_c = 15 mΩ
V_s = 2.5 volts

(a) D.C. Conditions

Direct duty PWM modulator:

$$\frac{D}{V_c} = \frac{1}{V_s}$$

Power circuit, buck-boost, discontinuous mode:

$$\frac{V_o}{V_i} = D.\sqrt{\frac{RT}{2L}}$$

Therefore:

$$\frac{V_o}{V_c} = V_i \cdot \sqrt{\frac{R.T}{2.L}} \cdot \frac{1}{V_s}$$

So:

$$\frac{V_o}{V_c} = 26 \text{ dB for } V_i = 10, \; R = 15\,\Omega$$
$$= 19 \text{ dB for } V_i = 10, \; R = 3\,\Omega$$
$$= 30 \text{ dB for } V_i = 15, \; R = 15\,\Omega$$
$$= 23 \text{ dB for } V_i = 15, \; R = 3\,\Omega$$

(b) Small Signal Transfer Function

$$\frac{v_o(s)}{v_c(s)} = \frac{V_i}{V_s} \cdot \sqrt{\frac{R.T}{2.L}} \cdot \frac{\left(1 + \dfrac{s}{\omega_z}\right)}{\left(1 + \dfrac{s}{\omega_p}\right)}$$

where

$$f_p = \frac{2}{2.\pi.R.C}$$
$$= 10 \text{ Hz for } R = 3\,\Omega$$
$$= 2 \text{ Hz for } R = 15\,\Omega$$

$$f_z = \frac{1}{2.\pi.R_c.C}$$
$$= 1060 \text{ Hz}$$

(c) Error Amplifier Compensation

As the discontinuous mode buck-boost regulator has a single pole characteristic, the single pole error amplifier shown in Figure 3.40 will be used.

Crossover frequency $f_c = \dfrac{f_s}{10} = 10$ kHz

A pole to compensate for the filter capacitor zero is placed at

$$f_{p2} = \frac{f_z}{10} = 100 \text{ Hz}$$

thus increasing the overall phase lag to (90° + 45°), but still leaving a phase margin of 45°.

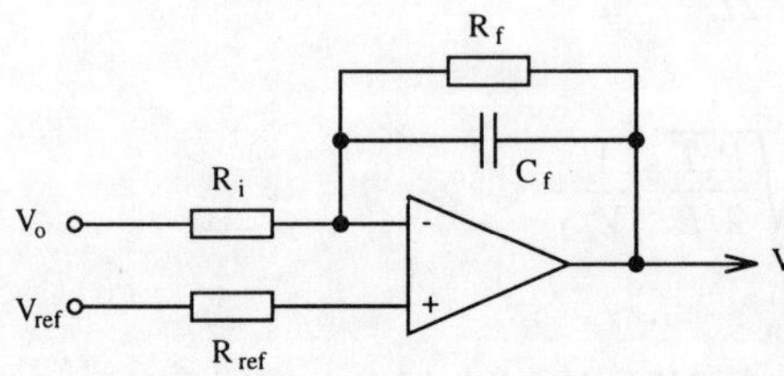

Figure 3.40 Error amplifier with single pole compensation

The overall plot can now be drawn, passing through the point (10 kHz, 0 dB), with the gradient reducing by 20 dB/decade at every pole, and increasing by 20 dB/decade at every zero. The overall curve in Figure 3.41 is drawn for case (a), as this is the most critical.

The required error amplifier d.c. gain = 80 - 23 = 57 dB.

Therefore:

$$20 \log_{10}\left(\frac{R_f}{R_i}\right) = 57$$

ie.

$$R_f = 741 \times R_i$$

If $R_i = 3\ \text{k}\Omega$
$R_f = 2.2\ \text{M}\Omega$

The error amplifier pole is at 100 Hz, therefore:

$$f_{p2} = 100 = \frac{1}{R_f . C_f}$$

Therefore:

$$C_f = 723 \text{ pF}$$

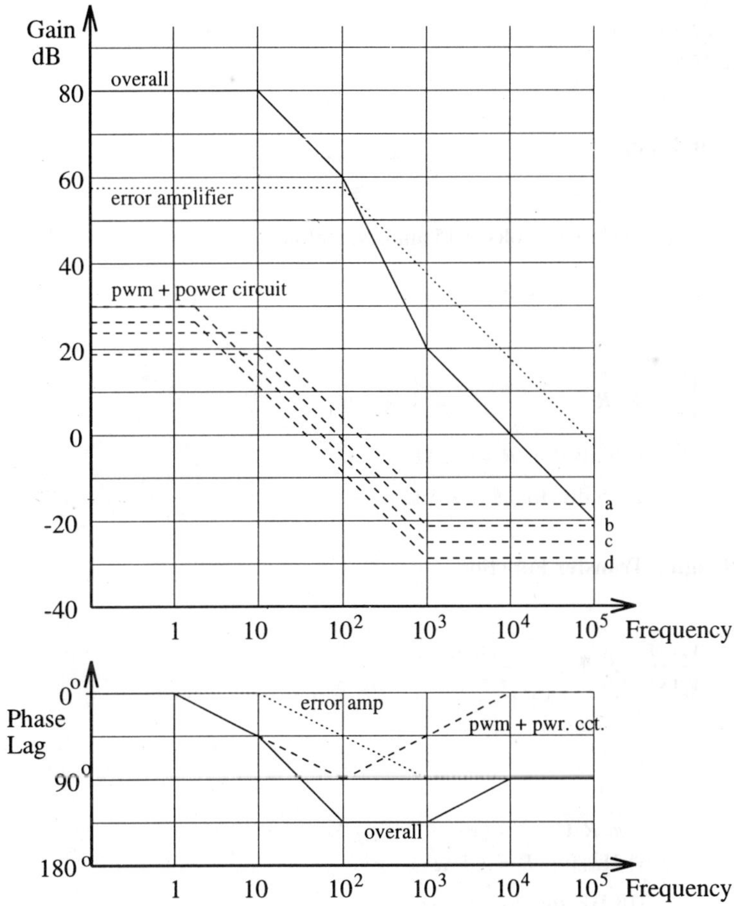

Figure 3.41 Complete Bode plot for Buck-boost converter with direct duty control

EXAMPLE CALCULATION 2

SMPS Specification

Buck regulator, continuous mode, current mode control.
Frequency = 100 kHz (ie. T = 10 microseconds).
Input: 10 volts.
Output: 5 volts, 2 amps to 10 amps.
L = 10 μH
C = 1,000 μF

$R_c = 25\ \text{m}\Omega$

Current control factor:

$$K = \frac{I_{L(max)}}{V_{c(max)}}$$

(a) D.C. Conditions

$$V_o = K.V_c.R$$

Maximum V_c clamped to 2.5 volts at 15 amps, therefore:

$$K = \frac{I_L}{V_c} = \frac{15}{2.5} = 6$$

So:

$$\frac{V_o}{V_c} = K.R$$

$$= 9.5 \text{ dB for } R = 0.5\ \Omega$$

$$= 23.5 \text{ dB for } R = 2.5\ \Omega$$

(b) Small Signal Transfer Function

$$\frac{v_o(s)}{v_c(s)} = K.R.\frac{\left(1+\frac{s}{\omega_z}\right)}{\left(1+\frac{s}{\omega_p}\right)}$$

where:

$$f_p = \frac{1}{2.\pi.R.C}$$

$$= 64 \text{ Hz for } R = 2.5\ \Omega$$

$$= 318 \text{ Hz for } R = 0.5\ \Omega$$

$$f_z = \frac{1}{2.\pi.R_c.C}$$

$$= 6.4 \text{ kHz}$$

(c) Error Amplifier Compensation

As the continuous mode buck regulator with current mode control has a single pole characteristic, the single pole error amplifier will be used as shown in Figure 3.42.

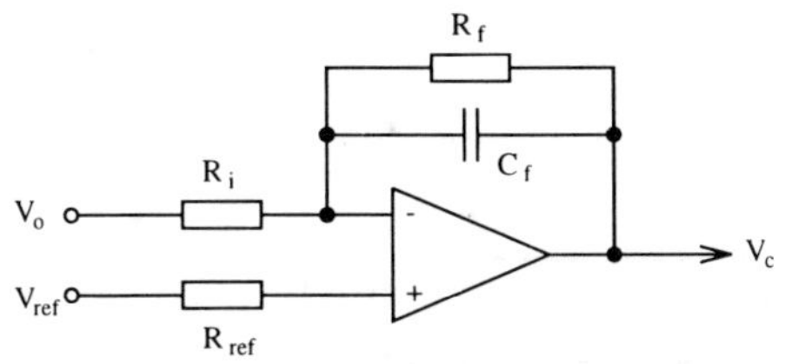

Figure 3.42 Error amplifier with single pole compensation

Crossover frequency, $f_c = \dfrac{f_s}{10} = 10$ kHz

A pole to compensate for the filter capacitor zero is placed at

$$f_{p2} = \frac{f_z}{10} = 640 \text{ Hz}$$

thus increasing the overall phase lag to (90° + 45°), but still leaving a phase margin of 45°.

The error amplifier plot can now be drawn (Figure 3.43), with a gain of 16 dB at 10 kHz (pwm + power circuit gain at 10 kHz is -16dB from graph). The d.c. gain of the error amplifier can be seen to be 40 dB.

The overall plot can now be drawn, passing through the point (10 kHz, 0 dB), with the gradient reducing by 20 dB/decade at every pole, and increasing by 20 dB/decade at every zero. The overall d.c. gain is 64 dB ($R = 2.5\Omega$) or 50 dB ($R = 0.5\Omega$).

Error amplifier gain = 40 dB, therefore:

$$20 \log_{10}\left(\frac{R_f}{R_i}\right) = 40$$

ie:

$$R_f = 100 \times R_i$$

If: $R_i = 3$ kΩ
Then: $R_f = 300$ kΩ

The error amplifier pole is at 640 Hz, therefore:

$$f_p = 640 = \frac{1}{R_f . C_f}$$

Therefore:

$$C_f = 5.2 \text{ nF}$$

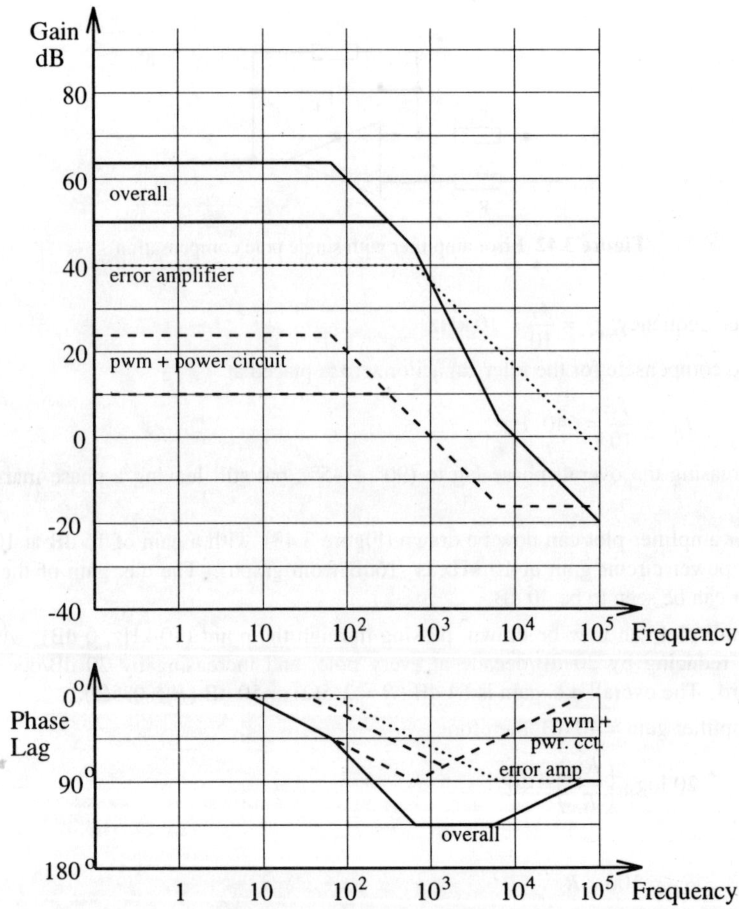

Figure 3.43 Complete Bode plot

SECTION 4

PRACTICAL SMPS DESIGN CONSIDERATIONS

4.1 ELECTROMAGNETIC INTERFERENCE (EMI) AND SCREENING

Introduction

Switched mode power conversion has many advantages making it very desirable, or even essential in some applications. Its one major drawback is the generation of high frequency electrical noise associated with the fast switching waveforms in the power regulator. In most applications it is necessary to filter out this noise and prevent it radiating from the power supply by the use of screens.

EMI is generated by rapidly changing electric or magnetic fields. Common sources of EMI are electric motors (particular commutator motors), relays and switches where rapid changes of current flow produce a broad range of interference frequencies.

As switched mode power supplies are continually switching current, they are potentially major sources of EMI (linear supplies generate much less). The square wave output of a switched mode supply is designed to have very steep rise and fall times to minimise the transistor switching losses, but the steeper the edges the greater the harmonic content, and the greater the likelihood of EMI being a problem.

It is necessary that switched mode power supplies are designed to minimise EMI and that they can operate in close proximity with other electronic equipment, without interfering with its operation. They should also be resistant to interference from external or internal sources, in other words they should be Electromagnetically Compatible (EMC) with other systems.

Figures 4.1 and 4.2 illustrate how EMI can arise. Initially, with the switch open, there is an electric field only around the wire connected to the battery. This is a static field and does not induce interference in surrounding circuits.

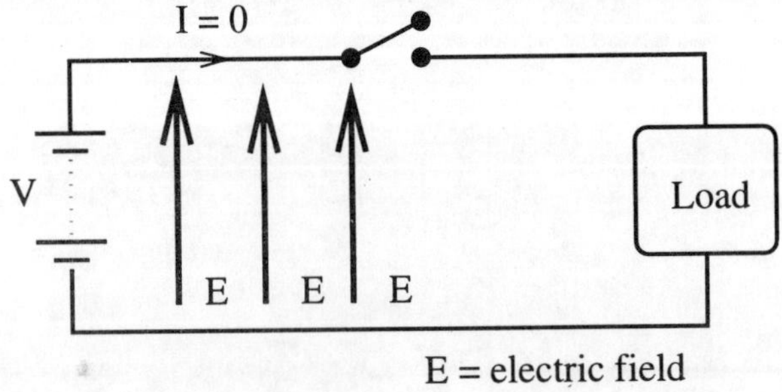

Figure 4.1 Simple switching circuit with switch open

When the switch is closed, magnetic fields are established around the conductors and an electric field is established in the right hand half of the circuit.

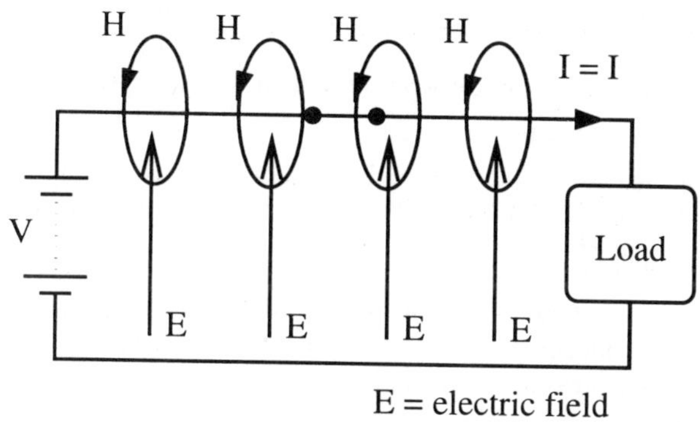

Figure 4.2 Simple switching circuit with switch closed

The establishment of the field flux in the space around the wires involves rapid changes of these fields. These changing or moving fields may intersect other conductors in nearby circuits, inducing unwanted voltages and currents, namely interference. The amount of interference produced by the circuit will depend on the rate of change of voltage and current in the circuit and also upon the size or geometry of the circuit. A large, spread-out, circuit will produce more interference than a small compact one for a given current or voltage change.

In the simple switched mode power supply circuit shown in Figure 4.3 it is possible to identify the areas that give rise to EMI by considering the changes in voltage and current in the circuit.

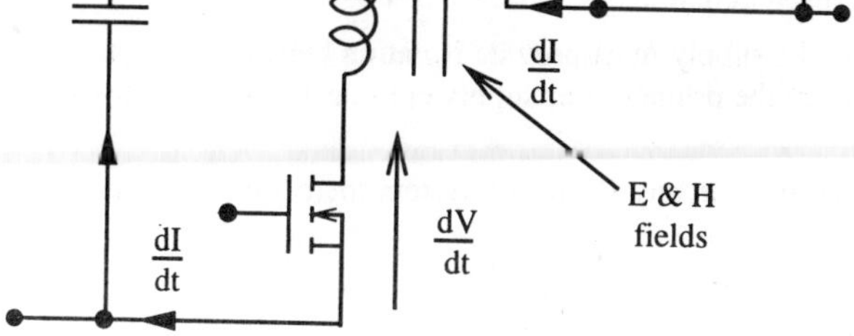

Figure 4.3 Simple SMPS circuit showing sources of EMI

The area around the switching transistor has high values of $\frac{dV}{dt}$ associated with it, while the conductors from the reservoir capacitor have high $\frac{dI}{dt}$ values. Both can provide severe interference if appropriate steps are not taken.

Another possible source of interference is the circuitry associated with the rectifier diodes. Here, the rectification action of the diodes gives rise to discontinuous changes in current and hence high $\frac{dI}{dt}$ values.

EMI can be transmitted by electrical conductors, electric coupling (capacitive) or magnetic coupling (inductive) or by free space radiation. Figure 4.4 illustrates the potential EMI problem areas in a switching supply.

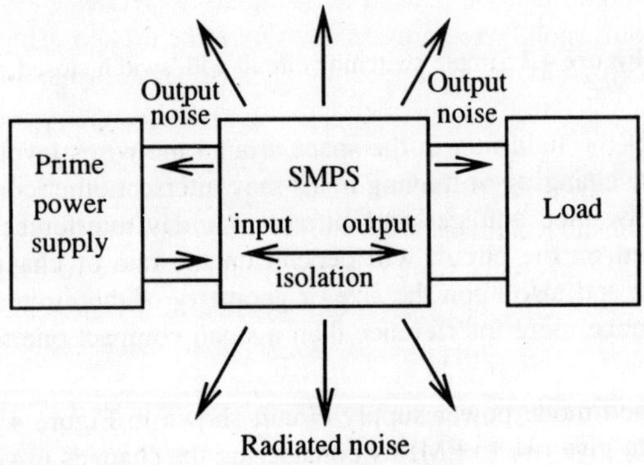

Figure 4.4 The potential EMI problem areas in a SMPS

They are:

- Noise output on the output connections to the load.
- Noise output on the input power connections.
- Direct free space radiation.
- Additionally the supply must provide isolation between its input and output and not pass noise from the prime power supply onto the output and vice-versa.

For EMI to be a problem in any electronic system there are three requirements.

- There must be a source of interference.
- There must be a transmission medium.
- There must be a susceptible receiver.

Removing any one of these will cure the problem, but ideally all three should be eliminated to avoid unexpected problems when the equipment is in use.

In order to solve an EMI problem it is important to realise that there two ways in which noise is transmitted or propagates in an equipment. It can be:

- Conducted noise carried along wiring;
- Radiated noise transmitted through space between wires.

To eliminate a noise problem there are three steps that should be taken. Firstly, the noise should be reduced at source by reducing the values of $\frac{dV}{dt}$ and $\frac{dI}{dt}$ in the circuit if possible. Attention should also be paid to reducing stray electric and magnetic fields by careful layout. Secondly, conducted noise paths should be broken using frequency filters; and finally radiation should be contained by the use of screens. In the next section consideration will be given to the implementation of these measures.

Electromagnetic Screening or Shielding

Another important consideration in the design of switched mode power supplies is the prevention of radiated interference from the supply entering into surrounding systems and wiring. This is achieved by paying careful attention to screening and grounding throughout a design. Switching regulators can generate noise up to frequencies in the VHF range. These frequency components are easily radiated from packages that are not RF tight, in other words the circuitry of the supply should be fully enclosed in a grounded, conducting case. In addition all leads for input, output and control functions must be adequately filtered at the point of entry to the case. All lids and covers should be bonded onto the main chassis using RF gasket material. For optimum screening the enclosure should be thought of as being electrically water-tight.

When planning screening for a supply it is necessary to know the type of field that is being shielded against. The characteristics of the field are determined by the nature of the source. A source with a high current and low voltage will have a near-field that is predominately magnetic, while one that has a high voltage and low current has a predominately electric field. The electric and magnetic fields must be considered separately. Electric fields are relatively easy to shield against by using a metal sheet of good electrical conductivity, as the prime shielding mechanism is reflection.

To understand the principles of screening it is useful to have some insight into the nature of an electromagnetic field. This is shown in graphical form in Figure 4.5. At a distance of up to $\frac{\lambda}{2\pi}$ from the source is the so-called near-field region where the characteristics of the field are determined by those of the source. If the source is predominantly a high voltage (high impedance) one the near-field is predominantly electric. If the source is predominantly a high current (low-impedance) one then the field will be predominantly magnetic in nature.

For any electromagnetic wave, a wave impedance can be calculated from the ratio of the electric and magnetic fields

$$Z_W = \frac{E}{H}$$

A predominantly electric field will have a high wave impedance and a magnetic field will have a low wave impedance.

As the distance from the source increases beyond $\frac{\lambda}{2\pi}$ the wave impedance approaches that of free space and the radiated energy propagates as a plane electromagnetic wave.

$$Z_W = \frac{E}{H} = \eta_o = 377\Omega$$

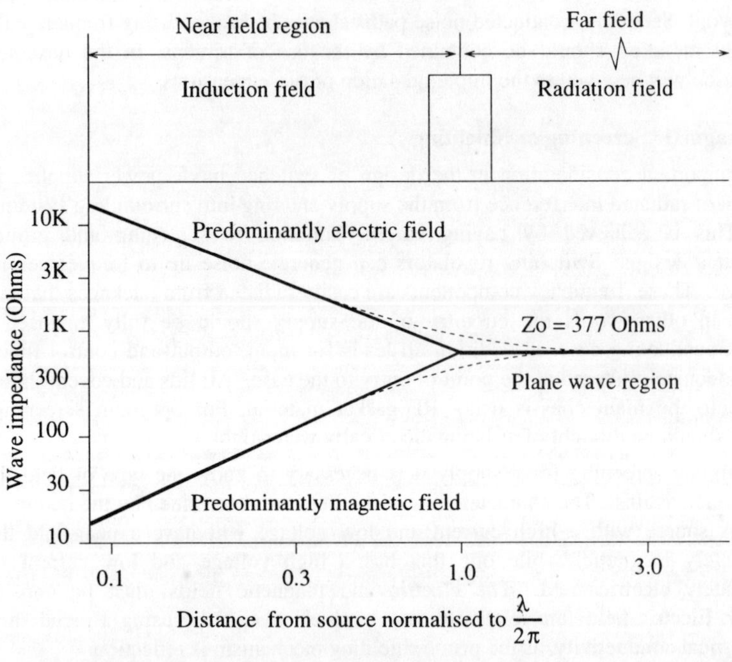

Figure 4.5 Wave impedance depends on the distance from the source and whether the source is electric or magnetic

Screening Effectiveness

An electromagnetic screen works in two ways. Firstly, it serves to reflect the unwanted field and, secondly, energy transmitted through the screen is absorbed and hence attenuated. The total attenuation provided by the screen is the sum of the absorption loss and the reflection loss.

total attenuation = absorption loss + reflection loss

Absorption Loss

When an electromagnetic wave passes into a lossy medium its amplitude decreases exponentially as shown in Figure 4.6.

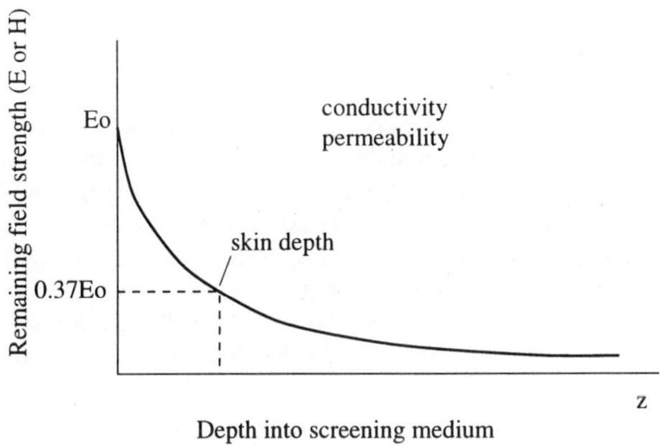

Figure 4.6 Skin depth in a lossy medium

$$E_1 = E_o e^{-\alpha z}$$
$$H_1 = H_o e^{-\alpha z}$$

Where α determines the "skin depth" and z is the thickness of the screen. α is the attenuation constant of the material. (α is the reciprocal of the skin depth in the material.)

Attenuation Constant for an E/M Wave in a Conductor

An expression for the the propagation constant γ can be derived from Maxwell's equations.

$$\gamma = \sqrt{j\omega\mu(\sigma + j\omega\varepsilon)}$$

where ω = radian frequency

μ = permeability ($\mu_o \mu_r$)

ε = permittivity ($\varepsilon_o \varepsilon_r$)

σ = conductivity

the medium is conducting, therefore $\sigma \gg j\omega\varepsilon$

$$\gamma = \sqrt{j\omega\mu\sigma}$$

$$\alpha + j\beta = \sqrt{\frac{(1+j)^2}{2}\,\omega\mu\sigma} \qquad \left(j = \frac{(1+j)^2}{2} \right)$$

$$\alpha + j\beta = (1+j)\sqrt{\frac{\omega\mu\sigma}{2}}$$

$$\alpha = \sqrt{\frac{\omega\mu\sigma}{2}}$$

Reflection Loss

Reflection loss can be calculated from a knowledge of the wave impedances in the screen and the wave impedance of the surrounding medium. In order to maximise the loss through the screen, the amount of the signal reflected from the screen should be high and the amount of signal transmitted should be small. A useful analogy is to think of the matching at the junction of two transmission lines of different characteristic impedances. In the case of a screen, in order to maximise reflection, it is necessary to ensure that the wave impedance of the screen is radically different from that of the surrounding air. Figure 4.7 shows the relationship between the incident and transmitted fields at the boundary between two media.

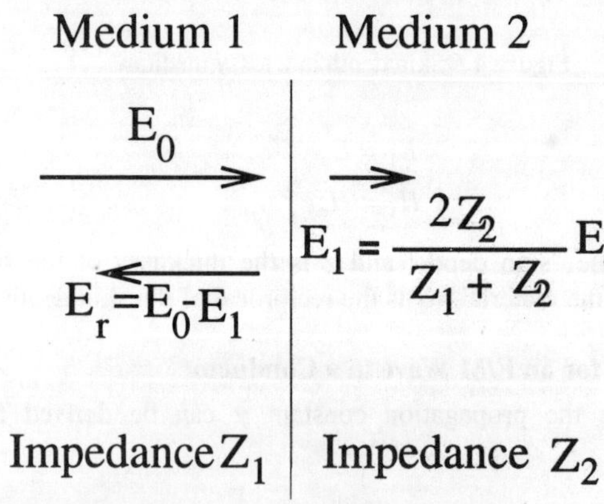

Figure 4.7 Transmission at the boundary between two media

$$E_1 = 2\frac{Z_2}{Z_1 + Z_2} \cdot E_o$$

$$H_1 = 2\frac{Z_1}{Z_1 + Z_2} \cdot H_o$$

Figure 4.8 shows the relationship between the incident and transmitted fields through a sheet of metal, used as a screen.

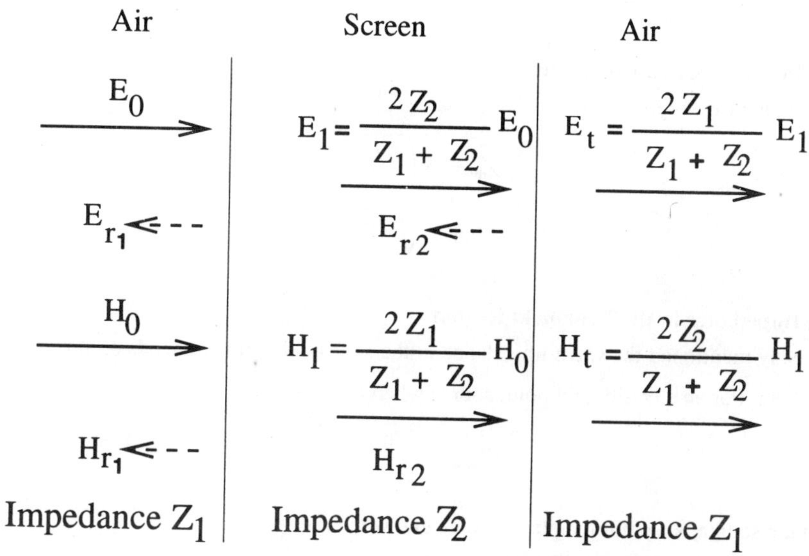

Figure 4.8 Transmission through a screen

Therefore the total attenuation through a sheet is

$$\frac{E_t}{E_o} = \frac{4Z_1Z_2}{(Z_1 + Z_2)^2}$$

$$\frac{H_t}{H_o} = \frac{4Z_1Z_2}{(Z_1 + Z_2)^2}$$

Wave Impedance of a Generalised Electromagnetic Medium

An expression for the wave impedance of a lossy medium can be derived from Maxwell's equations.

$$Z_W = \sqrt{\frac{j\omega\mu}{\sigma + j\omega\varepsilon}}$$

Wave Impedance in an Insulator

In an insulator $\sigma \ll j\omega\varepsilon$ and hence

$$Z_W = \sqrt{\frac{\mu}{\varepsilon}}$$

In free space where $\mu = \mu_o$ and $\varepsilon = \varepsilon_o$

$$Z_W = \sqrt{\frac{\mu_o}{\varepsilon_o}} = \text{intrinsic impedance of free space} \doteq 377\Omega$$

Wave Impedance in a Conductor

In a conductor $\sigma \gg j\omega\varepsilon$

$$Z_W = \sqrt{\frac{j\omega\mu}{\sigma}}$$

$$|Z_W| = \sqrt{\frac{\omega\mu}{\sigma}}$$

Wave Impedance in the Near-field Region

As already mentioned the wave impedance in the near-field region depends on the source of the field. For an electric field point source when $r < \frac{\lambda}{2\pi}$

$$|Z_W|_e = \frac{1}{2\pi f \varepsilon r}$$

When the source is a point magnetic source and when $r < \frac{\lambda}{2\pi}$

$$|Z_W|_m = 2\pi f \mu r$$

Screening Guidelines

The following points should be borne in mind when planning enclosures and shields.

- Electric fields are relatively easy to screen. In both cases the main mechanism is reflection. For good reflection it is necessary to use a good conductor such as copper. Attenuation levels of around 150-200 dB are relatively easily obtained.
- Magnetic fields are more difficult to contain. Reflection loss is generally low ($\leq$ 10 dB) as the near-field wave impedance is low and comparable to that of a metal sheet. The main mechanism has to be absorption, so it is necessary to use thick screens of a material with high relative permeability, μ_r. The commonest solution is to use mild steel which has a relative permeability of around 1000. There are also special alloys such as mu-metal that have permeabilities of around 10,000 that can be used to solve magnetic field problems. These have some drawbacks, however, as they tend to lose their magnetic properties when worked and are not as effective at frequencies in excess of around 1 kHz.
- An alternative approach to dealing with magnetic screening is to provide a "magnetic short circuit" around the area to be screened. This has the effect of bypassing the lines of magnetic flux. To provide the short circuit it is necessary to completely enclose the area with a material which has a high permeability.

- A useful general purpose screen is provided by plated steel. Here, the high permeability of steel is available to combat magnetic fields, and a high conductivity plating such as copper, tin or zinc provides good electric field screening.
- In practice it is difficult to fully enclose a unit such as a power supply in a metal box, as some provision must be made for cooling either by convection or forced air cooling. This necessitates the provision of holes for the air to pass through. The shielding effectiveness of a square grid of side *l*, of round holes of diameter d, and pitch c is

$$S = 20 \log \frac{c^2 l}{d^3} + 32 \frac{l}{d} + 3.8 \ dB$$

where S, the shielding effectiveness, is the improvement in shielding over a square hole of side *l*. This assumes that the holes are acting as short waveguides above cut-off; ie. $d < \frac{\lambda}{2\pi}$, where λ is the wavelength at the frequency of interest.
- Other areas to pay particular attention to in the design of screens are the joints and seams in cases and also the seating and electrical bonding of lids and covers. If a lid or joint is not tight fitting it is relatively easy for it to act as a slot antenna, making it an excellent radiator and receiver of interference. To avoid this, the use of conducting gaskets is recommended in all joints and covers.
- Actual screening effectiveness obtained in practice is usually determined by the leakage at the seams and joints, not by the material itself.
- The maximum dimension (not area) of a hole or gap determines the amount of leakage, eg. slot radiator.
- A large number of small holes results in less leakage than a larger hole of the same total area.

EMI Reduction at Source

The requirement for efficient power conversion requires rapid switching of current and voltage by the main switching transistor. This gives rise to high $\frac{dI}{dt}$ and $\frac{dV}{dt}$ values which cause EMI. The major source of EMI in a switched mode power supply is around the main switching transistor. The abrupt transitions of switching current and voltage shock excite ringing or oscillations in the parasitic capacitances and inductance of transformers, chokes and wiring. In order to reduce this interference at source, a slight trade-off can be made with efficiency by deliberately reducing the speed of the current changes, $\frac{dI}{dt}$, and voltage changes, $\frac{dV}{dt}$, at the switching devices. This can be achieved by the addition of small series inductors to limit $\frac{dI}{dt}$ and small shunt capacitors to limit $\frac{dV}{dt}$ as shown in Figure 4.9.

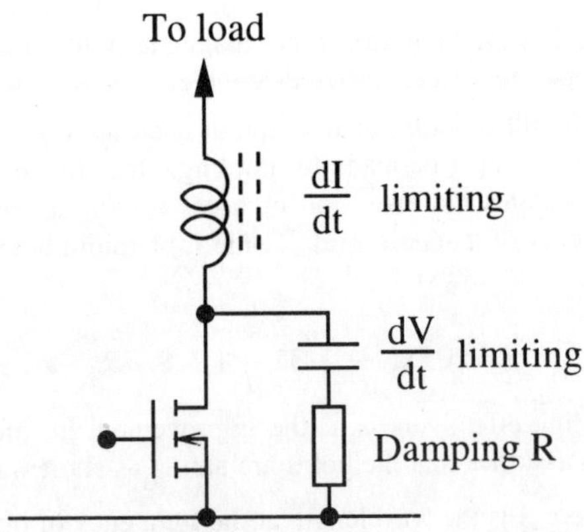

Figure 4.9 $\frac{dI}{dt}$ and $\frac{dV}{dt}$ limiting components

This solution will give a slight increase in the power dissipated in the switching device.

Another source of interference is the fast fall time current spikes which occur when diodes are reverse biased. Typically, a fast recovery diode will "snap off" in around 10 ns. This can result in ringing and radiation in the very high frequency region.

The fast fall time current spikes arising from diode snap-off can be controlled by the use of "soft recovery" diodes or by the incorporation of a low value ceramic capacitor connected across the diode. A small trade-off can be made with efficiency by using small RF inductors in series with the main switching transistors to limit the switching edges, thereby giving a substantial reduction in EMI at source. Additionally, the circuitry should be contained in a grounded metal screening enclosure in order to prevent radiated interference. Usually effective suppression is only achieved by using both filtering and screening together, as neither is fully effective on its own.

Wiring Layout

Another area that repays close attention for EMI reduction at the initial design stage is the physical layout of the supply. All leads carrying rapidly switched currents and voltages should be kept as short as possible to minimise radiation. Excessive wiring length increases inductance and capacitance, encouraging unwanted voltage drops. It is particularly important to pay special attention to the switching paths in the supply. Excessively long wiring can act as an aerial causing unwanted electric and magnetic fields, which easily couple into other wiring. Examples of good and bad wiring layouts are shown in Figure 4.10. In addition, high current and high voltage wiring should be kept away from sensitive parts of the circuit such as the voltage reference and the low-level sense circuits in the regulator. In practice this will mean placing the main switching devices close to the transformer and choke, and also the provision of screening.

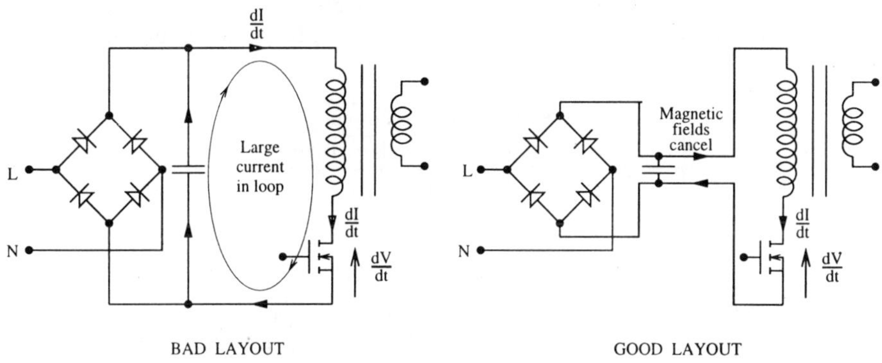

Figure 4.10 Examples of good and bad wiring layouts

EMI FILTER COMPONENTS

Filtering of the input and output leads to contain EMI within an SMPS is an important aspect of interference control. The components available for this purpose are capacitors, inductors and feed-through capacitors and filters. These must be chosen with care and appropriate types picked for the frequencies at which the filtering is to be effective. The most important consideration for choosing a component for this application is the value of its "parasitics". Take, for example, the capacitor equivalent circuit shown in Figure 4.11.

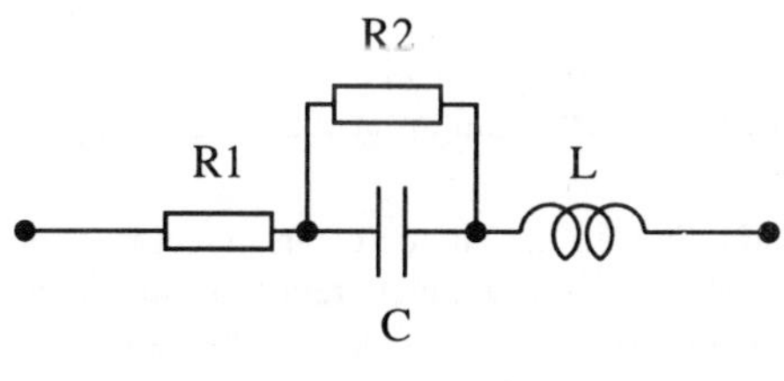

Figure 4.11 Capacitor equivalent circuit

This has series inductance, L, arising from the leads and the physical construction of the component and resistances associated with its losses. It is important that the effects of the parasitics are small at the frequency of interest if the capacitor is to be effective at decoupling or bypassing.

Capacitors for EMI suppression and filtering should have good high frequency properties and a low series inductance. The most useful types are disc and plate ceramic components. These have excellent high frequency properties with good high voltage properties. It is important to consider the effect of lead length on the layout of the filter and the effectiveness of the bypass capacitors. The table below gives the self-resonant frequency for ceramic capacitors of different values with different lengths of leads.

Table 4.1 Self-resonant frequency MHz		
capacitance pF	0.25in leads	0.5in leads
10,000	12	-
1,000	35	32
500	70	65
100	150	120
50	220	200
10	500	350

It is important to use capacitors whose self-resonant frequency is well above the frequencies at which bypassing or decoupling is to be effective.

At switching frequencies where a higher capacitance is required than is available from ceramic types, polycarbonate or polypropylene types are the most effective.

Inductors

Inductors may be classified by their core type. The most general types are the air-cored varieties and the magnetic core types. Magnetic core types can be further subdivided depending on whether the core is open or closed. Designing EMI filters would not be a problem if the inductors were ideal. Unfortunately they have stray capacitance arising from adjacent turns and stray resistance from the wire of which it is wound.

In a low pass filter configuration the inductor will only be effective if it is operated well below its self-resonant frequency; thus, ideally, only the smallest inductance should be used that will give the necessary attenuation, at the lowest frequency at which the filter has to reject.

Another important consideration in the choice of an inductor is its stray magnetic field. Closed core types, eg. toroids, have a much reduced surrounding magnetic field as compared to air or the open cored types. Consequently they are much less prone to radiate or receive signals by means of stray magnetic coupling. If a toroidal inductor cannot be used it may be necessary to provide shielding by enclosing the winding in a grounded metal box.

4.2 EMI SUPPRESSION IN SMPS

CONDUCTED EMI SUPPRESSION

The Bifilar Wound Choke

A useful component for filtering power supply lines between equipments is the bifilar wound choke. It is especially useful when common mode or ground noise is a problem, and it finds almost universal use in switched mode power supplies. It consists of a bifilar winding placed on the core to form a broadband transformer which allows equal and opposite currents to flow through its windings while suppressing unequal opposite currents such as ground noise. Because of the bifilar winding, no net flux is set up in the core when the currents are balanced; therefore balanced currents do not encounter any inductance. When unbalanced currents flow there is a net flux giving an inductance, and the choke opposes such currents. An additional advantage of the balanced configuration is that in normal operation the core is kept well away from saturation. Figure 4.12 illustrates the use of a bifilar choke between a supply and a load.

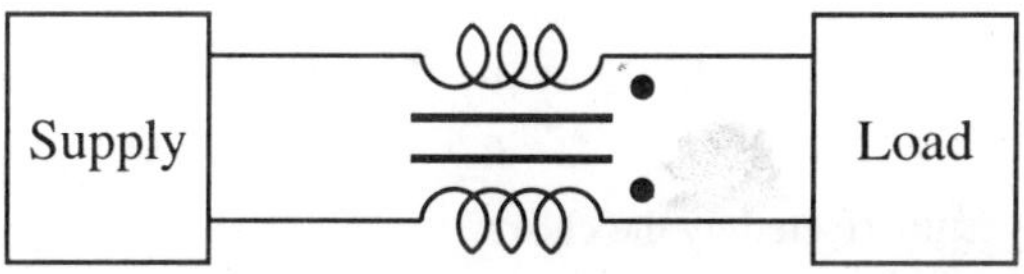

Figure 4.12 A bifilar choke used to block EMI between a supply and a load

Bifilar chokes are used to break ground loops, as shown below. Figure 4.13 shows an equivalent circuit of a bifilar choke including an interfering ground potential.

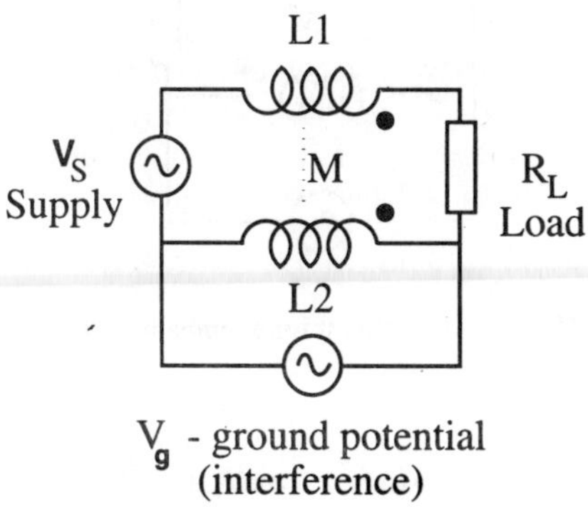

Figure 4.13 Equivalent circuit of a bifilar choke

For a balanced supply only (no ground noise), neglect V_g; the equivalent circuit becomes:

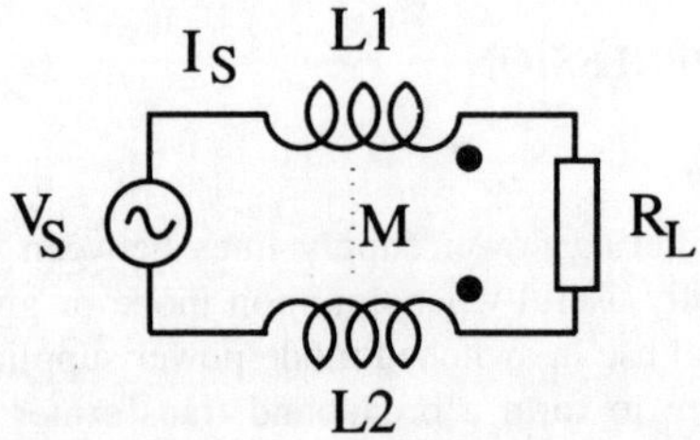

Figure 4.14 Equivalent circuit for a balanced supply only

$$V_s = j\omega(L_1 + L_2)I_s - 2j\omega MI_s + I_sR_L$$

where:

$$L_1 = L_2 = M$$

Therefore:

$$I_s = \frac{V_s}{R_L}$$

The balanced supply is unaffected by the choke.

For an unbalanced (ground) voltage the circuit becomes:

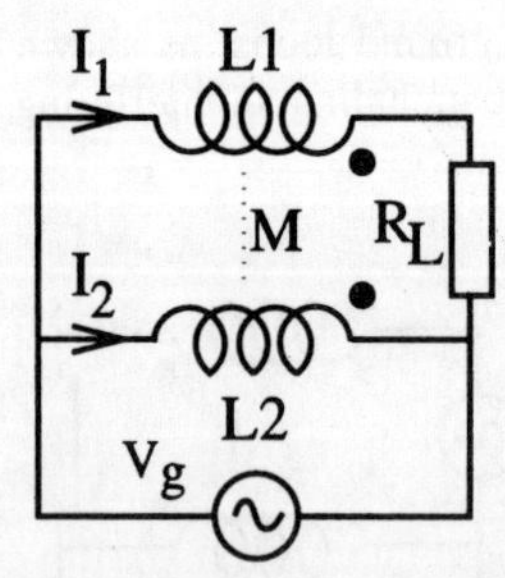

Figure 4.15 Equivalent circuit for an unbalanced supply only

For outer loop:

$$V_g = j\omega L_1I_1 + j\omega MI_2 + I_1R_L$$

For inner loop:

$$V_g = j\omega L_2 I_2 + j\omega M I_1$$

But:

$$L_1 = L_2 = M = L \quad (say)$$

Therefore:

$$I_1 R_L = 0$$

Therefore there is no current in R_L due to V_g.

In order to determine suitable values of inductance for a bifilar choke there are two formula that are important. Firstly,

$$\omega_{mains} \geq \frac{5R}{L}$$

where ω_{mains} is the mains radian frequency, L is the winding inductance and R is the resistance of the winding. Secondly, to maximise the effect of the choke,

$$L \gg \frac{R}{\omega_{interference}}$$

where $\omega_{interference}$ is the lowest frequency of interference signal that the choke is required to block.

Ferrite Beads

Ferrite beads are a simple and convenient way to increase the high frequency loss in a conductor, without affecting its low frequency and d.c. properties. They are small cylinders of a lossy ferrite material, with an axial hole through the centre.

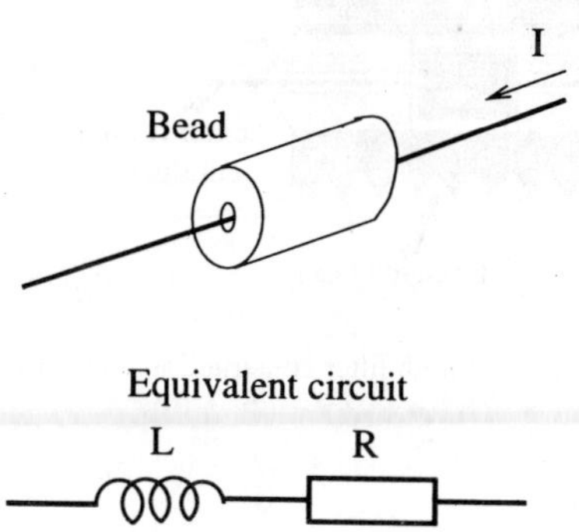

Figure 4.16 Ferrite bead

They can easily be slipped over the leads of components to provide attenuation of high frequency signals. They are most effective above 1MHz and when properly used can give effective high frequency decoupling and shielding. They are particularly useful in applications where a high current is flowing and it is not possible to insert a resistor in the circuit. Figure 4.16 is the equivalent circuit of a ferrite bead at high frequencies.

The resistive component arises from the loss component of the ferrite. Ferrite beads are most useful for damping out high frequency oscillations and "ringing" in switching circuits. They are also useful for blocking high frequency noise on power lines. The impedance of most beads is limited to around 100 Ω, making them most effective in low impedance lines, such as power supplies and switching circuits. Typically, ferrite beads are used in conjunction with shunt capacitors to form low pass filters to block EMI on lines. Care should be taken in their use not to introduce any spurious resonances into a circuit which could exacerbate an interference problem. Another point that is often overlooked is that the ferrite must not be saturated.

Feed-Through Filters

Feed-through filters are useful components for EMI suppression. They consist of a central ferrite bead to supply series inductance between two coaxial ceramic capacitors formed from a high dielectric ceramic material. These are manufactured by several companies and are available in a variety of voltage and current ratings, covering a range of frequencies. They are available as both L and pi low-pass sections and are convenient to use. Figure 4.17 shows the construction of a typical feed-through filter.

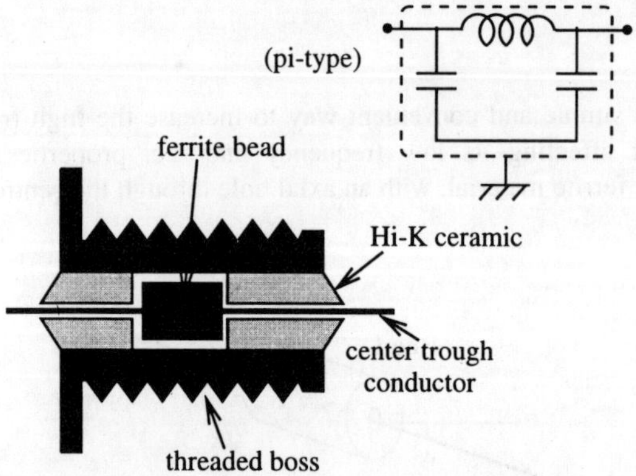

Figure 4.17 Feed-through filter construction and equivalent circuit

Input Filters

The interference problem is most severe at the input of a switched mode power supply. At the output there is generally a low pass filter section, to remove the switching frequency ripple, and this serves to attenuate high frequency noise. It is usually only necessary to add a relatively simple single section LC low pass RF filter on the output lines in order to meet most EMI output specifications.

The filtering at the input must be capable of blocking the switching frequency ripple and all of its harmonics well into the MHz region of the spectrum. This ensures that no interference is fed back into the prime power supply. Typically, to meet most input noise specifications a mains input filter such as that shown in Figure 4.18 is used.

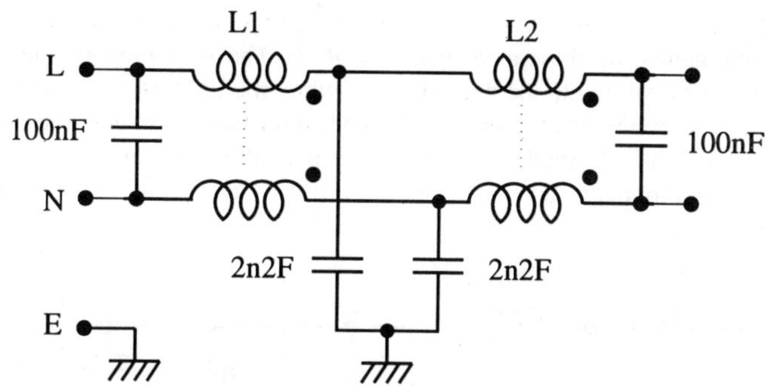

Figure 4.18 A typical mains input filter

In this input filter two bifilar, or common mode, chokes are used along with four bypass capacitors. The values of the chokes depend upon the switching frequency and the amount of attenuation required. The value of the ground bypass capacitors is limited by the amount of earth leakage current that is acceptable. Normally this is close to 2.2nF or 4.7nF.

At the output the filtering problem is normally easier as there is already a low-pass filter to smooth the output current. Typically, for a switching frequency of 40kHz, a single section low-pass filter comprising a 100μH inductor and a 47μF capacitor will be effective for blocking the switching frequency. At harmonics in the MHz range, where EMI is usually a problem, the stray inductance of the capacitor will make it ineffective as a bypassing component.

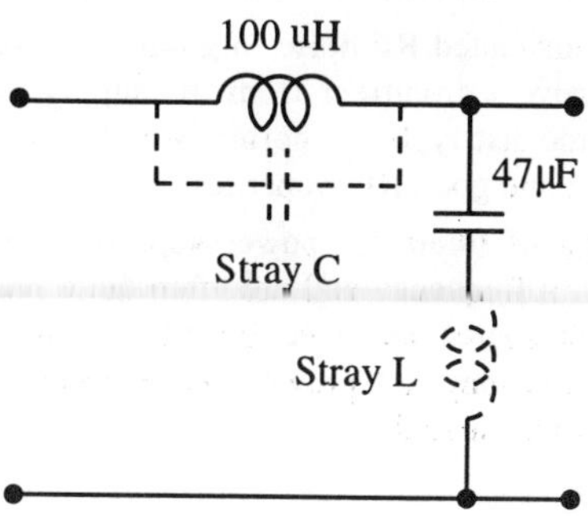

Figure 4.19 A typical LC output filter showing strays

The inter-turn capacitance of the choke will appear in parallel with its inductance and eventually may bypass it at high frequencies, providing very little attenuation of EMI. The effect of these parasitics is shown in Figure 4.19.

The solution to this problem is to use two filter sections, one to perform the low frequency filtering at the switching frequency and a second section to remove the high frequency components, as illustrated in Figure 4.20. The switching frequency filter is placed from the positive line to the negative line, while the EMI filter is placed from each line to ground as shown below. Typically, the EMI filter would use ceramic capacitors of values around 10-100nF. A small series inductor can be added if required. In this way the high frequency components are bypassed to ground, while the low frequencies are bypassed line to line.

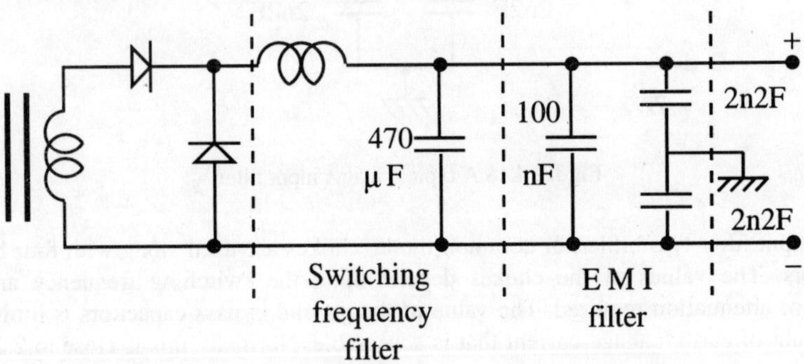

Figure 4.20 LC output filter with additional high frequency bypass components

Components for use in such filters should be chosen carefully. The inductors must be designed so that they are not magnetically saturated at the current levels drawn from the supply. The RF inductors are often wound on cores of a lossy material such as powdered iron to give them a dissipative component at high frequencies.

The capacitors bypass the unwanted RF noise to ground. These must be chosen so that they do not pass an excessive a.c. current from the supply as this constitutes an a.c. ground leakage path. Ceramic disc types are normally preferred in this application as they have a low series inductance and good RF properties.

One problem in the design of filters for power supplies is that the source and load impedances vary widely with frequency and are often quite reactive. Most filter design techniques assume constant source and load impedances which are usually resistive. Filters designed on this basis may not provide the expected attenuation noise simply because they are incorrectly terminated.

GROUNDING

Grounding is an important aspect of interference control. There are two configurations commonly used for grounding within equipment. These are shown in Figures 4.21 and 4.22.

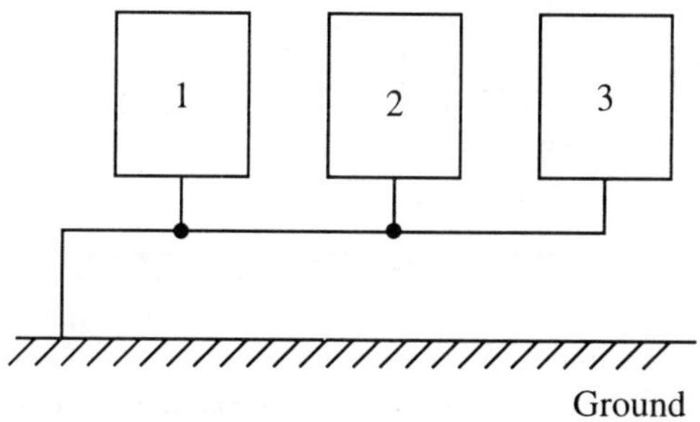

Figure 4.21 Series connection - single point

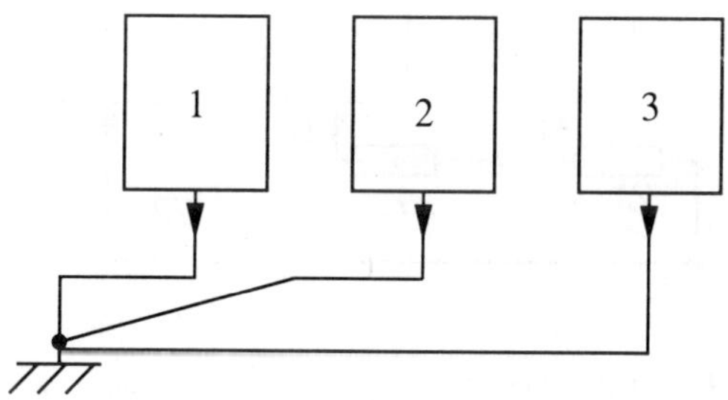

Figure 4.22 Parallel connection - single point

Two points should be borne in mind when discussing grounding:

- Separate ground points on a chassis are seldom at the same potential;
- All conductors and wires have a finite impedance.

Inclusion of these points gives a different appearance to Figure 4.21, as can be seen in Figure 4.23. The first point dictates that a common single point earth is desirable; unfortunately, in practice this tends to mean that a number of common impedance paths are introduced into the earth returns for units 1, 2 and 3. A situation where this occurs commonly is in printed circuit boards which pick up all their connections including ground through an edge connector. This can result in excessively noisy grounds especially if one of the stages is a high powered stage.

At low frequencies where wiring inductance is not a problem the solution is to use a single point grounding scheme, such as that shown in Figure 4.24.

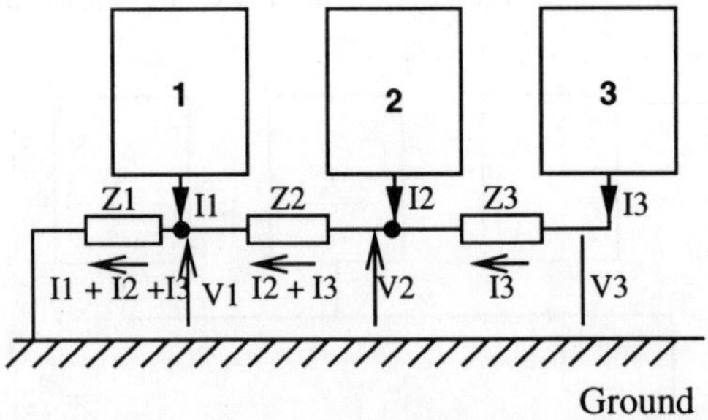

Figure 4.23 Series connection - single point, plus parasitic resistances

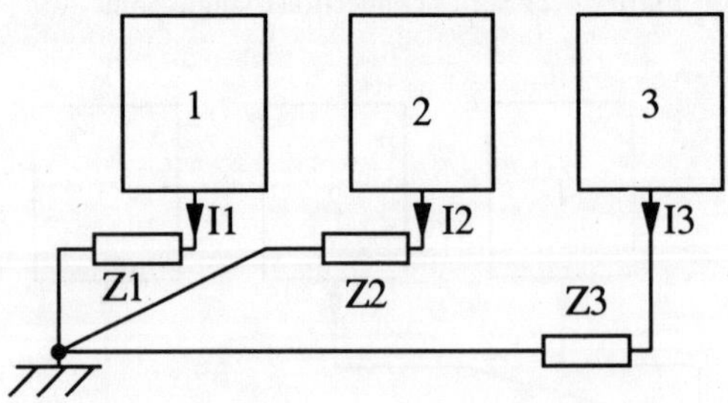

Figure 4.24 Parallel connection - single point, plus parasitic resistances

This scheme avoids the problems of common ground return paths and impedances; however it is cumbersome and can necessitate long ground connections.

For frequencies above around 1MHz a low impedance ground plane is good practice especially on printed circuit boards. Here multi-point grounding is the preferred method, provided the ground connections are kept short.

The importance of choosing grounding points carefully can be seen in Figure 4.25. The gate of the transistor is driven from the secondary of a pulse transformer to provide mains isolation for the control electronics. In the first circuit the lower connection from the secondary of the gate drive transformer includes a length of common wire connection which carries the source current. At the switching frequencies in common use this wire could have a significant inductance causing a voltage drop to occur along its length. This voltage could easily be large enough to cause faulty turn-on cycles in the MOSFET. By making the transformer connection directly to the source of the transistor this problem can be avoided.

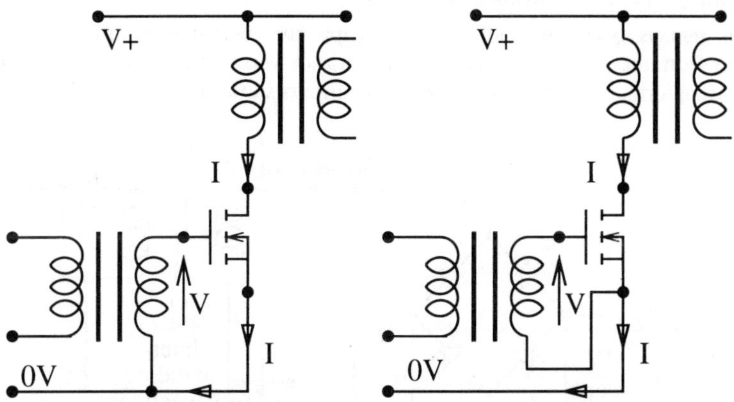

Figure 4.25 Method of avoiding faulty turn on cycles due to wiring inductance

In practice, it is often impossible to stick rigorously to one grounding scheme or another and the following guidelines should prove useful.

- Never combine noisy, "high power" circuit grounds with ones for "low powered" signal circuitry.
- Group ground leads selectively, ie. place high power grounds together and keep low power grounds together.
- Provide separate grounds for chassis, case and a.c. power ground when required for safety.

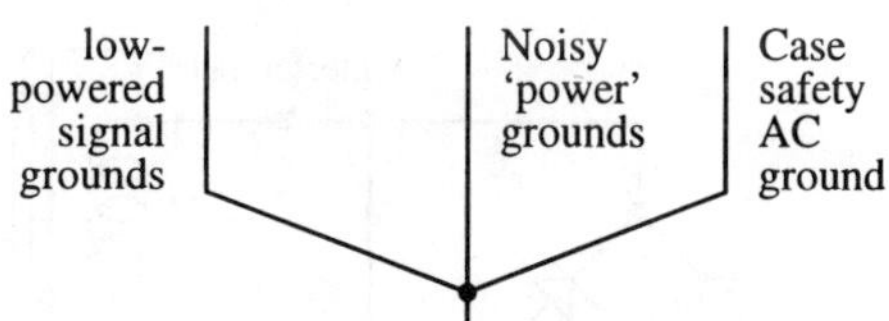

Figure 4.26 Grounding guidelines

A further point to watch out for in a design, when planning the earthing or grounding, is to avoid the unintentional inclusion of earth loops. These are closed circuit loops, often produced inadvertently, which act as pick-up loops for interfering signals induced by stray magnetic fields. If such loops are unavoidable their area should be minimised.

Electrostatic Screens in Transformers

One point that is often overlooked is the capacitive coupling of noise across the transformer from the primary to the secondary or vice-versa. The effect of this coupling across the transformer is to produce the ground currents shown in Figure 4.27.

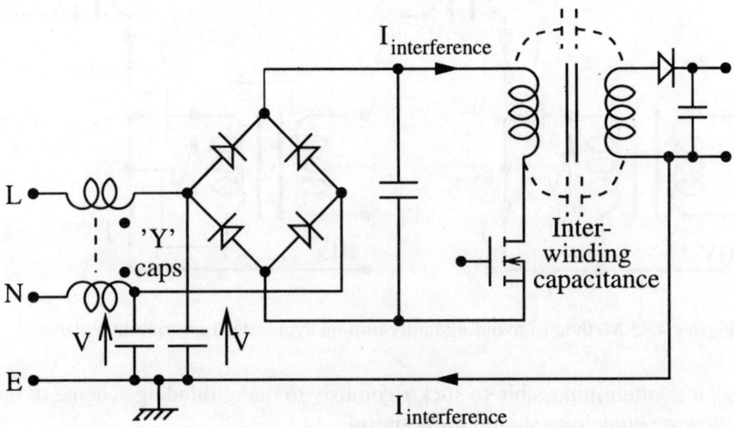

Figure 4.27 Ground currents caused by transformer inter-winding capacitance

The return path for these is through mains supply and the "Y" capacitors. Ideally the current in the mains-to-ground impedance should be kept to a minimum. As the value of the filter capacitors is limited by safety considerations, the only remaining option is to reduce the ground current itself.

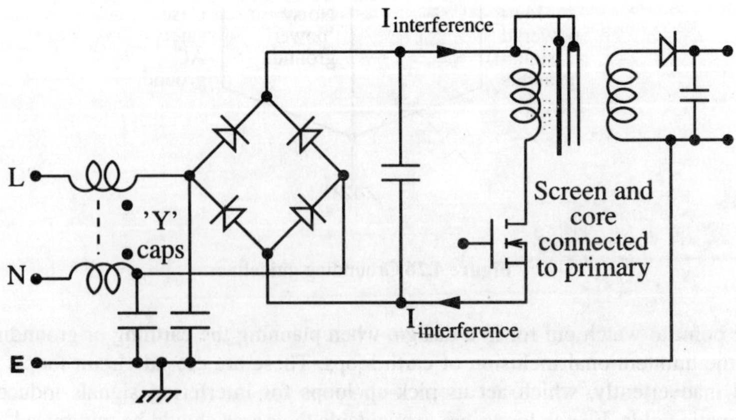

Figure 4.28 Transformer screen used to break ground current path

This can be achieved by incorporating a Faraday screen into the transformer and connecting it back to the primary circuit. In this way the ground noise circuit path is broken and the noise current is returned to the primary as shown in Figure 4.28.

The screen is implemented by winding a layer of copper tape between the primary and secondary in such a way that it does not provide a "shorted turn". The copper tape has no effect on the magnetic coupling between the primary and the secondary.

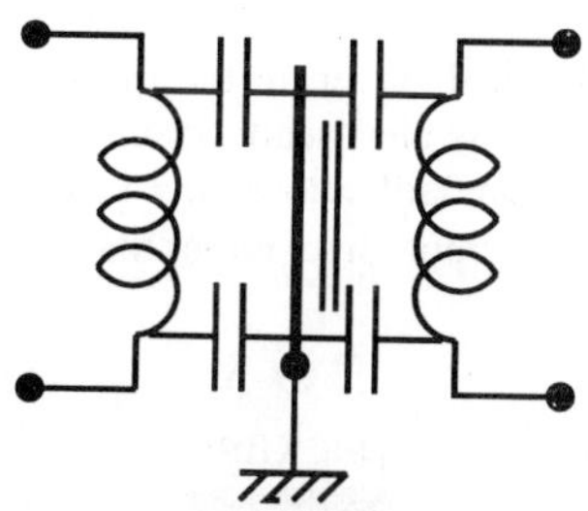

Figure 4.29 Use of screen between primary and secondary of transformer

Another source of unwanted noise can arise from currents coupled to ground through the transformer core if it is clamped to the chassis ground. The solution is to electrically connect the core to the primary side of the transformer.

Switching Transistor Mounting and Heatsinking

The primary noise sources in a power supply are the power switching transistors.

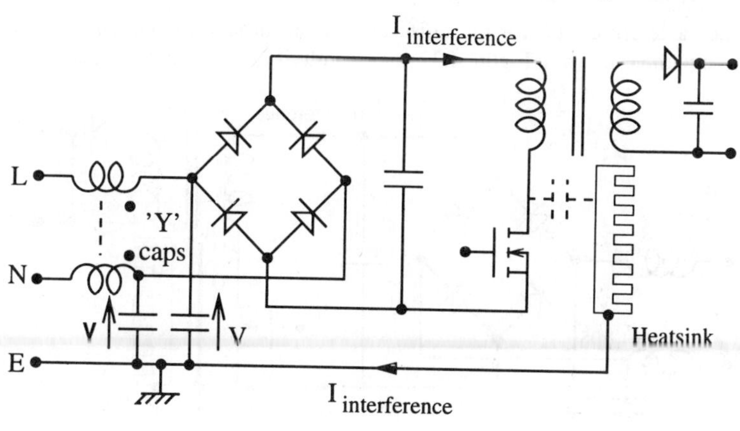

Figure 4.30 Ground currents arising from heatsink capacitance

Unfortunately, they must be mounted in such a way as to dissipate their heat into the chassis, which usually sets up ground currents. A method must be employed to mount them so that they are free to dissipate heat and not induce ground currents. The capacitance of a TO-3 transistor package mounted on a heatsink with a mica washer is typically of the order of 100pF. Given a 200 volt input with almost perfect switching at 20kHz: over 1mA at 1MHz could flow in the ground. The ground current path is shown in Figure 4.30.

The solution is to mount an electrical screen in the form of a copper foil, between the transistor and the heatsink. The foil is electrically insulated by mica waskers, from both the transistor and the heatsink, but still allows the passage of heat. This screen is connected back to the prime power supply line, rather than ground.

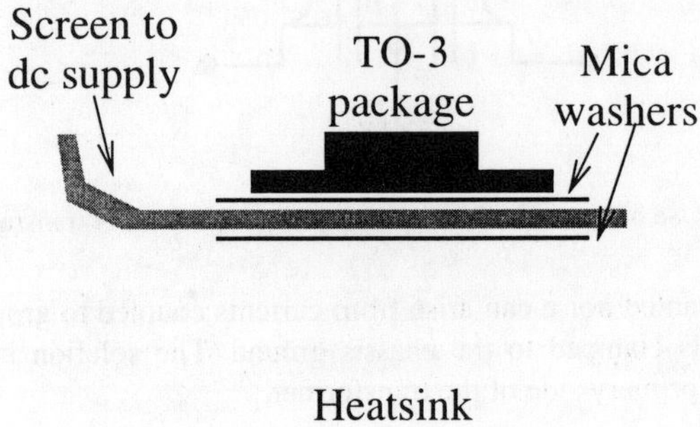

Figure 4.31 Transistor heatsink screen

This provides a return circuit for the noise other than through the chassis. The screen current return path is shown in Figure 4.32, along with a typical mounting arrangement.

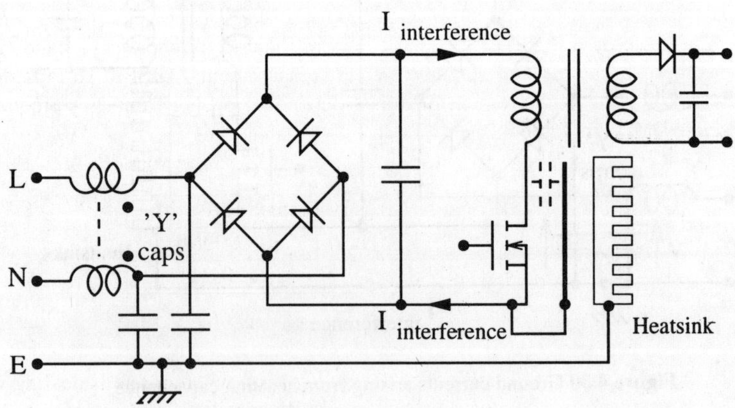

Figure 4.32 The use of transistor heatsink screen to break ground current path

4.3 EMI MEASUREMENT AND SPECIFICATIONS

B All electronic and electrical equipment generates some electrical noise. These noise emissions must be kept below statutory levels. There are different national and international organisations that specify acceptable noise limits from electronic equipment including switched mode power supplies. For computer and information technology equipment BS6527 applies as does the European standard EN55022. These are based on the International Electrotechnical Commission (IEC) and CISPR publication 22. In the US the FCC (Federal Communications Commission) rules apply, in Germany VDE0871 applies. Broadly, the different national limits are similar.

The methods of specification and measurement of interference and noise are defined internationally by the CISPR (Comité International Spécial des Perturbations Radioélectriques). CISPR publication 16 (which is reproduced as BS727) gives detailed information on the specification and measurement of EMI, including the techniques that should be used for the measurements. The different national standards are all based on the guideline definitions in CISPR 16.

Noise Measurements

Noise or interference can take many forms from occasional impulses to continuous sinusoidal signals. It is important that the specification of an interference signal takes this into account. The specifications of interference have been worked out by the CISPR and are given in the document "Specification of radio interference measuring apparatus and measurement methods", CISPR Publication 16, 1977. (They are also available in BS727). These documents also give details of the apparatus and techniques to be used to measure EMI.

Continuous sinusoidal signals are reasonably easy to specify in terms of the *rms* power they contain, provided the impedance level is known or defined. Impulsive noise is much more difficult to specify as it occupies a wide bandwidth and its power can vary widely with time. The power in a broadband signal is proportional to the measuring bandwidth. To overcome these problems and standardise the measurements, CISPR 16 lays down fixed bandwidths for the measurement of noise, depending on the frequency frequency range. These are shown in Table 4.2.

Table 4.2 CISPR Noise Measurement Bandwidths

3-150kHZ	0.15-30MHz	30-1000MHz
200Hz	9kHz	120kHz

Noise Units

The units for the measurement of noise vary depending upon whether one is dealing with conducted or radiated noise. Conducted noise is usually specified in terms of dBμV, ie decibels with respect to 1 μV. A figure of 60dBμV represents a voltage of 1 mV. The levels are specified for known impedance levels (either 50 or 150 Ω) to give known power levels.

Radiated noise is defined in terms of the electric field strength of the signal, in units of volts per metre. Again it is usually expressed in terms of dBμV/m.

Types of Noise Measurement

Three different measures of noise are defined in CISPR 16. They are average noise, peak noise and quasi-peak noise. Each is applicable to different situations.

Average Noise

This is defined as the average value of the envelope of the signal passing through the filters of the measuring receiver. It is not a useful measure for impulsive noise and is used only for narrowband (CW) signals where all of the energy is contained in one frequency.

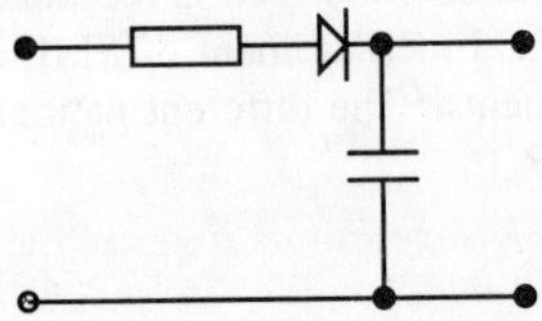

Figure 4.33 Peak detector circuit

Peak Noise

This is the peak of the noise energy in the measurement bandwidth and is useful for impulsive noise which covers a wide frequency range. The measurement is done with a detector, of the form shown in Figure 4.33, which responds to, and holds, the maximum amplitude of the signal occurring in the receiver bandwidth.

Quasi-Peak Noise

If noise is impulsive, an interfering signal which has a high pulse repetition frequency (PRF) will have a greater subjective annoyance than one which has a low PRF. A high level of interference that only occurs occasionally will be less annoying than a low level which is much more frequent. This is the basis of the quasi-peak noise measure. CISPR 16 defines curves which relate the subjective annoyance and the PRF of interfering signal in different bandwidths. Figure 4.34 reproduces the curve for a receiver bandwidth of 120kHz which is applicable in the frequency range 30-1000MHz.

The lower the PRF of the interfering signal, the greater the difference between the peak signal and its quasi-peak value. At PRFs greater than the measurement bandwidth, the signal loses its broadband nature and the quasi-peak and the peak values become the same. (In this situation the receiver is capable of resolving the individual peaks in the interfering signal's spectrum, assuming that we are dealing with a constant PRF.) At low PRFs, around 1Hz, there is a difference of around 40dB between the peak and quasi-peak values. As the PRF rises to around 10kHz the quasi-peak and peak values approach each other and become virtually the same.

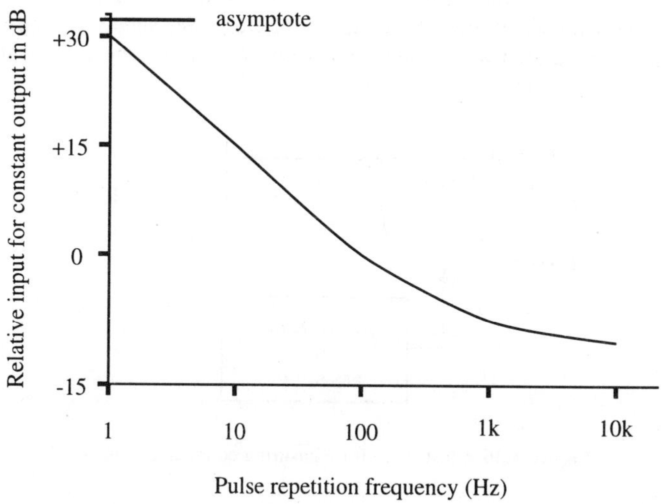

Figure 4.34 Curve for conversion between peak and quasi-peak values

It is arguable whether quasi-peak measurements are very useful for SMPS where the switching frequency is likely to be in excess of 10kHz and the bulk of the noise produced will be at harmonics of the switching frequency. Figure 4.35 shows a schematic for a simple quasi-peak detector.

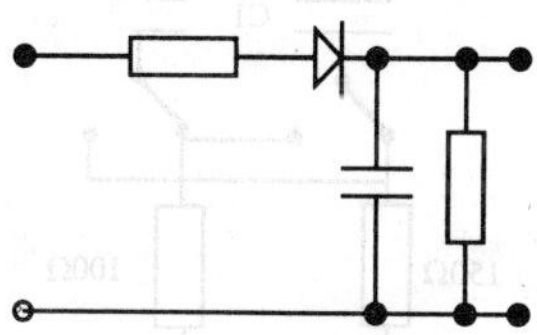

Figure 4.35 Quasi-peak detector circuit

EMI - Conducted Noise and Radiated Noise

There are two main EMI specifications that must be checked out, that for conducted noise and that for radiated noise. Usually, if a design includes adequate screening and the conducted noise is kept under control by means of appropriate filters, radiated noise is not too much of a problem.

Conducted Noise

The set-up used for measuring conducted noise is shown in Figure 4.36. The SMPS is powered from the mains via a Line Impedance Stabilisation Network (LISN). A circuit of a typical LISN is shown in Figure 4.37. The function of this circuit is to connect a specified RF terminating resistance of 150 Ω across each mains input terminal of the SMPS to ground, over which the RF voltage from the power supply can be measured. This RF voltage is measured with a calibrated noise receiver or a spectrum analyser with a 50Ω input impedance and a closely specified bandwidth.

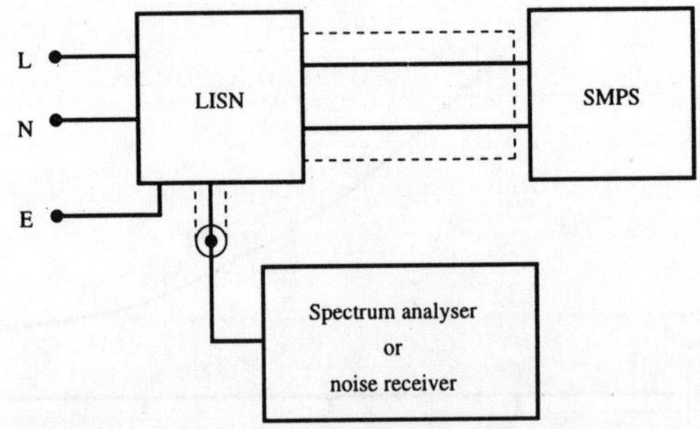

Figure 4.36 A test setup for measuring conducted noise

The LISN can be switched to measure the RF voltage on the line or the neutral connection. The figure below shows a simplified schematic circuit for a LISN.

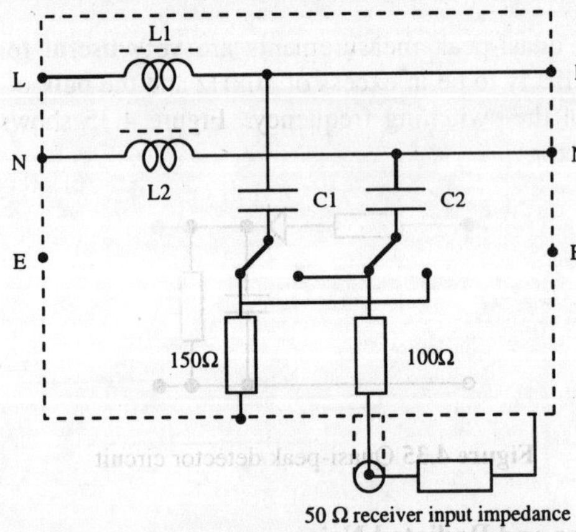

Figure 4.37 Simple schematic for a LISN

The levels of conducted noise that are permitted by EN55022 class B are shown in Table 4.3.

Table 4.3 Conducted interference - EN55022 class B limits		
Frequency range	level (quasi-peak)	level (average)
0.15-0.5MHz	66-56dBμV*	56-46dBμV*
0.5-5.0MHz	56dBμV	46dBμV
5-30MHz	60dBμV	50dbμV
*Level varying linearly with log frequency		

The levels permitted by the German national specification VDE0871 are shown in Table 4.4.

Table 4.4 Conducted interference - VDE class B limits				
Frequency range	Bandwidth	Level(quasi-peak)	Sensor	Limit (dBm)
10kHz to 150kHz	200Hz	79dBμV at 10kHz to 57.5dBμV at 150kHz*	150ΩLISN or 50ΩLISN	-28 to -49.5
150kHz to 500kHz	9kHz	54dBμV	150Ω LISN	-53
500kHz to 30MHz	9kHz	49dBμV	150Ω LISN	-59
*Level varying linearly with log frequency				

A comparison of the different permitted levels of EMI is shown in in Figure 4.38.

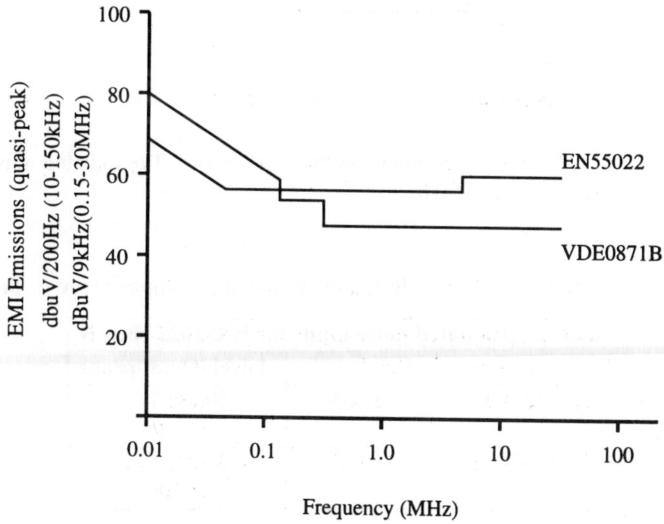

Figure 4.38 The different limits for conducted EMI

The vertical scale is in dBμV, that is decibels above 1μV, so 60dBμV is 1mV. As mentioned previously, there are some minor variations in the different national specifications but a power supply is acceptable in all countries if the RF voltage at its input terminals at frequencies above 150kHz is less than +54dBμV or 500μV.

Radiated Interference

Radiated interference is normally specified in terms of the acceptable maximum field strength in volts/metre at a given distance from the equipment. Measurements are normally carried out using a testing range known to be free from reflections and extraneous signals. The power supply is set up in normal operation and a spectrum analyser or tunable noise receiver is used with a calibrated aerial to measure the electromagnetic field strength at different frequencies. Figure 4.39 shows a typical radiated noise measurement set-up.

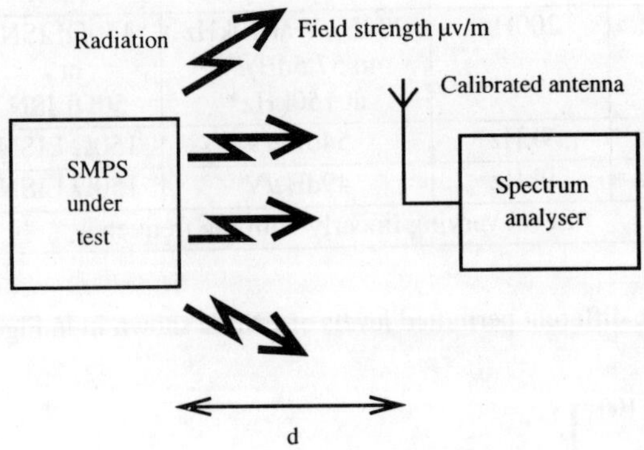

Figure 4.39 The setup for measuring radiated EMI

The levels defined for EN55022 are shown in the table below. The radiated noise is only specified at frequencies above 30MHz

The limits specified in EN55022 for information technology equipment are in Table 4.5.

Table 4.5 Radiated noise limits for EN55022 class B

Frequency range	Bandwidth	Level (Quasi-peak)
30-230MHz	120kHz	30dBμV/m at 10m
230-1000MHz	120kHz	37dBμV/m at 10m

The radiated noise limits for VDE0871 are given in Table 4.6.

Table 4.6 VDE0871 class B EMI field strength limits for radiated noise

Frequency range	Bandwidth	Level	Recommended antenna
10-150kHz	200Hz	50μV/m at 30m	Magnetic loop 60cm per side maximum
150kHz to 30MHz	9kHz	50μV/m at 30m	Magnetic loop as above or 1m vertical rod
30MHz to 470MHz	120kHz	50μV/m at 10m	Balanced dipole tuned to 80MHz or higher, 1 to 4m height above ground
470MHz to 1GHz	120kHz	200μV/m at 10m	Balanced dipole - plane polarised; Directional plane polarised antenna may be used.

In order to make reliable radiated field strength measurements, great care is required to ensure that the measurements are made correctly. Ideally a test range should be set up which is free of reflecting objects and is above a perfectly conducting ground. This is not always possible in practice and the CISPR documents give practicable set-ups which will suffice to get measurements of reasonable accuracy. The important point is to keep reflecting objects well clear of the test unit and the aerial. Figure 4.40 schematically shows the area that must be kept free of reflecting objects for radiated EMI measurements.

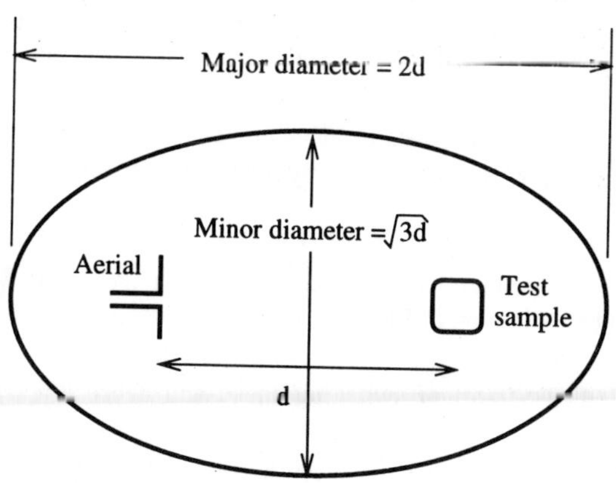

Figure 4.40 Test range set up showing clear area around aerial and test sample

Aerials for Radiated Noise Measurement

The spectrum analyser, or noise receiver, measures the voltage at its input terminals. In order to measure a radiation field it is necessary to use an aerial to convert the field into a signal voltage that can be applied to the measuring device.

The incident field in dBμV/m is related to the antenna voltage by

$$E(dB\mu V/m) = V(db\mu V) - K$$

where K is the antenna factor, which is given by

$$K = 20\log f(MHz) - G(dB) - 29.78$$

for a 50Ω system. G is the power gain of the aerial and f is the measuring frequency. The gain of an "ideal" isotropic aerial is 1 (G(dB) = 0). Half-wave dipoles have a gain of 1.64 over isotropic. For any aerial the gain will depend on the frequency.

Noise Measurement Equipment - Spectrum Analyser or Noise Receiver?

There are two types of equipment that can be used for EMI measurements: spectrum analysers and noise receivers. Each have advantages and disadvantages. Spectrum analysers generally are the lower cost solution to the problem but have some disadvantages. They usually only have peak detectors and the results have to be carefully interpreted to get good quasi-peak results. Another problem with spectrum analysers is that they are more prone to overload at the input. This input circuitry is generally broadband and has to cope with all of the noise present simultaneously. With quasi-peak measurements, the peaks can be up to 40dB above the actual peak value. This means that the input has to cope with very high signal levels, which can cause non-linearity and give erroneous results.

Specialised noise receivers have inputs which have frequency pre-selection fitted to give a very high dynamic range. This is important to get accurate measurements. They also have filters which correspond to the CISPR bandwidths, as well as specialised peak and quasi-peak detectors, which again meet CISPR requirements.

Probably the spectrum analyser is best for development work and as a "look-see" device, but for final testing and qualification a noise receiver should be used.

Summary

The following are some points to consider at the design stages of a switch mode power supply to help with the reduction of EMI.

- Consider a slight trade-off of switching speed and hence efficiency for an easier EMI problem!
- Plan on a fully encased, grounded enclosure to screen and house the supply.
- Keep high $\frac{dI}{dt}$ and $\frac{dV}{dt}$ lines as short as possible to reduce the noise radiation.
- Keep the input and output leads as far as possible from the electric and magnetic noise generators.

- Keep switching paths simple to prevent the creation of excessive ground paths.
- Be careful with grounding.
- Provide shielding between the noise sources and sensitive input and output circuits, including sensitive voltage references.
- Minimise capacitive coupling into the chassis.
- Provide effective RF filtering on all input and output connections from the screened enclosure.
- Consider a Faraday screen in the main transformer.

4.4 INPUT RECTIFIERS WITH UNITY POWER FACTOR

Introduction

New EC regulations in the form of EN60555 part 2 are being introduced which will severely limit the harmonic currents equipment is allowed to draw from the mains supply. This regulation is based on the IEC recommendation IEC555-2 which is the basis of the British Standard BS5406. Table 4.7 gives the IEC555-2 recommendations.

Table 4.7 IEC555-2 Recommendations

Harmonic Order	**Permissible Current**	**Maximum permissible current**
n	**mA/W**	**A**
	Odd harmonics	
3	3.4	2.30
5	1.9	1.14
7	1.0	0.78
9	0.5	0.40
11	0.35	0.33
13	0.3	0.21
15 & up	$\frac{3.85}{n}$	$0.15 \times \frac{15}{n}$
	Even harmonics	
2	1.8	1.08
4	0.7	0.42
6	0.5	0.30
>8	$\frac{3}{n}$	$\frac{1.80}{n}$

There are several reasons why the the harmonic content of the load current drawn for the supply should be minimised.

1. High peak currents make inefficient use of the supply. The supply will have to be rated to deliver the peak current even if the mean current is well below the peak. This limits the power that can be drawn from the supply to well below its full potential.
2. The high peak currents cause problems with electronic circuit breakers (ELCBs). These respond to peak currents and tend to trip out when the mains waveform becomes badly distorted.
3. Power factor degradation - the current peak is displaced from the voltage peak, resulting in a degradation of power factor. The power factor also depends on the form factor of the waveform, and the pulse nature of the current wave contributes to

the degradation.

4. The high harmonic content gives rise to a high neutral current in a three phase system, which can cause safety trips to come out.

Figure 4.41 shows how harmonics in the load current waveform drawn by a SMPS can arise. This common circuit draws very non-sinusoidal currents from the mains supply.

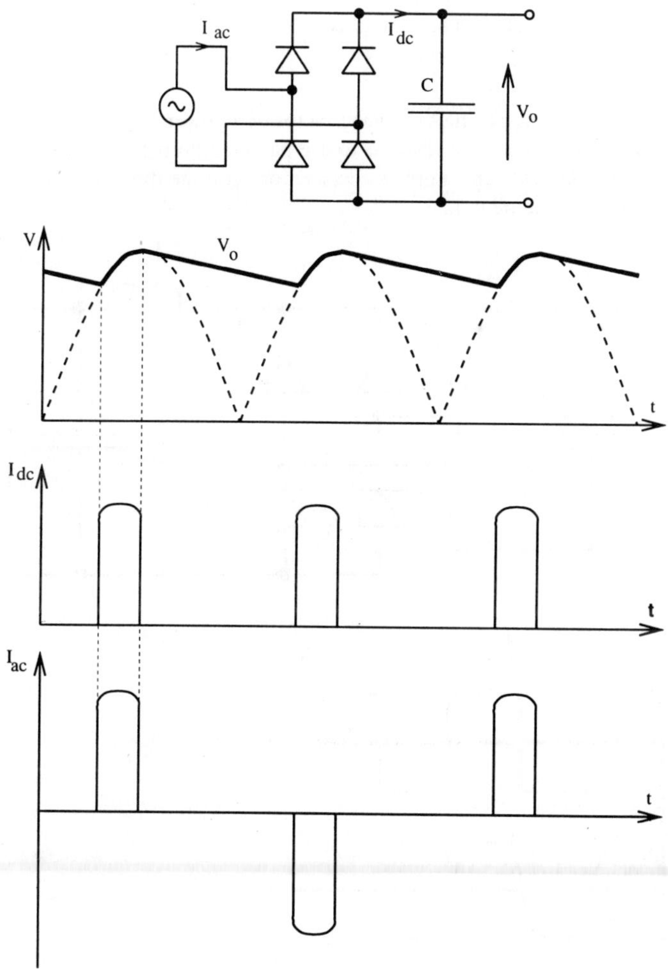

Figure 4.41 Typical SMPS input circuit and waveforms

If a smoother d.c. supply is desired, the capacitor C can be made larger. This has the effect of making the current spike narrower, and hence taller (to pass the same energy), making the harmonic problem worse.

There are two methods which can be used to reduce the harmonic content to acceptable levels:

1. Passive filtering which requires large, expensive passive filters (L-C) being added to the SMPS, or
2. Active filtering, which is far more complex.

Passive Filtering

The simplest approach to improving the power factor of a power supply and reducing the harmonic content of the current waveform is to use passive filtering. This can be done by the addition of inductors and capacitors in conjunction with the diode bridge. A suitable arrangement is shown in Figure 4.42.

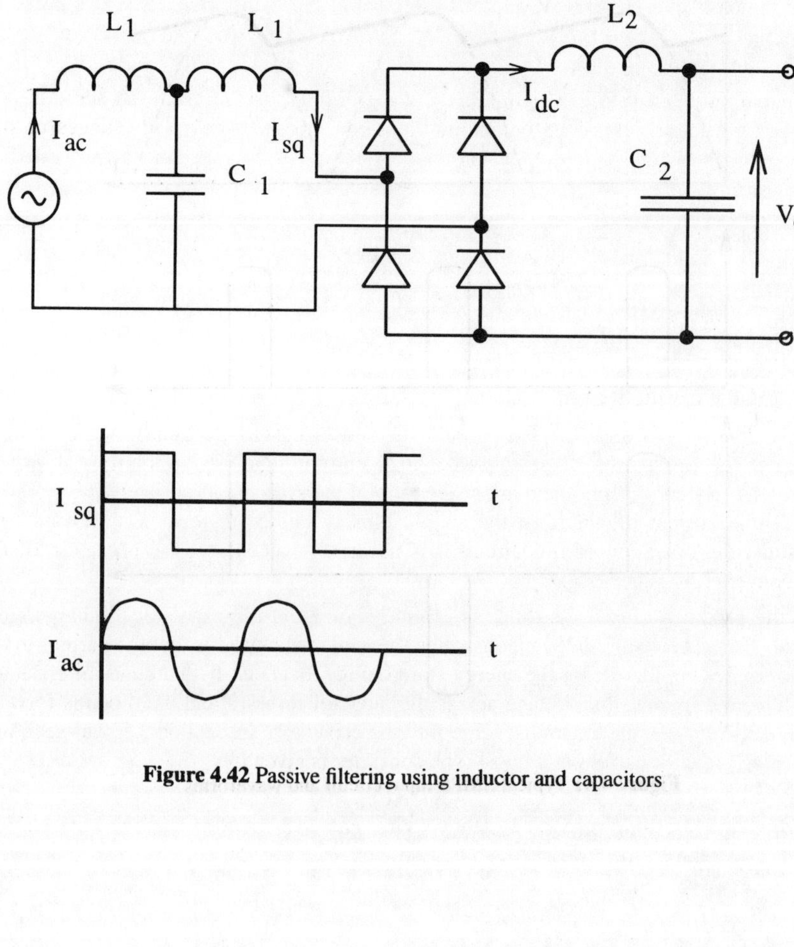

Figure 4.42 Passive filtering using inductor and capacitors

The choke L2 has the effect of "smoothing" the current drawn from the bridge. At the a.c. side of the bridge, the current is a square wave which is in phase with the mains voltage waveform. Some additional filtering in the form of L1, L1 and C1 help to reduce the harmonic content of the current waveform. Ideally the input filter should have a corner frequency of around 100Hz to block the 3rd, 5th etc. harmonics in the waveform.

The effect of adding the inductors and capacitor can be summarised as follows:

- The improved current waveform gives rise to an improved power factor.
- The output voltage regulation is degraded compared to the circuit without filtering. and it is also reduced by around 10%.
- The inductor L2 and the capacitor C2 form a low-pass filter which improves the voltage ripple level on the output.
- The overall efficiency is unaffected (barring resistive losses) by the addition of the inductor.

Typically the "smoothing inductor" will require to have a relatively high inductance, of several hundred mili-Henries. It must be effective at the mains frequency and it can be constructed on a silicon iron laminated core. It will be physically large and relatively heavy.

A further improvement in the input current waveform is possible from the addition of a low value capacitor across the output of the diode bridge. The disadvantages of this arrangement are weight, size, losses and the degradation of the output voltage regulation. It does, however, have the great advantage of simplicity, and may well be appropriate in power supplies handling powers less than say 100 -150W. In this situation the current carrying capacity of the inductor need not be too high and the resistive losses may be acceptable.

In power supplies required to handle higher powers the only real alternative is to use active shaping of the load current.

Active Load Current Shaping

A boost type d.c. to d.c. converter similar to that discussed Section 1 is the obvious choice for the production of a sinusoidal load current. The basic circuit is shown in Figure 4.43. By controlling the mark space ratio of the switch appropriately it is possible to make the current drawn from the supply closely approximate to a sine wave. To understand the operation of this circuit it is necessary to consider the operation of the boost converter in some detail.

When the switch is closed the diode is reverse biased and the capacitor discharges into the load. The other thing that happens when the switch is closed is that the current in the inductor builds up, increasing the energy stored in the magnetic field around the inductor. When the switch opens the voltage across the inductor reverses and the diode is forward biased, causing the inductor to discharge into the capacitor. In Section 1 it was seen that the average inductor current in a boost type converter is given by

$$I_{L(av)} = \frac{I_{load}}{(1 - D)}$$

By controlling the switching duty ratio, D, it is possible to control the input current drawn by the converter, $I_{L(av)}$.

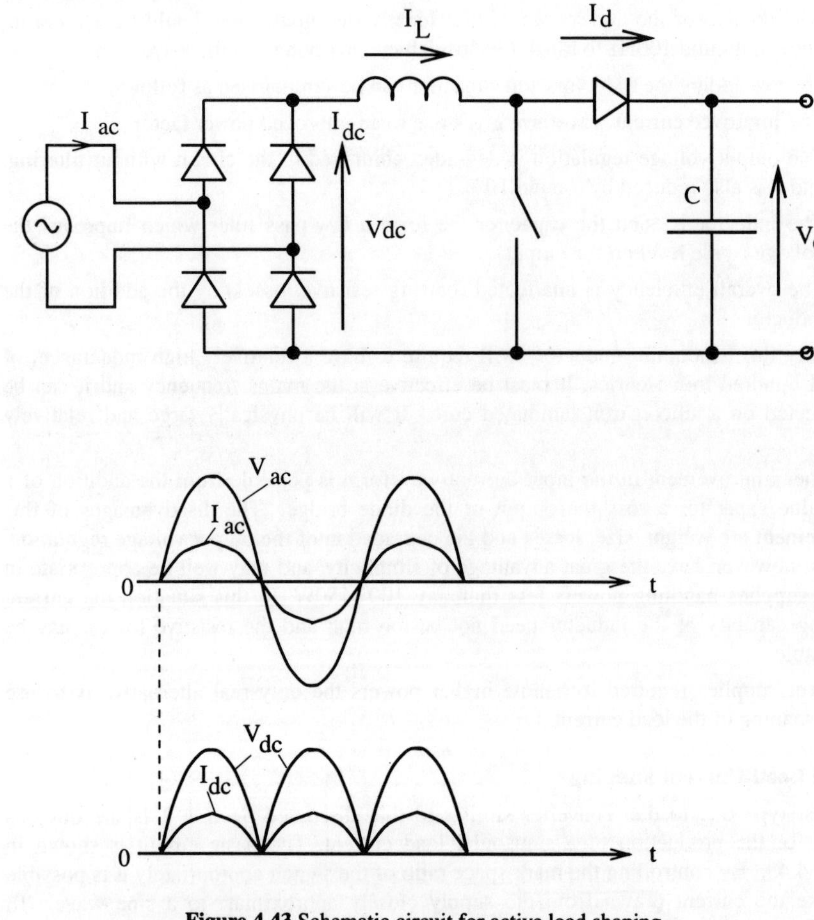

Figure 4.43 Schematic circuit for active load shaping

Because the current in the inductor cannot be changed discontinuously it is possible to build up a sinusoidal current in the inductor provided that the switch is driven at a frequency considerably in excess of the sine wave. Figure 4.44 shows a sinusoidal current drawn from a series of charge/discharge cycles of current through an inductor.

By controlling the mark-space ratio of the switch it is possible to arrange that the current in the inductor either rises or falls. By varying the switching cycle appropriately it is possible to synthesise a sinusoidal current waveform from the mains supply.

In order to ensure that the waveform is sinusoidal it is necessary to have three pieces of information.

1. The current from the supply must be sampled.
2. The input voltage sinewave must be available.
3. The output voltage must be sampled.

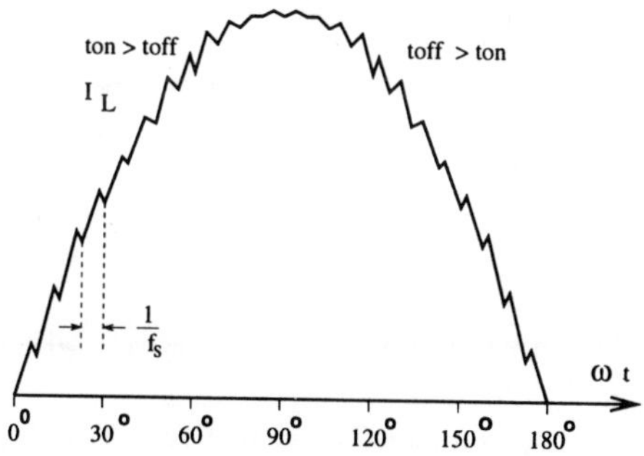

Figure 4.44 Current waveform from active current shaping

A suitable arrangement for doing this is shown in the block diagram in Figure 4.45.

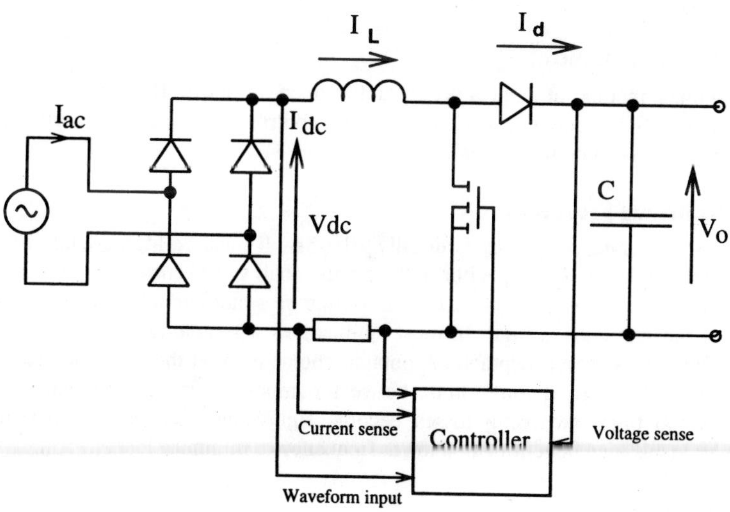

Figure 4.45 Schematic showing controller and necessary inputs for active load shaping

This circuit controls both the output voltage and the input current. The input current is controlled by the input voltage and the output voltage is controlled by comparison with a fixed reference.

The control block can be explained by reference to the block diagram in Figure 4.46.

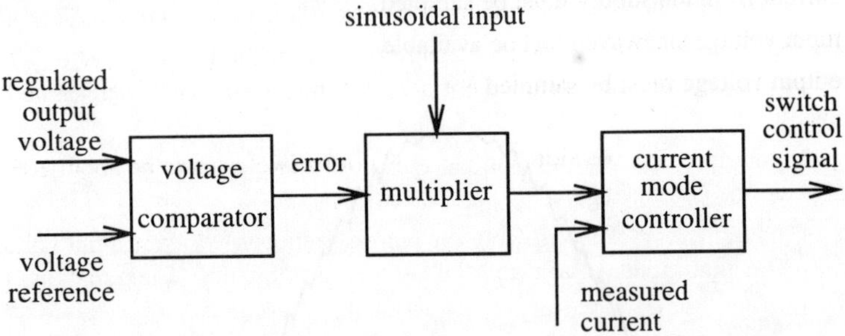

Figure 4.46 Schematic of controller block for active load current control

The output voltage is compared with a reference to give an error signal. This error is then multiplied with the incoming voltage waveform to produce one input of the current controller. This works by comparing this signal with a sample of the input current. If it is necessary to ramp the input current upwards, the control switch is switched on for longer during each cycle. If it is required to reduce the input current, the switch is held off for longer each cycle.

Constant Frequency Control

The commmonest method of control is constant frequency control. Here, the controller is driven at a fixed clock frequency, and input current control is provided by varying the on to off ratio of the switch control signal.

Choice of Switching Frequency

The choice of switching frequency is usually arbitrary. It must be high enough to make the values of the inductor and capacitor in the circuit small and to ensure that distortion of the input waveform is low. It must at the same time be small enough to ensure that the efficiency of the regulator is high. In most applications a switching frequency between 20kHz and 300kHz will be acceptable. A popular choice is to set the frequency to around 100kHz as this gives a good compromise between component size and efficiency. If the frequency is too high, switching losses become significant. Converters operating at higher power levels may benefit from a lower frequency to minimise losses.

Inductor Selection

The inductor value determines the amount of high frequency ripple current in the input and its value is chosen to give a specific value of ripple current. The first step is to decide the maximum value of the input current sinewave. This occurs at minimum line voltage and is given by

$$I_{line(pk)} = \frac{\sqrt{2} \times P}{V_{in(min)}}$$

where P is the maximum input power which the converter is required to handle.

The maximum ripple current in a boost converter occurs when the duty cycle is 1:1. The peak value of the inductor current does not occur at this point as it is determined by the input sinewave.

The peak-to-peak ripple current in the inductor is normally chosen to be about 20% of the maximum peak line current.

The value of the inductor is selected from the peak current at the lowest input voltage, the duty factor, D, at that input voltage and the switching frequency. The equations for this are as follows:

$$D = \frac{V_o - V_{in}}{V_o}$$

$$L = \frac{V_{in} \times D}{f_s \times \Delta I}$$

where ΔI is the peak-to-peak ripple current.

The high frequency ripple current is added to the line current peak so that the maximum current in the inductor is the line current peak plus half of the peak-to-peak ripple current. The inductor must be designed to handle this current.

Output Capacitor

The factors involved in the selection of the output capacitor are the switching frequency ripple current, the second harmonic ripple current, the d.c. output volatge, the output ripple voltage and the hold-up time. The total current through the capacitor is the rms value of the switching frequency ripple current and the second harmonic of the line frequency current.

If hold-up time for the output is not specified or not critical, the capacitor should have a value of around 0.2μF/watt of output power. If a hold-up of say two cycles of the supply is required, then a much higher value of capacitor is required, typically 1-2μF/watt of output.

Switch and Diode Ratings

The switching device must have a current rating that is at least equal to the peak current in the inductor and a voltage rating at least equal to the output voltage. The same is true for the output diode. It must also be fast enough to keep its own losses low.

Observations on sinusoidal input circuits

- The output voltage contains a 100Hz ripple content at twice the line frequency. The feedback control circuit cannot compensate for this without distorting the input current waveform.

- If the switching frequency is kept to a low level then a laminated iron core inductor can possibly be used, which will be smaller due to its higher saturation flux density, compared to one made with high frequency ferrite materials.
- A higher switching frequency allows the use of a smaller inductance value, but it must not be so high that switching losses become a problem.
- Inrush limiting is still required with this configuration while the capacitor charges.

Other Advantages of Active Input Current Shaping

- The DC voltage can be stabilised to a nearly constant value for large variations of line voltage.
- The components in the subsequent converter can be derated as the voltage and current ratings are known and fixed.
- Because of the absence of large peak currents in the input, the ratings of EMI filters can be reduced.
- For equal ripple in output voltage, only one third to a half the output capacitance is required compared to a conventional supply, resulting in a reduced size.
- The energy efficiency of such a circuit is typically 96% compared to a figure of 99% for the conventional arrangement with active current shaping.

References

1. Unitrode UC3854 data sheet

2 Unitrode application note U-134 "UC3854 Controlled Power Factor Correction Circuit Desgn"

4.5 PROTECTION AND MANAGEMENT OF SMPS

In the design of a power supply it is prudent to provide protection circuitry to protect against extreme and abnormal operating conditions that will inevitably occur when the supply is in use. These can occur in the form of output short circuits and excessive loads or high voltage transients on the input supply line. Many of the components in a power supply are handling powers greatly in excess of their dissipation capability. Under fault conditions it is quite possible that they may start to dissipate this power, leading to their rapid failure. The power supply designer has no control over these faults and therefore must incorporate circuitry to accommodate them safely. This falls into four broad categories:

- overcurrent protection
- overvoltage protection
- inrush protection
- device protection and snubber circuits

OVERCURRENT PROTECTION

In order to provide current-limiting, some means of sensing overcurrent conditions must be provided.

The normal method of providing current-limiting in an inverter or power supply regulator is to provide an output current sensor driving a feedback path that is used to control the output current. Below a critical threshold level the feedback does not affect the output current, but above the threshold a high resistance path is introduced into the circuit to control the current. In a switched mode power supply the commonest method of achieving current limiting is to control the mark space ratio of the switching transistors. Under fault conditions the transistors can be switched off.

The purpose of current-limiting is two-fold: firstly to limit the dissipation in the regulator components to safe values and thereby prevent damage to them, and secondly to provide some protection to circuits and systems being powered by the supply.

Three types of current-limiting are normally used. Firstly, the straightforward current limiter merely prevents the current rising above a critical value by dropping the output voltage to zero. This characteristic is represented in Figure 4.47.

This is relatively simple to implement but can have the disadvantage that under overcurrent conditions it can still over dissipate the regulator device. A second, more effective, solution is to use a foldback current limiter with the current voltage characteristic in Figure 4.48.

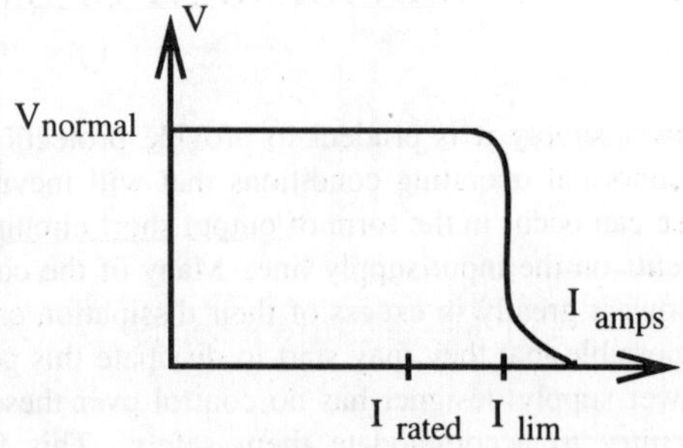

Figure 4.47 A typical current limiting V-I characteristic

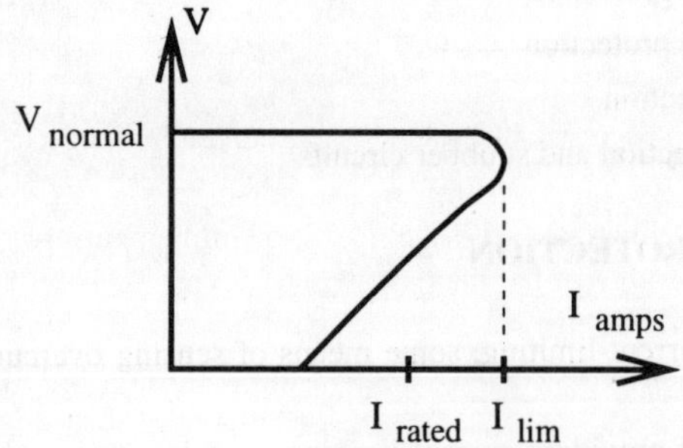

Figure 4.48 A typical foldback current limiting V-I characteristic

Thirdly, cycle-by-cycle protection is a useful method of output current limiting in an SMPS. It is usually implemented by means of a current transformer placed in the primary circuit of the main switching transformer as shown in Figure 4.49. In this way a signal is fed back to the controller circuit, which is used to reduce the pulse width under overcurrent conditions. Under short circuit conditions the output can be switched 'off completely by removing the drive from the main switching device. It has the advantage of fast operation on a cycle-by-cycle basis and can be implemented with few extra components. Most SMPS controller ICs incorporate it as a standard facility.

Some provision must be made for restarting the power supply. Either the supply is latched off under fault current conditions and stays off until the mains power is interrupted to reset the supply, or the supply can be designed to start up periodically to see if the fault is still present. The method of restarting chosen will depend on the application for the supply.

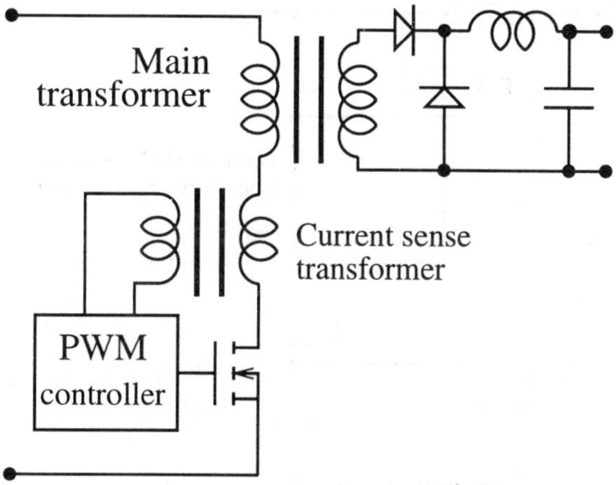

Figure 4.49 Cycle-by-cycle current limiting

An alternative method, illustrated in Figure 4.50, of implementing overcurrent sensing is to use a resistor in the source of the main switching device. This will provide a lower cost means of current sensing.

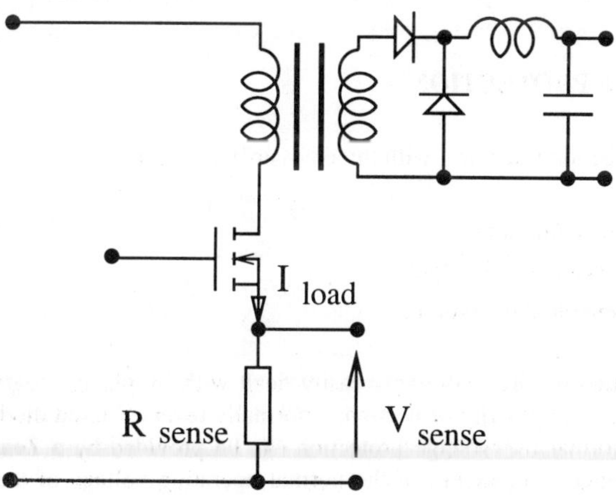

Figure 4.50 Use of a current sensing resistor

Another method of current sensing is to use a series resistor and employ the voltage drop across it to turn on a transistor as shown in Figure 4.51.

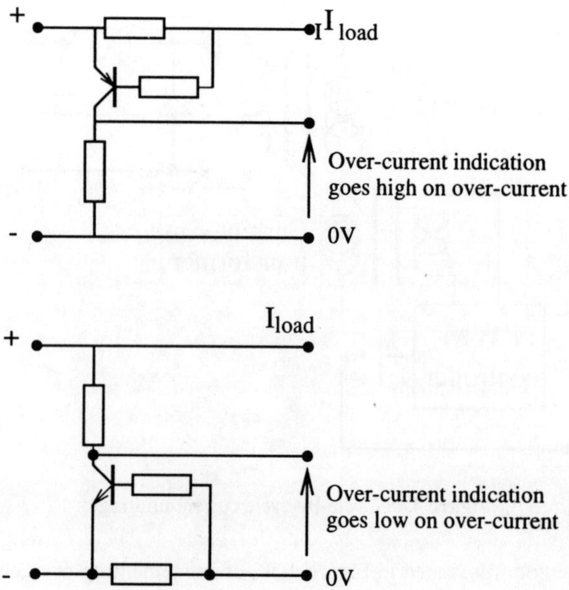

Figure 4.51 Use of a series current sensing resistor

OVERVOLTAGE PROTECTION

Overvoltage protection must deal with three possible situations:

- Reverse voltage on output
- External overvoltage on output
- Internally generated overvoltage

The first two situations are reasonably easily dealt with by placing "catcher" diodes on the output. For reverse polarity protection, a normally reverse biased diode can be placed on the output. Normal overvoltage protection can be provided by a Zener or avalanche diode whose voltage is in excess of the normal operating voltage of the power supply. Diodes for both types of protection must be amply rated to cope with the anticipated fault conditions.

It is important that a power supply does not give out an abnormally high voltage under fault conditions. If it did so it could easily damage the circuitry which it is powering. There are two widely used schemes for overvoltage protection in SMPS, namely inverter-inhibiting protection and crowbar protection.

Turning first of all to inverter-inhibiting protection, a block diagram of this scheme is shown in Figure 4.52.

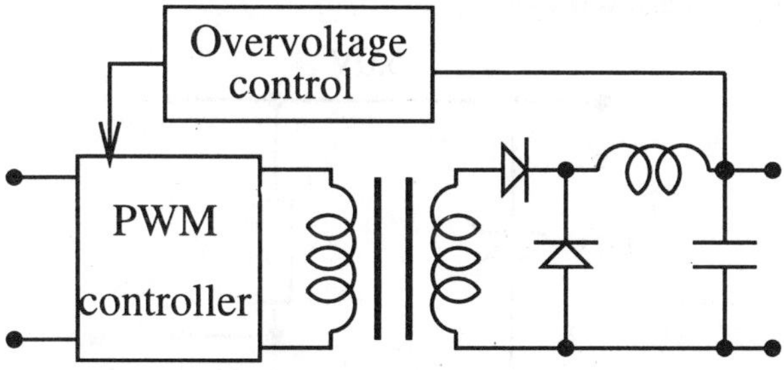

Figure 4.52 Inverter inhibiting overvoltage protection

The d.c. output voltage is monitored by the overvoltage control circuit. This is usually some form of comparator which is set to trigger under overvoltage conditions. Its output is used to switch off the pulse width modulator (PWM), thereby shutting down the power supply, in much the same way as was done for cycle-by-cycle current limiting. One problem with this system of overvoltage protection is that the energy stored in the filter capacitor must be dumped into the load, possibly causing damage.

To get round this problem we can use the "crowbar" circuit shown in Figure 4.53.

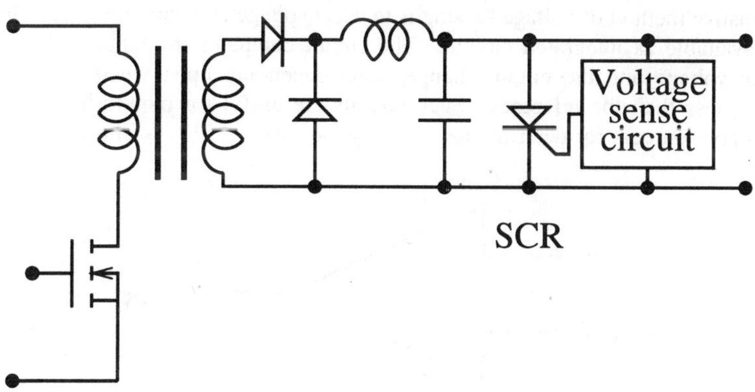

Figure 4.53 Crowbar overvoltage protection

This can be made to shut down the power supply very quickly, within a few microseconds. It operates by sensing the output voltage and when an overvoltage occurs, the silicon control rectifier (SCR) is fired, shorting the output. This scheme depends upon the power supply having adequate current limiting and the SCR being rated to withstand the short-circuit current along with the discharge surge from the output filter capacitor.

Another simple method of sensing an overvoltage condition is to use a Zener diode to control the turn-on point of a transistor as shown in Figure 4.54. This circuit has the advantage of simplicity and versatility.

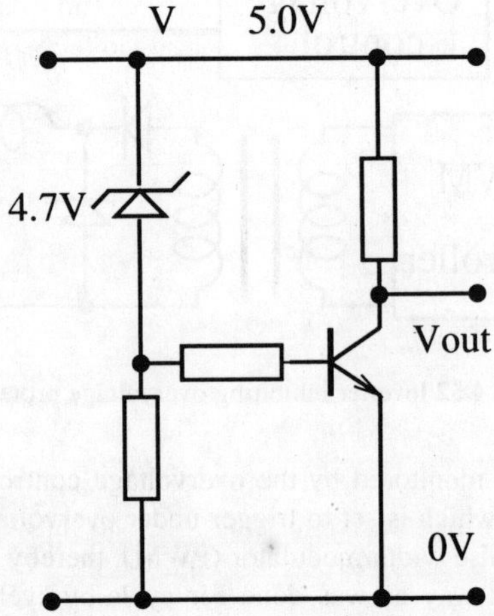

Figure 4.54 A simple overvoltage detection circuit

An alternative method of voltage sensing is to use a voltage comparator circuit. These are widely available as integrated circuits. The circuit compares the input voltage with a reference voltage and the output changes state depending upon whether the input is greater or less than the reference. Such circuits are useful for monitoring the state of power supply outputs for determining "power good" status. This is illustrated in Figure 4.55.

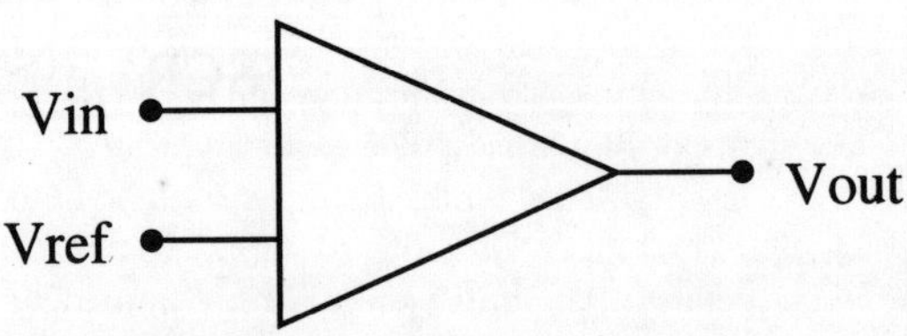

Vin > Vref : Vout high

Vin < Vref : Vout low

Figure 4.55 A voltage comparator

INRUSH PROTECTION

The input filter smoothing capacitor used in many switched mode power supplies causes a potential problem. Figure 4.56 shows a typical input circuit of an SMPS. Included in the circuit are the parasitics associated with the capacitor and the wiring.

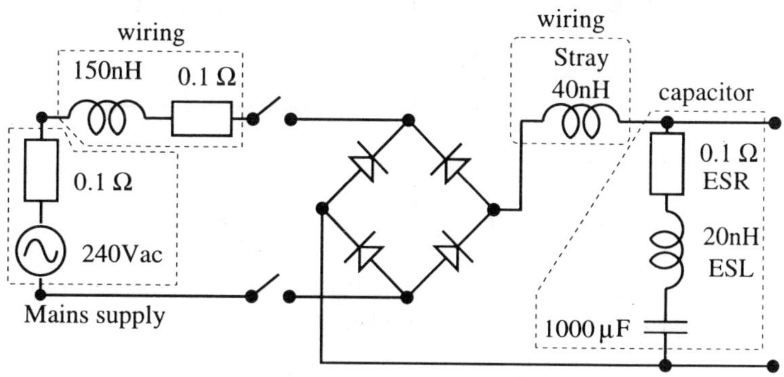

Total resistance = 0.3 Ω

Total inductance = 150nH

Input voltage = 240V rms

Inrush current = 100s of amps

Figure 4.56 Typical input circuit showing parasitic inductances and resistances

The filter capacitor is deliberately chosen to have a high capacity and a low equivalent series resistance (ESR). On application of power it appears very close to a perfect short circuit, causing a very high current surge until it is charged. These current surges can exceed the ratings of the diodes in the input rectifier by many times, destroying them. This inrush current surge can be of very short duration and hence may not contain enough energy to open circuit breakers or blow fuses. The exact amplitude of the surge will vary depending on when, in the input voltage cycle, the input switch is closed; however, it is necessary to design for the worst case when the switch closes at the maximum of the voltage waveform. The magnitude of an inrush surge is only limited by the resistance and inductance of the wiring associated with the input circuit and the ESR of the capacitor. Typically, inrush currents can reach many hundreds of amperes.

Two methods of inrush protection are shown in Figures 4.57 and 4.58. The circuit in Figure 4.57 uses a resistor to limit the peak surge current. It has the advantage of simplicity but suffers from the drawback that it reduces efficiency due to losses in the resistor.

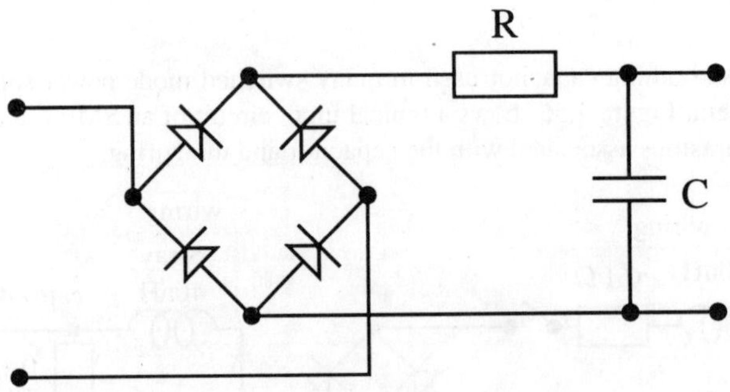

Figure 4.57 A simple resistive surge limiter

An alternative is to use a thermistor as shown in Figure 4.58. This component has a high resistance when cold and a low resistance when hot.

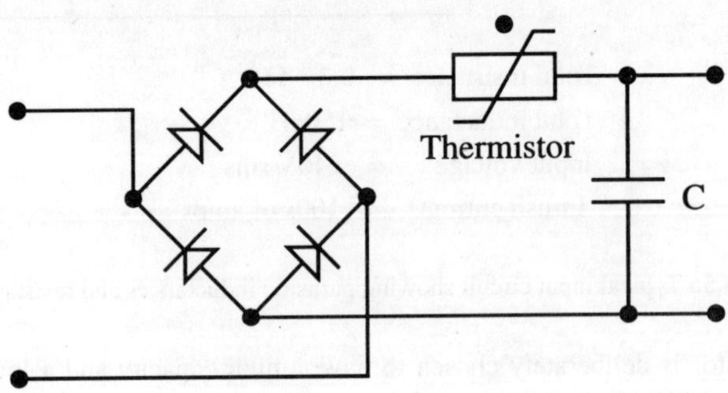

Figure 4.58 A thermistor surge limiter

On switch-on the thermistor is cold and in its high resistance state, thereby limiting the initial current. The current causes the thermistor to self-heat, reducing its resistance once the inrush period is over. This overcomes most of the efficiency problems associated with the resistor method, but gives rise to new problems when "dropouts" occur on the prime power supply, caused by the thermal time constant of the thermistor. During a dropout, the thermistor may not get sufficient time to cool to its high resistance state and will not afford protection to the circuit when the supply comes on again.

A better solution is to use a resistor that is switched out of circuit as the voltage across the capacitor builds up. The classic method of doing this is with a relay whose coil senses the capacitor voltage. A faster acting solution is to use a silicon controlled rectifier (SCR) or a TRIAC to switch out the resistor. The circuit in Figure 4.59 shows such a scheme.

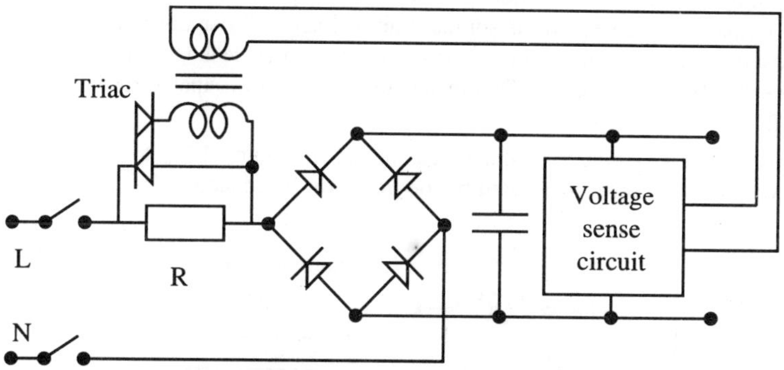

Figure 4.59 Triac switched inrush protection

The circuit chosen will depend on the type of prime power supply in use, the degree of protection required for the input circuitry and the overhead of including the additional circuitry. It is worth remembering that the inclusion of effective protection will contribute to the reliable operation of the unit.

SNUBBERS AND DEVICE PROTECTION

Turn-Off Snubber Circuits

Snubber circuits are used to reduce the losses in switching transistors by altering the waveforms around them.

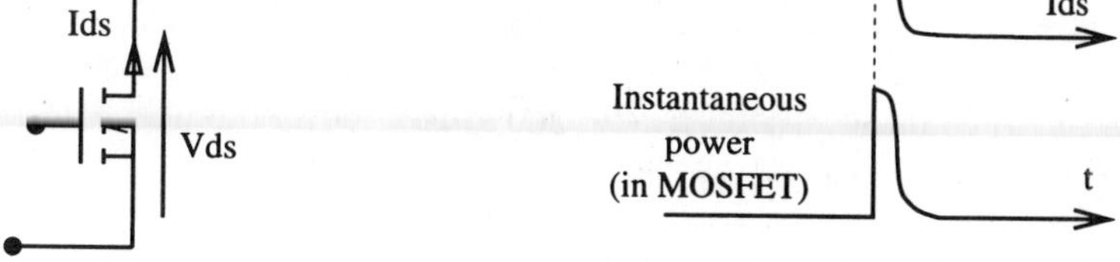

Figure 4.60 MOSFET switching circuit without turn-off snubber

To understand the need for a snubber consider the simple circuit shown in Figure 4.60. When the transistor is turned off the source-drain voltage will rise instantaneously, but the drain current will flow until the energy stored in the leakage inductance of the transformer has been discharged. This means that power is dissipated in the transistor at switch-off.

If a snubber circuit is added to the transistor, as in Figure 4.61, to slow the rise in collector voltage, the power dissipated by the transistor is reduced.

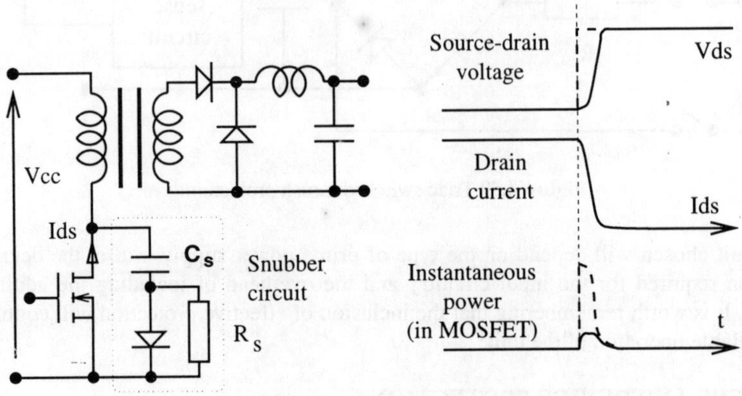

$C_s = Ids \dfrac{t_f}{Vcc}$ $\quad t_f$ = fall time on current switching waveform

$R_s = \dfrac{t_{on}}{2C_s}$ $\quad t_{on}$ = on time of MOSFET

Figure 4.61 MOSFET switching circuit with turn-off snubber

The operation of the snubber is as follows. Capacitor C_s holds V_{ds} low during current turn-off, as the diode is forward biased. Resistor R_s is chosen to discharge C_s in less than the minimum on-time, t_{on}. Hence, the time constant R_sC_s is chosen to be a half of t_{on}.

$$C_s = i_c \frac{t_f}{V_{ds}}$$

$$R_s = \frac{t_{on}}{2C_s}$$

where t_f is the device switching time.

Turn-On Snubber Circuits

Again, the turn-on snubber is used to limit the power dissipation during switching. It is mainly useful when the transformer leakage inductance does not provide sufficient delay between the fall in V_{ds} and I_{ds} at turn-on.

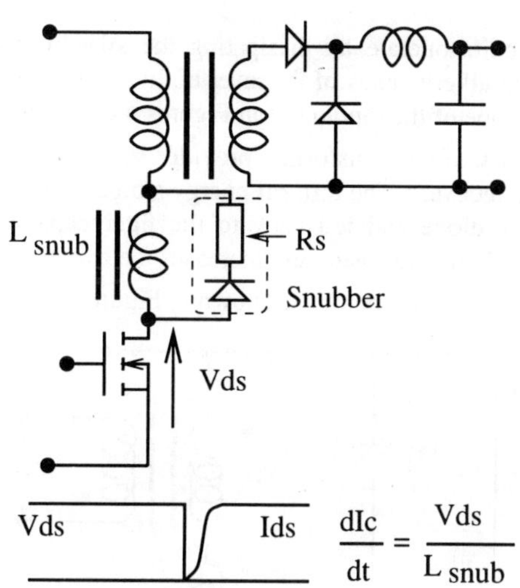

Figure 4.62 Turn-on snubber circuit

The circuit in Figure 4.62 shows a typical turn-on snubber circuit. During turn-on the series inductor serves to isolate the transistor from the load, permitting the transistor to turn on before it passes significant current. The rate of rise of the source-drain current $\frac{dI_{ds}}{dt} = \frac{E_{in}}{L_{snubber}}$. The resistor diode network around the snubber inductance provides a current discharge path to dissipate the energy stored in the inductor during the off period. It is worth noting that snubber circuits do not reduce the overall dissipation in a power supply, but do reduce the dissipation of the switching device. They work by dissipating the switching energy in the snubber resistor rather than the device.

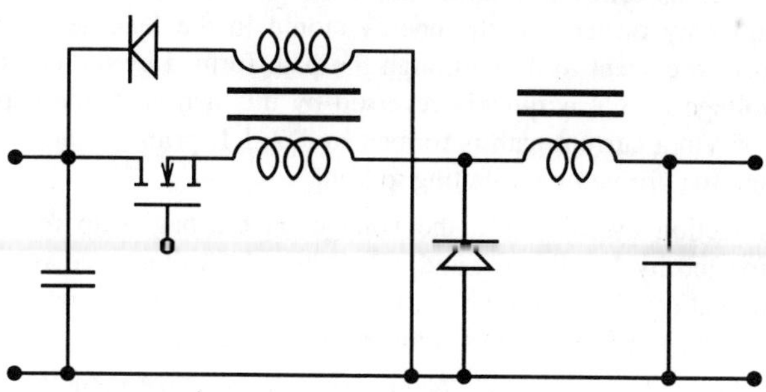

Figure 4.63 A simple non-dissipative snubber

Active Snubbers

All of the snubber circuits operate by dissipating the switching energy in a resistor, thereby lowering the overall efficiency of the inverter. In order to provide snubber circuits that are non-dissipative, one of the topologies in Figures 4.63 and 4.64 can be used.

In Figure 4.63 the primary of the transformer provides inductance to limit current surges due to the diode reverse recovery. The turn-off energy stored in the transformer primary is coupled to the recovery diode and fed back to the filter capacitor. This prevents the dissipation of the energy in the transistor and increases the overall efficiency.

Another non-dissipative snubber topology is shown in Figure 4.64.

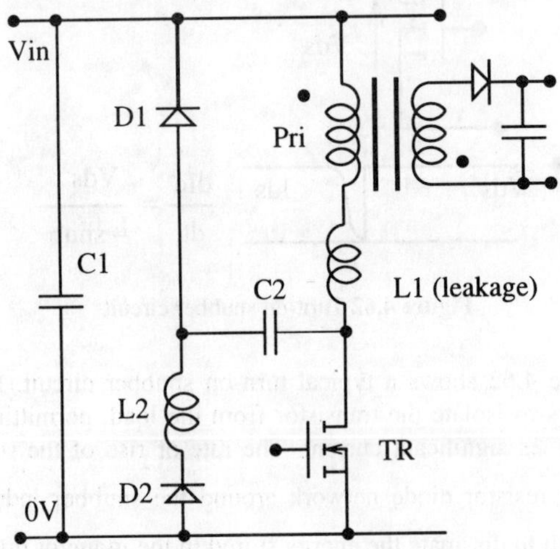

Figure 4.64 Another non-dissipative snubber

The circuit operates as follows: assume that TR is on and that C2 is charged to -Vin. When TR is suddenly turned off, the energy stored in the leakage inductance of the transformer causes a current to flow through the path formed by the circuit C2, D1 and primary. The voltage on C2 is quickly reversed by this action. If the capacitor voltage rises in excess of Vin a current path is formed by D2, L1, primary and C1. C2 will then discharge through the primary contributing to Vout.

During the conduction cycle of TR, the voltage on C2 begins to reverse due to the resonant path formed by L1, D2, C2 and TR. When the voltage across C2 has reached -Vin it is clamped at this level and the current in L1 now flows through D1 and D2 back to C1 changing at the rate Ein/L1, thus completing a full cycle.

The value of this circuit is that it puts the energy in the leakage inductance back into the filter capacitor rather than dissipating it. L1 is the leakage inductance of the transformer and C2 is determined from

$$t_{on} = \pi(L1C2)$$

Device Protection

High voltage MOSFETs have the major advantage over bipolar junction devices that they do not suffer from secondary breakdown and generally they do not need to be provided with voltage clamping devices across their source/drain connections. They are, however, quite vulnerable at their gate electrodes. The gate region in the transistor is formed from a layer of silicon dioxide which is only a few thousands of Angstroms thick, which is susceptible to electrical breakdown. In general the gate breakdown voltage on most MOSFETs is around 20 volts. It is a wise precaution to provide some form of gate protection circuit which will limit the maximum gate voltage to a value below the breakdown voltage. An arrangement for doing this is shown in Figure 4.65. Two Zener or avalanche diodes are placed back-to-back between the gate and the source of the transistor.These are chosen so that their voltage is well below the minimum breakdown voltage that will be encountered for the gate.

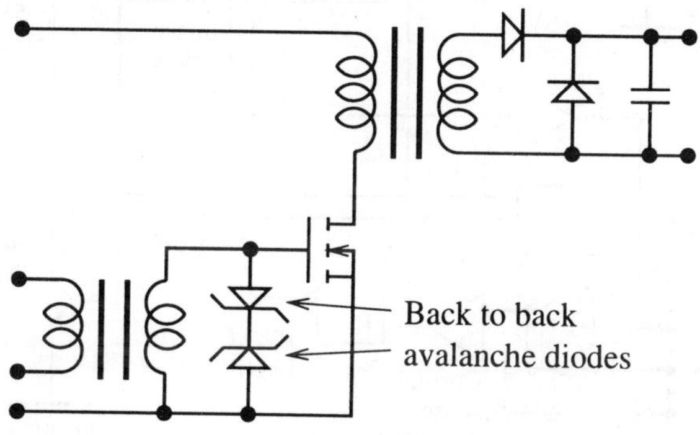

Figure 4.65 Gate protection using back-to-back avalanche diodes

The protection measures outlined in this section will considerably increase the complexity of a SMPS but they are well worth considering as they will greatly enhance its reliability.

POWER SUPPLY MANAGEMENT

Control Circuitry

This section will deal with a typical SMPS control integrated circuit and then consider the problem of powering the control circuitry. The designer of a SMPS has a wide range of integrated circuit controllers available from different semiconductor manufacturers. The decision whether to use an integrated circuit, or discrete circuitry, will depend on factors such as cost, ease of assembly and noise immunity. Integrated circuits are convenient for low and medium power SMPS, but they tend to have relatively poor amplifiers and poor noise immunity, which makes them less useful in high powered SMPS applications.

The UC3842 is a popular low-cost IC current-mode controller for SMPS and is typical of a wide range of such devices that are available. It comes in an eight pin DIL package. Figure 4.66 shows its block diagram.

The circuit blocks in the top half of the diagram are to provide the necessary internally regulated power rails for the circuitry. They also provide start-up sequencing to allow the IC to have a low start-up current of around 1mA. This makes it easier to power in a practical SMPS circuit for reasons that will be discussed in the next section. There is also an undervoltage lock out (UVLO) facility which shuts down the whole power supply when the input voltage (V1) drops below 16 volts.

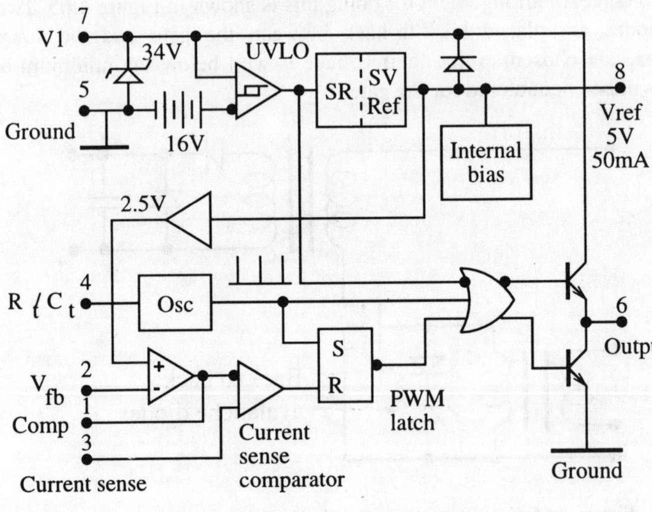

Figure 4.66 Block diagram of UC3842

Pins 5 and 7 are the power supply for the IC itself, which should lie in the range 16 to 34 volts. Pin 8 provides a 5 volt reference, capable of providing up to 50mA. Pin 4 has the timing resistor, R_t, and capacitor, C_t, attached to it. These components are used to set the switching frequency of the power supply. R_t is connected from pin 8 to pin 4 and C_t from pin 4 to ground. C_t charges up through R_t, from the 5 volt rail, and is then discharged by the oscillator circuitry in the IC. This cycle then repeats itself *ad infinitum*.

The sampled output voltage of the power supply is connected to pin 2 and a voltage representing the sampled output current is fed to pin 3. Pin 1 is to provide the output of the error amplifier and is for adding compensation feedback to optimise the response of the power supply to changes in load conditions. The S-R latch is used to vary the duty cycle of the switching waveform in response to differing loads. The output from the PWM latch is used to drive the totem pole output on pin 6. This output configuration is ideal for driving the capacitance of a MOSFET gate.

Powering the Control Circuitry

The provision of power for the control electronics in a SMPS can present a problem. It is not possible to take power from the regulated output, as the control circuitry must come up before the output voltage can build up. This means that power for the control circuit must be derived directly from the mains input and not via the control loop.

One solution to this problem is to provide a dropping resistor from the rectified mains supply to give a low voltage supply for the control electronics. This has the disadvantages that the circuitry is not isolated from the mains and that considerable power can be dissipated in the dropper resistor. In some applications, where low cost and simplicity are the over-riding considerations, this solution may be the most appropriate.

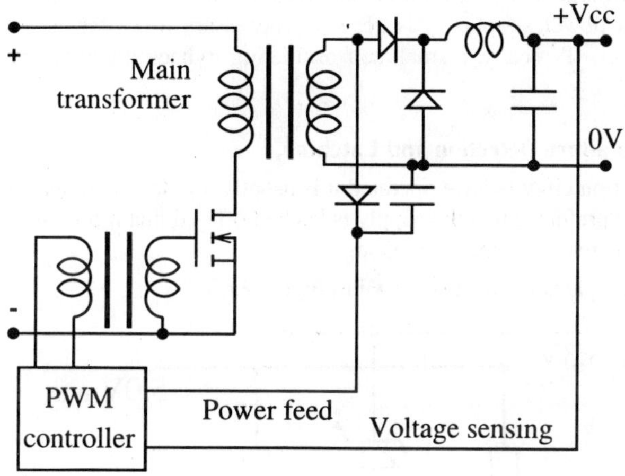

Figure 4.67 An alternative method of powering the control electronics

Another possibility is to use a low voltage step-down transformer from the 50Hz mains. This is a relatively expensive solution, which adds weight and bulk to a design. Remember that the 50Hz transformer may be nearly as large as the main switching transformer because of the frequency difference, despite the fact that it is only powering the control circuitry. This solution does have the advantage that it provides mains isolation for the control electronics.

In aerospace applications where the mains frequency is normally 400Hz this solution is more attractive, as the size of the transformer is considerably reduced.

A third method that can be used to power the control electronics is shown in Figure 4.67.

At initial switch-on the pulse-width modulator will not be running as its power supply will not be present. The pulse generator is used to supply a series of pulses to switch the MOSFET, allowing the main transformer to transmit sufficient power to start powering up the PWM, which then takes over the control of the power supply. The pulse generator can be powered directly from the mains as it does not require isolation. Usually the pulses are derived directly from the mains a.c. waveform. This scheme gives isolation and can be implemented at little cost. It is worth pointing out that it is best to use an IC like the UC3842, which has a low start-up current, for this scheme to work well.

Auxiliary Power Supplies

In some personal computer applications a "sleep" mode is required for the power supply such that it is powered down all bar a small standby supply which is used to maintain functions such as RAM memory. The advantages of such a scheme are twofold, in that it reduces the stress on the components of the computer and the supply, and it also saves energy. Typically, such auxiliary supplies are required to supply around 10W at efficiencies of around 50-60%. As it is difficult to maintain the efficiency at low levels of loading in most power supplies it is generally necessary to switch in a small auxiliary supply in parallel. Typically, a small self-oscillating flyback converter could be used in such a situation.

Power Supply Failure Detection and Latching.

Once the protection circuits have operated it is usually not desirable that the supply is left running and it is preferred that the supply is latched off and that it does not come on again until the power is removed and re-applied.

A suitable latching arrangement is shown in Figure 4.68.

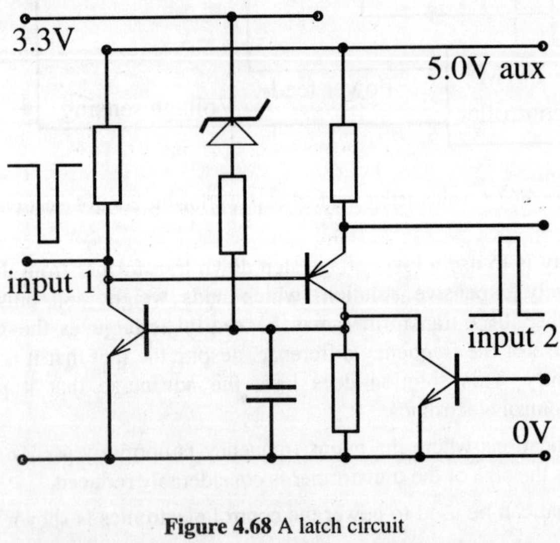

Figure 4.68 A latch circuit

This circuit is powered from an auxiliary 5 volt rail that is on continuously. It also allows detection of over-voltage conditions on the 3.3 volt rail shown. It can also be triggered by pulses of the polarity shown on its inputs. These pulses can be produced from under-voltage and over-current monitor circuits. The output is used to switch off the pulse width modulator, which shuts down the whole power supply. The only way to reset the latch and hence the power supply as a whole is to interrupt the mains supply and restart the supply.

4.6 RELIABILITY AND COOLING

RELIABILITY

For a power supply to be useful it must be reliable. The overall reliability of a system is strongly dependent on the reliability of its power supply. Usually a system can incorporate some degree of redundancy to enhance reliability but it is more difficult to incorporate redundant power supplies.

Reliability is a measure of the ability of a component or piece of equipment to perform its function, in an adequate manner, for a stated period of time. It is a necessary attribute for a product to be fit for the purpose for which it is designed and every bit as important as the actual functionality of the product.

The reliability of a component or system is only definitely known once it has failed. For a knowledge of reliability to be useful it must be possible to make predictions of the expected life in order to minimise the incidence of failures in service. Reliability, in an engineering sense, becomes the prediction of the life of a component or system based on knowledge of the previous failure history. Reliability is a "state of knowledge" rather than a "state of things".

In order to be able to predict the reliability of a component it is necessary to know its statistical failure rate. This knowledge is based on data gathered from either past operational experience of the component or from batch testing. For most most components the failure rate varies with time according to the well known "bath-tub" curve in Figure 4.69.

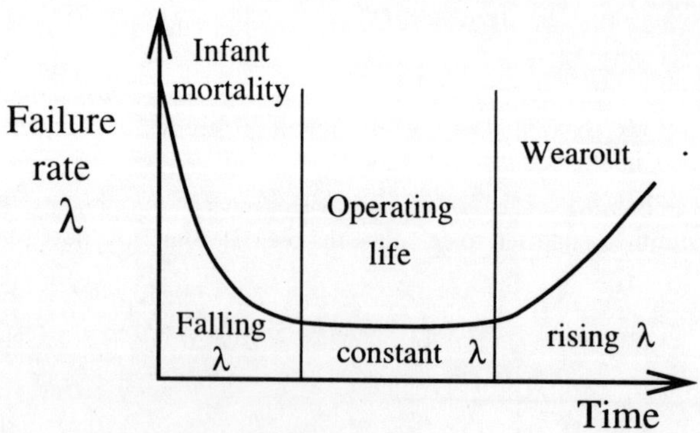

Figure 4.69 The bath-tub curve

During the early stages of life (region 1) the failure rate is high and decreasing. This is often referred to as the infant mortality period where components with inherent manufacturing weaknesses will fail prematurely. During the middle life period (region 2) the failure rate is constant and caused by random failures. This period is the useful life region. Finally the wearout region is reached where failures occur because of aging effects and the failure rate starts to slowly increase. In normal operation, semiconductor components do not generally reach this phase of operation. In practice, manufacturers try to make the infant mortality period as short as possible by careful quality control and process control during production. Additionally, parts may be subjected to a "burn-in" period before dispatch, to weed out potential failures, and they are only released when they are in their useful life period.

Quantifying Reliability

Various measures are used to quantify reliability, the commonest being failure rate, λ, and the mean time to failure, MTTF. These are related thus:

$$MTTF = \frac{1}{\lambda}$$

Typical values of failure rate for a high reliability part are around 10^{-8} failures per hour. Another measure often used is the mean time between failures, MTBF. Strictly this is the mean time between failures as the device goes through successive cycles of failure and repair, and is related to the MTTF thus:

$$MTBF = MTTF + repair\ time$$

For semiconductor parts, repair is not normally possible and the MTTF and MTBF are often used interchangeably.

The reliability, R(t), of a component is related to its failure rate and time, t, thus:

$$R(t) = e^{(-\lambda t)}$$

This assumes that the failure rate is constant and random. This assumption can be justified because of the many diverse forces leading to failure for complex parts. These conspire to produce, in effect, random failures.

To calculate the reliability of a system comprising many components, the individual failure rates are summed and used to calculate the overall reliability, thus:

$$\lambda_{total} = \lambda_1 + \lambda_2 + ... + \lambda_n$$
$$R_{total}(t) = e^{-(\lambda_{total} t)}$$

The degradation of semiconductors usually results from chemical reactions and physical processes which change the structure of devices on an atomic scale. The rate at which such reactions occur, and hence the degradation of the reliability with temperature, is well described by the Arrhenius equation:

$$R = R_o e^{\left(\frac{-\Delta E}{KT}\right)}$$

where

R = Reliability as a function of temperature

R_o = constant

ΔE = Activation energy

K = Boltzmann's constant

T = Temperature in degrees Kelvin

Typical values of activation energy, ΔE, are around 0.75ev; thus a 10 degree temperature rise will halve reliability.

Use can be made of this to overcome the infant mortality period (in the bath-tub curve) by raising the operating temperature to accelerate the failure rate. This process is often referred to as "burn-in". In this way, manufacturing faults leading to infant mortality can be overcome quickly and economically, before products are sold.

RELIABILITY PREDICTION

Methods of reliability calculation are outlined in the US Department of Defense MIL-HDBK-217E. This contains failure rate data on all types of components that have been cleared for US military use. These data have been built up from experience of component failures and also from the results of accelerated testing at elevated stress.

In the early stages of a project, before knowledge of the details of a circuit design is available, reliability is estimated by means of the Parts Count Method.

Parts Count Reliability Estimation

This method is useful before detailed information regarding the operating stresses of individual components is available. The information required for this method is as follows:

- Generic part types
- Numbers of each part type
- Part quality level
- Equipment environment

The overall failure rate for the equipment is calculated using the relation:

$$\lambda_{EQUIPMENT} = \sum_{i=1}^{n} N_i \left(\lambda_G \pi_Q \right)_i$$

where:

$\lambda_{EQUIPMENT}$ is the total equipment failure rate

λ_G is the generic failure rate for the ith generic part

π_Q is the quality level of the generic part

N_i is the number of the ith part type

n is the number of part types

These values are tabulated in MIL-HDBK-217E. This method requires only a minimum of information, as no details of component operating conditions are needed. It is intended to give a reasonable estimate of expected reliability at the planning stages of a project.

Part Stress Reliability Estimation

As a design progresses, more detailed design information is available and it is possible to estimate overall reliability by calculating the individual component failure rates. This method is known as Part Stress Analysis as it is based on the operating stress of each component.

A variety of different models are used depending on the component type; take, for example, discrete transistors and diodes:

$$\lambda_P = \lambda_b \left(\pi_E \times \pi_A \times \pi_Q \times \pi_R \times \pi_{S2} \times \pi_C \right)$$

where:

λ_P is the part failure rate

λ_b is the base failure rate

π_E is the environmental factor

π_A is the application factor (linear or switched)

π_Q is the quality factor (eg. JAN, JANTX etc.)

π_R is the power rating

π_{S2} is the voltage stress factor

π_C is the complexity factor (eg. dual, multiple emitter etc.)

A Cautionary Note

The use of the standard reliability prediction methods such as MIL-HDBK-217E can predict a higher MTTF than can actually be attained. MIL-HDBK-217E considers only static conditions and does not allow for transient conditions such as surges and spikes. Conversely, if a designer adds surge limiters, snubbers, soft-start circuitry, transient limiters and other protection devices, in order to obtain high actual reliability, MIL-HDBK-217E calculations will yield a lower MTTF, because of the extra complexity, than is attained in practice.

Be cautious of simple and inexpensive switch mode power supply designs with little protection and a high predicted MTTF!

Component Approval Systems

In order to build systems which have high reliability, which can be predicted with some confidence, it is necessary to use components of "approved quality". Several approval systems are in use and the choice will depend on particular customer requirements. One of the most widely used systems in the UK is the BS9000 system. It was established in the late 1960s for the independent inspection, approval and surveillance of manufacturers, distributors and test laboratories in the electronic component industry. For products destined for the Western European market, components approved to CECC quality levels should be used.

The BS9000 and CECC specification system consists of generic specifications which relate to families of components; for example, fixed resistors or semiconductor devices. They contain the terms, definitions, standard values for characteristics, test methods and information relating to quality assessment procedures.

COOLING CONSIDERATIONS

It was stated in the previous section that the temperature of a semiconductor device strongly influences its reliability. In particular the temperature of the actual semiconductor chip, rather than the package, is the controlling factor. To maximise reliability it is important to keep the device junction temperature as low as is reasonably possible.

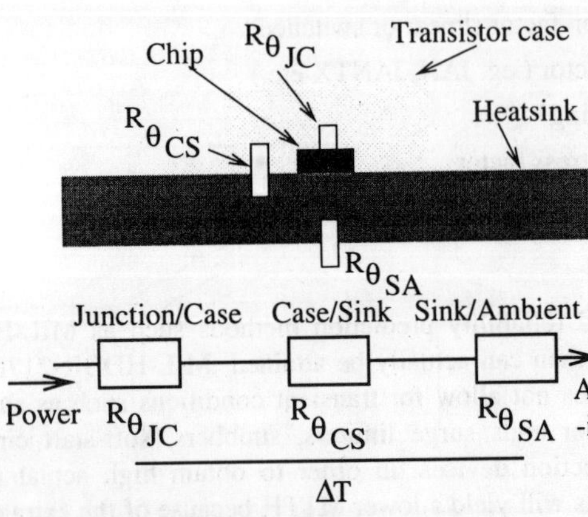

$$R_{\theta JA} = R_{\theta JC} + R_{\theta CS} + R_{\theta SA}$$

Figure 4.70 The junction to ambient thermal resistance of a transistor on a heatsink

The junction temperature, T_J, depends on the ambient temperature, T_A, the average power dissipation, P, and the junction to ambient thermal resistance, $R_{\Theta JA}$ (C/W), in the following manner:

$$T_J = T_A + PR_{\Theta JA}$$

This simple "d.c." thermal model is found to work well for switching power supplies since the waveforms are periodic and have a period much less than the thermal time constants involved.

The power dissipation is composed of three components in a switching regulator:

$$P = P_{blocking} + P_{conducting} + P_{switching}$$

Usually the power dissipated in the blocking state is negligible.

The junction to ambient thermal resistance $R_{\Theta JA}$ can be considered to consist of three separate components, connected in series, as shown in Figure 4.70. $R_{\Theta JC}$ is the junction to case thermal resistance, $R_{\Theta CS}$ is the case to heatsink thermal resistance and $R_{\Theta SA}$ is the heatsink to ambient thermal resistance.

$$R_{\Theta JA} = R_{\Theta JC} + R_{\Theta CS} + R_{\Theta SA}$$

The value of $R_{\Theta JC}$ is dependent on the internal structure of the transistor and its package and is determined by the semiconductor manufacturer. $R_{\Theta CS}$ and $R_{\Theta SA}$ are both determined by the mounting of the transistor. $R_{\Theta CS}$ is kept small by mounting the device using a heat conducting paste. $R_{\Theta SA}$ is determined by the size of the heatsink in use and depends on the surface area to volume ratio.

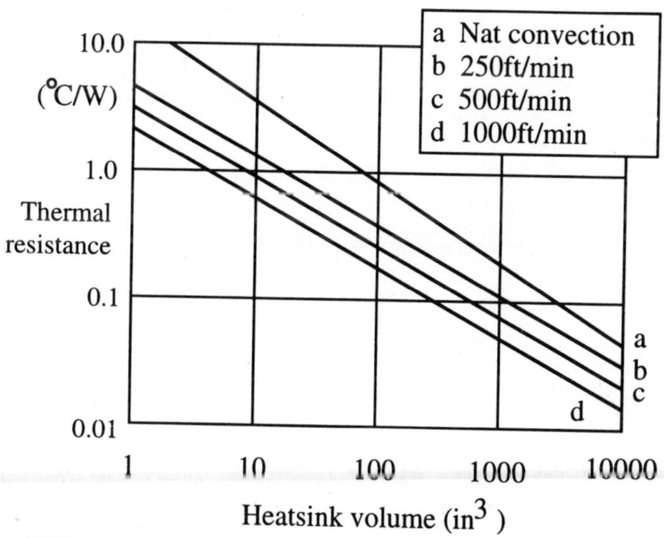

Figure 4.71 The thermal resistance of a heatsink as a function of volume and airflow

For most materials used as heatsinks, such as aluminium extrusion, the thermal resistance per unit surface area is around 800°C/watt/cm^2. Hence the thermal resistance is given by:

$$R_{\Theta SA} = \frac{800}{surface\ area} \quad °C/watt$$

The thermal conductivity of a heatsink can be improved by forced air cooling, and the graph in Figure 4.71 shows the thermal resistance versus volume of metal for different air flow rates. The surface to volume ratio for extruded aluminium heatsinks is relatively constant.

When specifying power devices care should be taken to select one with a suitable dissipation rating. Most manufacturers specify their devices at 25°C case temperature. In most situations where a device is dissipating a significant power it is not possible to keep the case at 25°C and devices should be derated according to the thermal resistance of the heatsink and mounting arrangements. Allowance must also be made for the internal ambient temperature of the equipment.

BIBLIOGRAPHY

1. N. Mohan, T.M. Undeland, W.P. Robbins, *Power Electronics: Converters, Applications and Design*, 2nd ed., Wiley, 1995.

2. K.K. Sum, *Switch Mode Power Conversion: Basic Theory and Design*, Dekker, 1984.

3. P.R.K. Chetty, *Switch Mode Power Supply Design*, TAB Professional and Reference Books, 1986.

4. B.W. Williams, *Power Electronics: Devices, Drivers, Applications and Passive Components*, 2nd ed.,Macmillan, 1992.

5. J. Vithayathil, *Power Electronics: Principles and Applications*, McGraw-Hill, 1995.

6. *Power Supply Design Seminar*, Unitrode, 1996.

7. *Product & Applications Handbook*, Unitrode Integrated Circuits, 1993.

8. J.G. Kassakian, M.F. Schlecht, G.C. Verghese, *Principles of Power Electronics*, Addison Wesley, 1991.

9. O. Kilgenstein, *Switched-Mode Power Supplies in Practice*, Wiley, 1989.

INDEX